EARLY STAGE 1

1

Alan McSeveny Rachel McSeveny Diane McSeveny-Foster

**Pearson Australia**
(a division of Pearson Australia Group Pty Ltd)
459–471 Church St, Level 1, Building B, Richmond, Victoria, 3121
PO Box 23360, Melbourne, Victoria 8012
www.pearson.com.au


First published 2023 by Pearson Australia
2027 2026 2025 2024
10 9 8 7 6 5 4 3 2 1



Publishers: Sophie Matta and Rachel Elliott
Project Manager: Michelle Thomas
Production Editor: Laura Rentsch
Editor: Katie Millar
Designer: Anne Donald
Proofreader: Laura Rentsch
Rights & Permissions Editor: Alice McBroom
Cover Design: Jennifer Johnston
Cover Art: Michael Barter
Illustrator: Michael Barter
Publishing Services Analyst: Jit-Pin Chong
Printed in Australia by Pegasus Media and Logistics

National Library of Australia Cataloguing-in-Publication entry

A catalogue record for this book is available from the National Library of Australia

ISBN 978 0 6557 0902 2
Pearson Australia Group Pty Ltd ABN 40 004 245 943

**Attributions**
We would like to thank the following for permission to reproduce copyright material.

The following abbreviations are used in this list:
t = top, b = bottom, l = left, r = right, c = centre.

123rf.com: Amorozov, p. 29 (didgeridoo); Coprid, p. 29 (paper rolls); Nanastudio, p. 29 (gift); Photoshkolnik, p. 29 (barrel); Terekhov, p. 29 (suitcase); Zoraa, p. 29 (cube).

Shutterstock: Azure1, p. 29 (cheese); Irin-K, p. 29 (soccer ball); CKP1001, p. 29 (party hat); Ifong, p. 29 (ice cream); Koosen, p. 29 (glass); Mega Pixed. p.29 (dice); Umberto Shtanzman, p. 29 (Earth); Vladnik, p. 117; Zovteva, p. 29 (tent).

**Acknowledgement of Country**
Pearson respects and honours Aboriginal and Torres Strait Islander Elders past, present and future. We acknowledge the stories, traditions and living cultures of the Traditional Custodians of the lands on which our company is located and where we conduct our business. Pearson is committed to honouring Australian Aboriginal and Torres Strait Islander peoples' unique cultural and spiritual relationships to the land, waters and seas and their rich contribution to society.

Aboriginal and Torres Strait Islander peoples are advised that this text may contain images, voices and names of deceased persons.

# What is Australian Signpost Maths NSW?

Australian Signpost Maths NSW is a mathematics program providing direction and support for teaching and learning. The series covers the content and skills presented in the NSW Mathematics Syllabus K–6, 2022.

A Student Book and an online Teacher Resource are provided for Kindergarten (Early Stage 1).

For Years 1 to 6 (Stages 1–3), a Student Book, an online Teacher Resource and a Mentals Book are provided for each year level. The online Teacher Resources provide a wealth of support for teachers.

The content has been carefully sequenced within each year level and across the K–6 series to take into account students' expected mathematical development. However, from the rich and varied material provided, teachers can develop individual learning programs to meet the needs of each student.

The Student Books are designed to support explicit teaching methods. Many group activities are provided in Activity, Investigation and Fun spots within the Student Books and the online Teacher Resource.

To maximise the benefits of the program, the Student Book, the online Teacher Resource and the Mentals Book should be used together.

Student Books

Mentals Books

Teacher Resource

# Structure of Australian Signpost Maths NSW

In the K–2 books, the worksheet pages covering all three strands are presented in a recommended order. Each unit of 4 pages usually begins with Number and algebra. The Contents cross-reference allows teachers to quickly find the pages where each concept has been covered.

Within the program, explicit teaching, working mathematically skills, language development and identification and treatment of weaknesses are given high priority.

### Identifying and addressing areas of need

Five progress tests are designed to identify each student's areas of need, and the follow-up program after each of the tests is designed to address these needs. A reference to the relevant worksheet page is given for each test question. A remediation record page is used to track the student's progress.

These testing resources can be found in the online Teacher Resource.

Parallel progress retests are provided for further testing after remediation has taken place. See pages 131 and 132 of this book for more information.

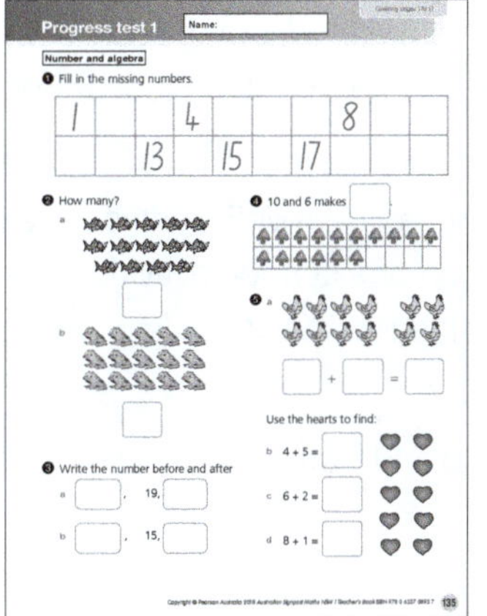

Progress test 1 Name:

Number and algebra

1 Fill in the missing numbers.

2 How many?

3 10 and 6 makes

Use the hearts to find:

4 Write the number before and after

Progress retest 1 Name:

Number and algebra

1 Fill in the missing numbers.

2 How many?

3 10 and 3 makes

Use the blocks to find:

4 Write the number before and after

# Special features of Australian Signpost Maths NSW

- **The traffic light icons**
  These are found on the top right of each worksheet page in the Student Books. They allow students to assess their own progress and give feedback to the teacher.
  - **Green:** I found this work easy.
  - **Orange:** I found some work on the page difficult.
  - **Red:** I don't understand the work on this page.

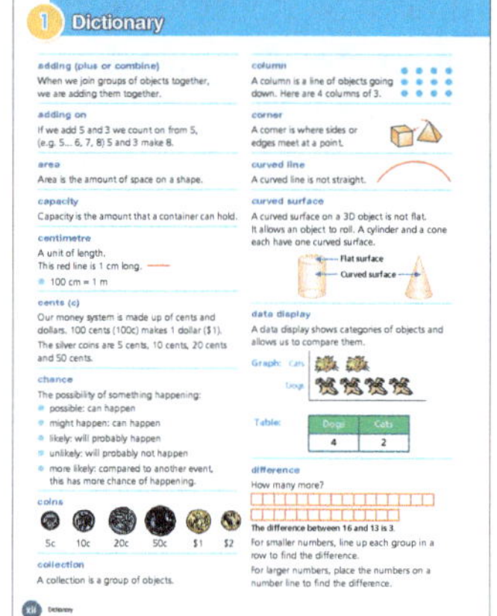


- **Dictionary**
  Terms used in the Student Book and terms that should be understood at this level are recorded here to provide a reference for students and teachers. This is found on pages xii–xvi of this book and in the online Teacher Resource.

- **ID cards (Years 1 to 6)**
  These cards review the language of Mathematics by asking students to identify common terms, shapes and symbols. They are designed to be reused and are found in the online Teacher Resource and in the front of the Mentals Books.

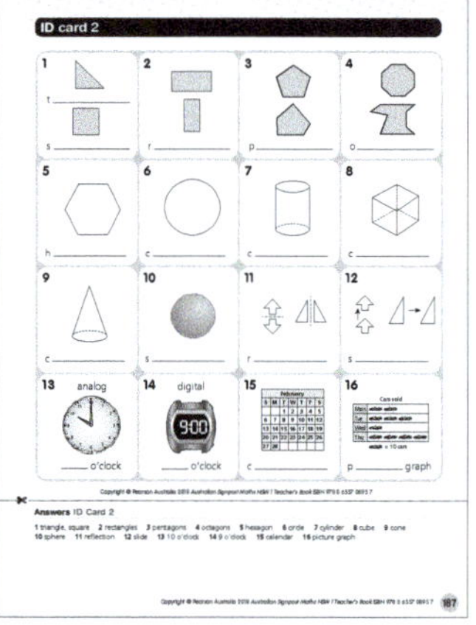


- **Progress tests**
  These allow the teacher to identify each student's strengths and needs. Cross-references for each question direct teachers and students to the pages where that work is introduced. Tables are provided to record the follow-up that takes place and parallel tests are provided for retesting. These tests can be found in the online Teacher Resource.

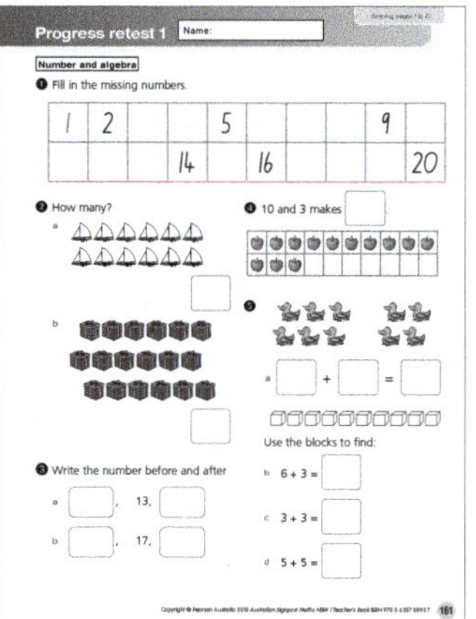


- **Year 1 Consolidation Booklet**
  This 30 page booklet is found in the online Teacher Resource. It is designed to reinforce work completed in class and provides practice of important skills and addition and subtraction facts. The booklet can be used when there is limited supervision or when a student finishes classwork early.

- **Answers**
  These are supplied in the online Teacher Resource.

- **Blackline Masters (BLM)**
  References are made to the Blackline Masters in the teaching suggestions provided for each student work page.

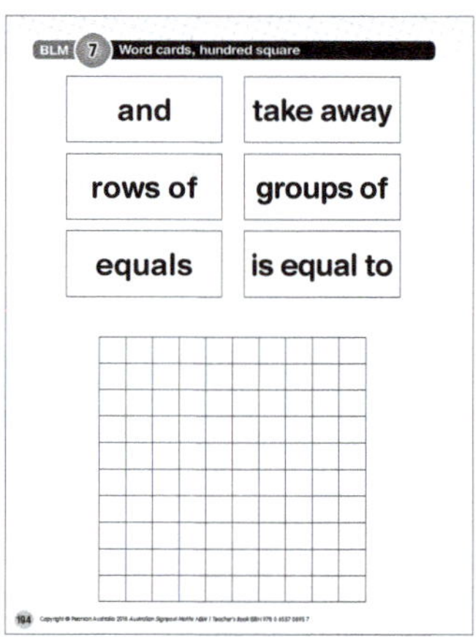


- **Differentiation**
  Each student work page has a Teacher Resource page to support it. Cross-references direct the teacher to pages where the concept is introduced and developed. These references may be from the Student Book for the previous year, current year or the next year.

  The Teacher Resource support pages provide additional learning activities for students who need remediation or extension activities. The Blackline Masters provide activities to support students of various learning abilities.

- **Cartoons**
  Cartoons are used to motivate and instruct.

## Australian Signpost Maths NSW icons

Signpost icons are used throughout the book as cues to the essential nature of exercises and activities, and as a guide to ways of engaging with them. These icons often indicate alternative or more concrete approaches to dealing with concepts.

This icon highlights **important rules and concepts** occurring throughout the book. It often appears with worked examples.

Investigations allow students to **explore and discover** maths concepts.

Activities provide **applications and enrichment**. These activities usually involve the use of concrete materials and partner or group work.

These enjoyable activities are used to **motivate and involve** students in mathematical pursuits. They usually involve games and puzzles.

## Structure of New South Wales Mathematics K–6

**The NSW Mathematics Syllabus content is presented in three strands.**

**1** Number and algebra
**2** Measurement and space
**3** Statistics and probability

**Working mathematically** pervades each of these strands.

**The Mathematics Syllabus can be found at:**
https://curriculum.nsw.edu.au/learning-areas/mathematics/mathematics-k-10

**Textbook Structure**
Within the Contents for Year 1, we show related pages using these categories:

| **Number and algebra** | **Measurement and space** | **Statistics and probability** |
|---|---|---|
| Numbers | 2D shapes / 3D objects | Data displays / chance |
| Addition / subtraction | Length / area / mass | |
| Sharing / grouping | Capacity / volume | |
| Patterns | Time / duration | |
| | Position | |

# Contents and syllabus overview

**KEY**

- Number and algebra
- Measurement and space
- Statistics and probability

| Page | Unit | Title | Strand | Number / algebra | Measurement / space | Statistics / probability | Content area | Numbers | Addition / subtraction | Sharing / grouping | Patterns | 2D shapes / 3D objects | Length / area / mass | Capacity / volume | Time / duration | Position | Data displays / chance |
|---|---|---|---|---|---|---|---|---|---|---|---|---|---|---|---|---|---|
| 1 | Thinking Skills | | Working mathematically pervades each of the strands. | | | | | | | | | | | | | | |
| 2 | 1A | Number revision | | ■ | | | | ● | | | | | | | | | |
| 3 | 1B | Number revision | | ■ | | | | ● | | | | | | | | | |
| 4 | 1C | Numbers to 20 | | ■ | | | | ● | | | | | | | | | |
| 5 | 1D | Shapes and patterns | | | ■ | | | | | | | ● | | | | | |
| 6 | 2A | Adding two groups | | ■ | | | | | ● | | | | | | | | |
| 7 | 2B | Addition sentences | | ■ | | | | | ● | | | | | | | | |
| 8 | 2C | Combinations up to 10 | | ■ | | | | | ● | | | | | | | | |
| 9 | 2D | Identifying objects | | | ■ | | | | | | | ● | | | | | |
| 10 | 3A | Numbers 11 to 20 | | ■ | | | | ● | | | | | | | | | |
| 11 | 3B | Numbers to 20 | | ■ | | | | ● | | | | | | | | | |
| 12 | 3C | Analog time | | | ■ | | | | | | | | | | ● | | |
| 13 | 3D | Digital and analog time | | | ■ | | | | | | | | | | ● | | |
| 14 | 4A | Numbers to 20 | | ■ | | | | ● | | | | | | | | | |
| 15 | 4B | Friends of 10 | | ■ | | | | | ● | | | | | | | | |
| 16 | 4C | Position language | | | ■ | | | | | | | | | | | ● | |
| 17 | 4D | Position language | | | ■ | | | | | | | | | | | ● | |
| 18 | 5A | Addition facts | | ■ | | | | | ● | | | | | | | | |
| 19 | 5B | Partitioning | | ■ | | | | | ● | | | | | | | | |
| 20 | 5C | Half past | | | ■ | | | | | | | | | | ● | | |
| 21 | 5D | Half past | | | ■ | | | | | | | | | | ● | | |
| Progress Test 1: Administer test (Teacher Resource, pages 135–137) then address weaknesses. | | | | | | | | | | | | | | | | | |
| 22 | 6A | Groups of 10 | | ■ | | | | ● | | | | | | | | | |
| 23 | 6B | Counting by tens | | ■ | | | | ● | | | | | | | | | |
| 24 | 6C | Counting by tens | | ■ | | | | ● | | | | | | | | | |
| 25 | 6D | Data displays | | | | ■ | | | | | | | | | | | ● |
| 26 | 7A | Subtraction | | ■ | | | | | ● | | | | | | | | |
| 27 | 7B | Subtraction | | ■ | | | | | ● | | | | | | | | |
| 28 | 7C | 3D objects | | | ■ | | | | | | | ● | | | | | |
| 29 | 7D | Objects in our world | | | ■ | | | | | | | ● | | | | | |

**KEY**

|  |  |
|---|---|
| ■ (blue) | Number and algebra |
| ■ (teal) | Measurement and space |
| ■ (orange) | Statistics and probability |

| Page | Unit | Title | Strand | Number / algebra | Measurement / space | Statistics / probability | Content area | Numbers | Addition / subtraction | Sharing / grouping | Patterns | 2D shapes / 3D objects | Length / area / mass | Capacity / volume | Time / duration | Position | Data displays / chance |
|---|---|---|---|---|---|---|---|---|---|---|---|---|---|---|---|---|---|
| 30 | 8A | Odd and even numbers | | ■ | | | | | | | ● | | | | | | |
| 31 | 8B | Addition to 20 | | ■ | | | | | ● | | | | | | | | |
| 32 | 8C | Units of length | | | ■ | | | | | | | | ● | | | | |
| 33 | 8D | Informal units of length | | | ■ | | | | | | | | ● | | | | |
| 34 | 9A | Counting on | | ■ | | | | | ● | | | | | | | | |
| 35 | 9B | Counting on | | ■ | | | | | ● | | | | | | | | |
| 36 | 9C | Analog and digital time | | | ■ | | | | | | | | | | ● | | |
| 37 | 9D | Digital and analog time | | | ■ | | | | | | | | | | ● | | |
| 38 | 10A | Addition to 20 | | ■ | | | | | ● | | | | | | | | |
| 39 | 10B | Larger numbers | | ■ | | | | ● | | | | | | | | | |
| 40 | 10C | Informal units of length | | | ■ | | | | | | | | ● | | | | |
| 41 | 10D | Measuring length | | | ■ | | | | | | | | ● | | | | |
| 42 | 11A | Numbers to 100 | | ■ | | | | ● | | | | | | | | | |
| 43 | 11B | Subtraction to 20 | | ■ | | | | | ● | | | | | | | | |
| 44 | 11C | Comparing capacities | | | ■ | | | | | | | | | ● | | | |
| 45 | 11D | Informal units of capacity | | | ■ | | | | | | | | | ● | | | |
| 46 | 12A | Addition sentences | | ■ | | | | | ● | | | | | | | | |
| 47 | 12B | Addition | | ■ | | | | | ● | | | | | | | | |
| Progress Test 2: Administer test (Teacher Resource, pages 139–142) then address weaknesses. | | | | | | | | | | | | | | | | | |
| 48 | 12C | Addition by counting on | | ■ | | | | | ● | | | | | | | | |
| 49 | 12D | Comparing capacities | | | ■ | | | | | | | | | ● | | | |
| 50 | 13A | Numbers to 120 | | ■ | | | | ● | | | | | | | | | |
| 51 | 13B | Numbers to 120 | | ■ | | | | ● | | | | | | | | | |
| 52 | 13C | The hexagon | | | ■ | | | | | | | ● | | | | | |
| 53 | 13D | Picture graphs | | | | ■ | | | | | | | | | | | ● |
| 54 | 14A | Subtraction | | ■ | | | | | ● | | | | | | | | |
| 55 | 14B | Subtraction | | ■ | | | | | ● | | | | | | | | |
| 56 | 14C | Comparing the mass of objects | | | ■ | | | | | | | | ● | | | | |
| 57 | 14D | Mass | | | ■ | | | | | | | | ● | | | | |
| 58 | 15A | Counting back | | ■ | | | | | ● | | | | | | | | |
| 59 | 15B | Counting back | | ■ | | | | | ● | | | | | | | | |
| 60 | 15C | Subtraction | | ■ | | | | | ● | | | | | | | | |
| 61 | 15D | Data displays | | | | ■ | | | | | | | | | | | ● |
| 62 | 16A | Doubles | | ■ | | | | | ● | | | | | | | | |
| 63 | 16B | Doubling and near doubling | | ■ | | | | | ● | | | | | | | | |
| 64 | 16C | Months of the year | | | ■ | | | | | | | | | | ● | | |
| 65 | 16D | Months and seasons | | | ■ | | | | | | | | | | ● | | |

**KEY**

|  |  |
|---|---|
| Blue | Number and algebra |
| Teal | Measurement and space |
| Orange | Statistics and probability |

| Page | Unit | Title | Strand | Number / algebra | Measurement / space | Statistics / probability | Content area | Numbers | Addition / subtraction | Sharing / grouping | Patterns | 2D shapes / 3D objects | Length / area / mass | Capacity / volume | Time / duration | Position | Data displays / chance |
|---|---|---|---|---|---|---|---|---|---|---|---|---|---|---|---|---|---|
| 66 | 17A | Patterns | | ■ | | | | | | | ● | | | | | | |
| 67 | 17B | Combinations for numbers | | ■ | | | | | ● | | | | | | | | |
| 68 | 17C | Object hunt | | | ■ | | | | | | | ● | | | | | |
| 69 | 17D | Recognising 3D objects | | | ■ | | | | | | | ● | | | | | |
| 70 | 18A | Difference | | ■ | | | | | ● | | | | | | | | |
| 71 | 18B | Difference between groups | | ■ | | | | | ● | | | | | | | | |
| 72 | 18C | The pentagon and octagon | | | ■ | | | | | | | ● | | | | | |
| 73 | 18D | Comparing areas | | | ■ | | | | | | | | ● | | | | |
| 74 | 19A | Place value | | ■ | | | | ● | | | | | | | | | |
| 75 | 19B | Numbers to 120 | | ■ | | | | ● | | | | | | | | | |
| 76 | 19C | Place value | | ■ | | | | ● | | | | | | | | | |
| 77 | 19D | Finding the nearest ten | | ■ | | | | ● | | | | | | | | | |
| 78 | 20A | Subtraction by counting on | | ■ | | | | | ● | | | | | | | | |
| 79 | 20B | Number relationships | | ■ | | | | | ● | | | | | | | | |
| 80 | 20C | Numbers to 100 | | ■ | | | | ● | | | | | | | | | |
| 81 | 20D | Chance words | | | | ■ | | | | | | | | | | | ● |
| 82 | 21A | Equal groups | | ■ | | | | | | ● | | | | | | | |
| 83 | 21B | Using groups | | ■ | | | | | | ● | | | | | | | |

Progress Test 3: Administer test (Teacher Resource, pages 144–147) then address weaknesses.

| Page | Unit | Title | Strand | Number / algebra | Measurement / space | Statistics / probability | Content area | Numbers | Addition / subtraction | Sharing / grouping | Patterns | 2D shapes / 3D objects | Length / area / mass | Capacity / volume | Time / duration | Position | Data displays / chance |
|---|---|---|---|---|---|---|---|---|---|---|---|---|---|---|---|---|---|
| 84 | 21C | Informal units of volume | | | ■ | | | | | | | | | ● | | | |
| 85 | 21D | Comparing volume | | | ■ | | | | | | | | | ● | | | |
| 86 | 22A | Numbers to 120 | | ■ | | | | ● | | | | | | | | | |
| 87 | 22B | Skip counting patterns | | ■ | | | | | | | ● | | | | | | |
| 88 | 22C | Volume | | | ■ | | | | | | | | | ● | | | |
| 89 | 22D | Halves and quarters | | | ■ | | | | | | | | ● | | | | |
| 90 | 23A | Equal groups | | ■ | | | | | | ● | | | | | | | |
| 91 | 23B | Using groups | | ■ | | | | | | ● | | | | | | | |
| 92 | 23C | Halves and quarters | | | ■ | | | | | | | | ● | | | | |
| 93 | 23D | Symmetry | | | ■ | | | | | | | ● | | | | | |
| 94 | 24A | Skip counting | | ■ | | | | | | | ● | | | | | | |
| 95 | 24B | Number patterns | | ■ | | | | | | | ● | | | | | | |
| 96 | 24C | Months of the year | | | ■ | | | | | | | | | | ● | | |
| 97 | 24D | Gather and display data | | | | ■ | | | | | | | | | | | ● |
| 98 | 25A | Number patterns | | ■ | | | | | | | ● | | | | | | |
| 99 | 25B | Counting by 2s, 5s and 10s | | ■ | | | | | | | ● | | | | | | |
| 100 | 25C | 2D shapes | | | ■ | | | | | | | ● | | | | | |
| 101 | 25D | Properties of shapes | | | ■ | | | | | | | ● | | | | | |

**KEY**

| | |
|---|---|
| ■ (blue) | Number and algebra |
| ■ (teal) | Measurement and space |
| ■ (orange) | Statistics and probability |

| Page | Unit | Title | Strand | Number / algebra | Measurement / 00space | Statistics / probability | Content area | Numbers | Addition / subtraction | Sharing / grouping | Patterns | 2D shapes / 3D objects | Length / area / mass | Capacity / volume | Time / duration | Position | Data displays / chance |
|---|---|---|---|---|---|---|---|---|---|---|---|---|---|---|---|---|---|
| 102 | 26A | Half of a group | | ■ | | | | | | ● | | | | | | | |
| 103 | 26B | Halves | | ■ | | | | | | ● | | | | | | | |
| 104 | 26C | Calendar | | | ■ | | | | | | | | | | ● | | |
| 105 | 26D | The calendar | | | ■ | | | | | | | | | | ● | | |
| 106 | 27A | Sharing | | ■ | | | | | | ● | | | | | | | |
| 107 | 27B | Sharing | | ■ | | | | | | ● | | | | | | | |
| 108 | 27C | The cube | | | ■ | | | | | | | ● | | | | | |

Progress Test 4: Administer test (Teacher Resource, pages 149–152) then address weaknesses.

| Page | Unit | Title | Strand | Number / algebra | Measurement / 00space | Statistics / probability | Content area | Numbers | Addition / subtraction | Sharing / grouping | Patterns | 2D shapes / 3D objects | Length / area / mass | Capacity / volume | Time / duration | Position | Data displays / chance |
|---|---|---|---|---|---|---|---|---|---|---|---|---|---|---|---|---|---|
| 109 | 27D | Giving directions | | | ■ | | | | | | | | | | | | |
| 110 | 28A | Grouping to share | | ■ | | | | | | ● | | | | | | | |
| 111 | 28B | How many groups? | | ■ | | | | | | ● | | | | | | | |
| 112 | 28C | Comparing areas | | | ■ | | | | | | | | ● | | | | |
| 113 | 28D | Area using units | | | ■ | | | | | | | | ● | | | | |
| 114 | 29A | Looking for tens | | ■ | | | | | ● | | | | | | | | |
| 115 | 29B | Relating addition and subtraction | | ■ | | | | | ● | | | | | | | | |
| 116 | 29C | Relating addition and subtraction | | ■ | | | | | ● | | | | | | | | |
| 117 | 29D | Comparing mass | | | ■ | | | | | | | | ● | | | | |
| 118 | 30A | Bridging to 10 | | ■ | | | | | ● | | | | | | | | |
| 119 | 30B | Bridging to 10s | | ■ | | | | | ● | | | | | | | | |
| 120 | 30C | Using coins in a data display | | | | ■ | | | | | | | | | | | ● |
| 121 | 30D | Reflecting a shape | | | ■ | | | | | | | ● | | | | | |
| 122 | 31A | Bridging to 10s | | ■ | | | | | ● | | | | | | | | |
| 123 | 31B | Sliding a shape | | | ■ | | | | | | | ● | | | | | |
| 124 | 31C | Counting back | | ■ | | | | | ● | | | | | | | | |
| 125 | 31D | Left and right | | | ■ | | | | | | | | | | | ● | |
| 126 | 32A | Using partitioning | | ■ | | | | | ● | | | | | | | | |
| 127 | 32B | Using partitioning to add | | ■ | | | | | ● | | | | | | | | |
| 128 | 32C | Chance | | | | ■ | | | | | | | | | | | ● |

Progress Test 5: Administer test (Teacher Resource, pages 154–157) then address weaknesses.

| Page | Unit | Title | Strand | Number / algebra | Measurement / 00space | Statistics / probability | Content area | Numbers | Addition / subtraction | Sharing / grouping | Patterns | 2D shapes / 3D objects | Length / area / mass | Capacity / volume | Time / duration | Position | Data displays / chance |
|---|---|---|---|---|---|---|---|---|---|---|---|---|---|---|---|---|---|
| 129 | 32D | Following directions | | | ■ | | | | | | | | | | | ● | |
| 130 | 33A | Gather and organise data | | | | ■ | | | | | | | | | | | ● |

| Page |  | |
|---|---|---|
| 131 | Identifying and addressing areas of need | |
| 133 | **BLMs 1** Number lines/charts | **2** Number bond houses |
| 135 | **3** Number bonds (addition) | **4** Addition and subtraction facts |

# Contents cross-reference

## Number and algebra

## Measurement and space

| 1 | Geometric measure | Pages |
|---|---|---|
| | Position: Describing position | 16, 17, 109, 125 |
| | Giving and following directions | 109, 125, 129 |
| | Ordinal numbers | 39, 75, 99, 105 |
| | Left and right | 16, 17, 125 |
| | Length: Describing and comparing lengths | 32, 33, 40, 41, 89, 92 |
| | Using units of length | 40, 41 |
| | Halves and quarters | 89, 92, 102, 103 |
| **2** | **Two-dimensional spatial structure** | **Pages** |
| | 2D shapes: Sorting, describing and making shapes | 5, 52, 72, 100, 101 |
| | Circle, triangle, square, rectangle, quadrilateral, hexagon, pentagon, octagon | 5, 52, 72, 100, 101 |
| | Symmetry, reflecting, sliding | 93, 121, 123 |
| | Area: Describing and comparing areas | 73, 112, 113 |
| **3** | **Three-dimensional spatial structure** | **Pages** |
| | 3D objects: Describing and sorting 3D objects | 9, 28, 29, 68, 69, 108 |
| | Volume: Describing and comparing volumes | 84, 85, 88, 108 |
| | Comparing internal volumes (capacity) | 44, 45, 49 |
| | Stacking, packing and building to compare volumes | 88, 108 |
| **4** | **Non-spatial measure** | **Pages** |
| | Mass: Describing and comparing the weight of objects | 56, 57, 117 |
| | Time: Describing, comparing, sequencing time, calendar | 12, 21, 36, 104, 105 |
| | Months and seasons | 64, 65, 96, 104, 105 |
| | Telling time on the hour and half-hour using analog and digital clocks | 12, 13, 20, 21, 36, 37 |

## Statistics and probability

| 1 | Data | Pages |
|---|---|---|
| | Collecting information | 33, 61, 97, 130 |
| | Using data displays | 25, 53, 61, 97, 120 |
| **2** | **Chance** | **Pages** |
| | Identify, describe possible outcomes | 81, 128 |

# 1 Dictionary

### adding (plus or combine)

When we join groups of objects together, we are adding them together.

### adding on

If we add 5 and 3 we count on from 5, (e.g. 5... 6, 7, 8) 5 and 3 make 8.

### area

Area is the amount of space on a shape.

### capacity

Capacity is the amount that a container can hold.

### centimetre

A unit of length.
This red line is 1 cm long.

- 100 cm = 1 m

### cents (c)

Our money system is made up of cents and dollars. 100 cents (100c) makes 1 dollar ($1).

The silver coins are 5 cents, 10 cents, 20 cents and 50 cents.

### chance

The possibility of something happening:

- possible: can happen
- might happen: can happen
- likely: will probably happen
- unlikely: will probably not happen
- more likely: compared to another event, this has more chance of happening.

### coins

5c

10c

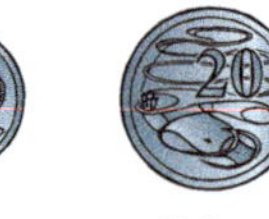
20c

50c

$1

$2

### collection

A collection is a group of objects.

### column

A column is a line of objects going down. Here are 4 columns of 3.

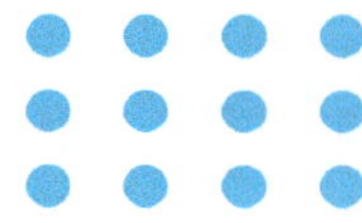

### corner

A corner is where sides or edges meet at a point.

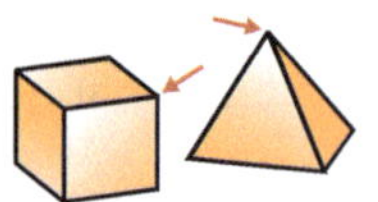

### curved line

A curved line is not straight.

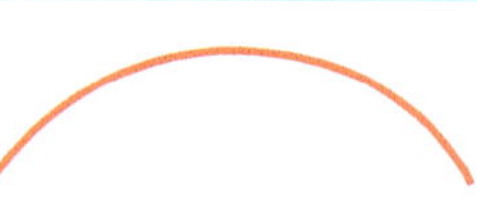

### curved surface

A curved surface on a 3D object is not flat. It allows an object to roll. A cylinder and a cone each have one curved surface.

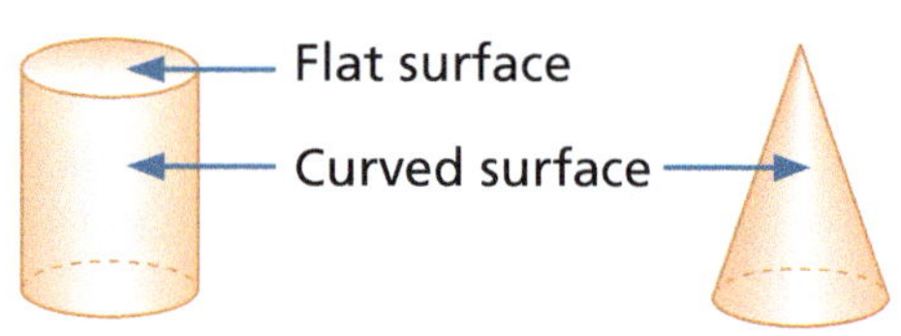


### data display

A data display shows categories of objects and allows us to compare them.

**Graph:** Cats, Dogs

**Table:**

| Dogs | Cats |
| --- | --- |
| 4 | 2 |

### difference

How many more?

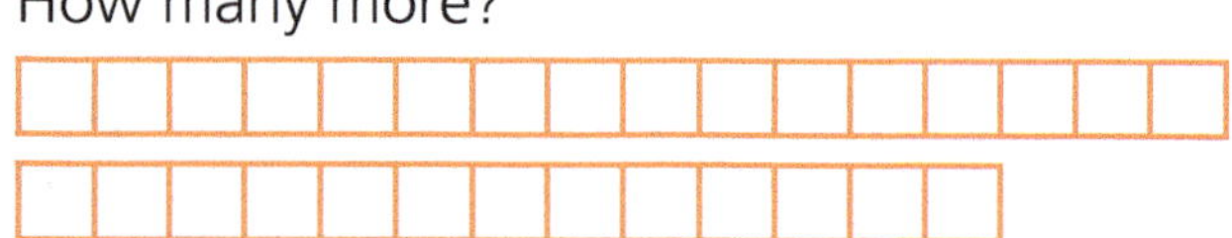

**The difference between 16 and 13 is 3.**

For smaller numbers, line up each group in a row to find the difference.

For larger numbers, place the numbers on a number line to find the difference.

## dollars ($)

Our money system is made up of cents and dollars.

100 cents (100c) makes 1 dollar ($1).

The gold coins are $1 (1 dollar) and $2 (2 dollars).

The notes are $5, $10, $20, $50, $100.

## double

Double means the same thing twice.

Double 4 means 4 + 4 = 8

## edge

An edge is where two faces of a 3D object meet.

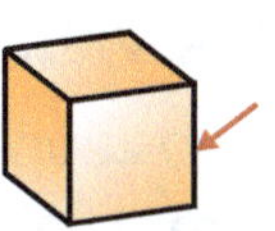

## equal groups

Groups that have the same number of members.

## equals sign =

The equals sign means "makes" or "is equal to" or "is the same as" (e.g. 2 + 3 = 4 + 1).

## estimate

A good guess.

## face

A flat surface that has straight sides (e.g. the side of a box).

## flat surface

A face on a 3D object.
It is not curved.
It allows an object to slide.

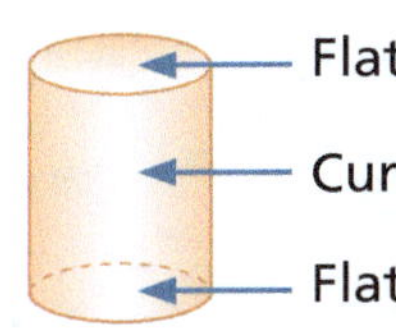


A cylinder has 2 flat surfaces, one on each end, and one curved surface.

## friends of ten

Numbers that add together to make 10.
The friends of 10 are 1 and 9, 2 and 8, 3 and 7, 4 and 6, 5 and 5, 6 and 4, 7 and 3, 8 and 2, 9 and 1.

## graph

See *data display*.

## half

One of two equal parts.

One half of the rectangle is coloured.

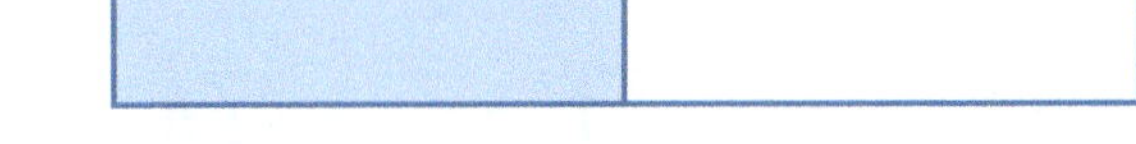

## halfway point

The halfway point is the middle position.

## hefting

To compare masses by lifting them with your hands.

## left and right

Left 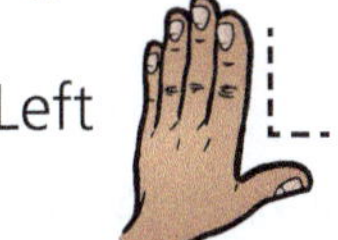 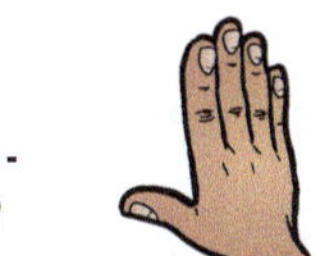 Right

The left hand makes an "L" for left.

## length words

| distance | long | tall |
|---|---|---|
| deeper | longer | taller |
| higher | short | thicker |
| lower | shorter | thinner |

## mass words

| heavy | light | weigh |
|---|---|---|
| heavier | lighter | weight |
| heaviest | lightest | balanced |

## notes

## number bonds

Pairs of numbers that add to make a specific number (e.g. 0 and 4, 1 and 3, and 2 and 2 all make 4).

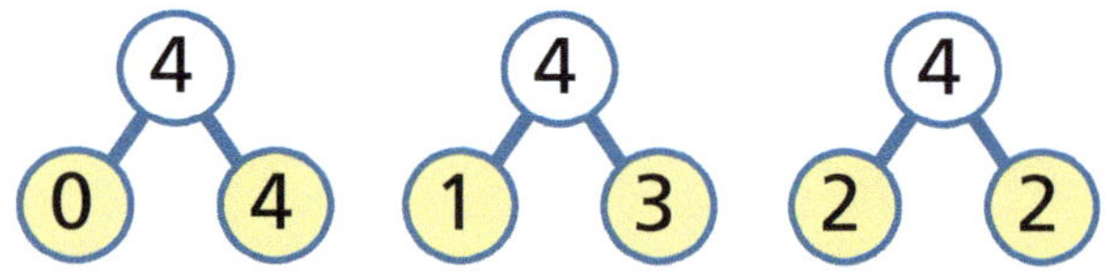


## number line

A number line is a line that shows numbers in order. Number lines can be used for many things (e.g. counting, adding and subtracting).

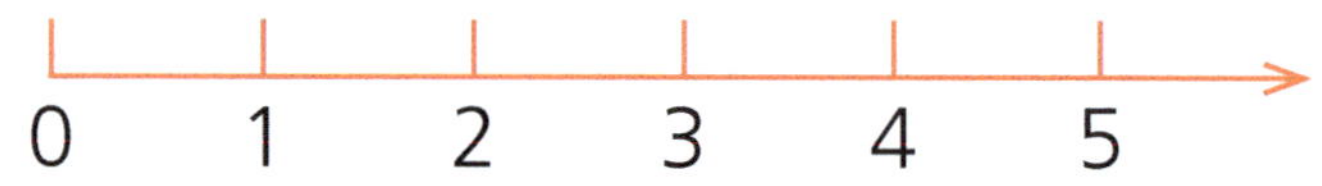


## number sentence

A number sentence uses numerals and symbols (e.g. 4 and 6 makes 10. This can be written as 4 + 6 = 10).

## numeral

A numeral is a written number symbol such as 7, 18, 92, 120.

## odd and even numbers

Odd numbers end in 1, 3, 5, 7 or 9 (e.g. 49).

Even numbers end in 2, 4, 6, 8 or 0 (e.g. 32).

## ordinal number

Ordinal numbers describe the order or position of something (e.g. 1st, 2nd, 3rd, 4th, 5th).

## partitioning

Partitioning is when a group of objects is broken up into two parts. The more objects there are in the group, the more different combinations can be made.

(e.g. The number 8 can be partitioned as 7 and 1, 6 and 2, 5 and 3, and 4 and 4.)

## pattern

A pattern is a group of numbers, objects, shapes, colours, sounds or actions that are repeated over and over again.

## place value

The position of each digit of a numeral holds a different value.

## place-value blocks

These are used to represent numbers.

ones block

tens block

hundreds block

42 shown as

113 shown as

## quarter

One of four equal parts.

One quarter of the rectangle is coloured.

### reflection (or flip)

A mirror image.

### right and left

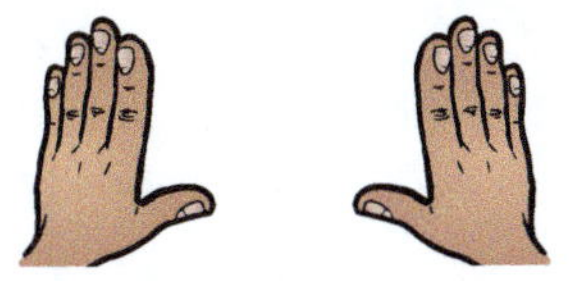

- Left
- Right

### row

A row is a line of objects going across. Here are 2 rows of 5.

### sharing

When sharing, we make sure that each share is the same size.

2 people could share these 6 balls. Each person would get 3 balls.
If two groups are not the same, we can make fair shares by moving items from the larger group to the smaller group.

### slide

Moving a shape in any direction without changing the size or orientation.

### straight line

A straight line has no bends or curves.

### symmetry

A shape has symmetry when one side is the mirror-image of the other. It can be folded so that the two halves match, exactly.

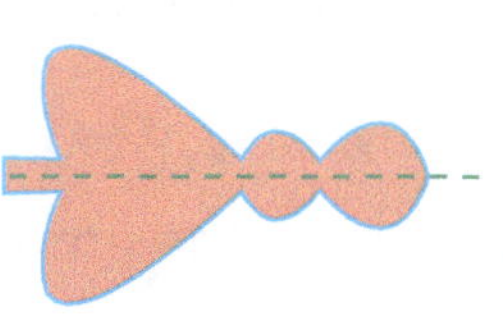

### take away (subtract or minus)

When we remove objects from a group we call this "take away".

### tally marks

Tally marks are used to keep count. Groups of 5 are used.

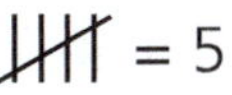


### three-dimensional (3D) objects

3D objects are three-dimensional. They have length, width and height.

spheres (ball-shaped objects) are curved and round. They can roll.

cubes (box-shaped objects) have 6 square faces. They can slide.

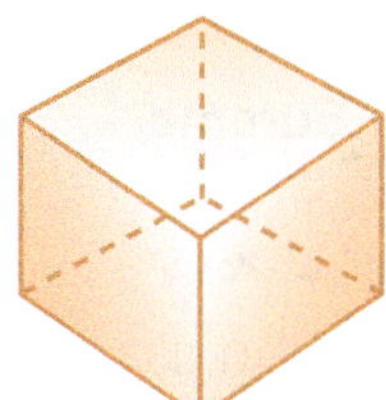

cylinders (can-shaped objects) have 2 flat surfaces and 1 curved surface. They can roll and slide.

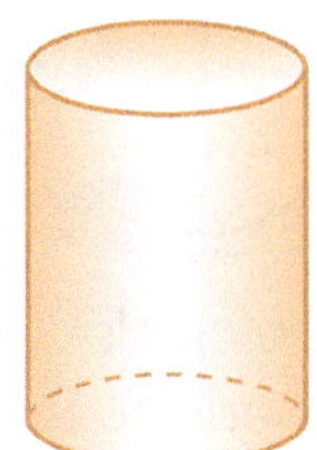

cones (cone-shaped objects) have 1 flat surface and 1 curved surface. They can roll and slide.

prisms

A prism has rectangular faces joining two identical bases at both ends.

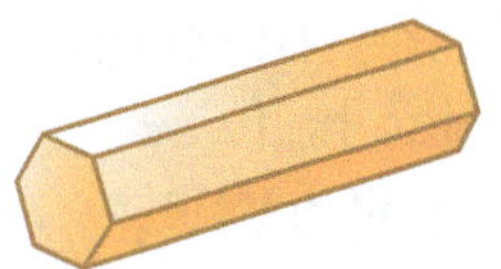

hexagonal prism

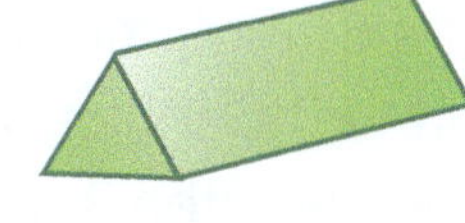

triangular prism

## time words

| morning | | day | |
|---|---|---|---|
| afternoon | | night | |
| **Days** | | | |
| Sunday | Monday | Tuesday | Wednesday |
| Thursday | Friday | Saturday | |
| **Months** | | | |
| January | February | March | April |
| May | June | July | August |
| September | October | November | December |
| **Seasons** | | | |
| Summer | Autumn | Winter | Spring |

- clocks

analog clock digital clock

3 o'clock

- o'clock

When the long hand (minute hand) is pointing to 12, the time is an "o'clock" time. The short hand (hour hand) points to the hour (e.g. the hour hand above is pointing to the 3 so it is 3 o'clock).

half past 3

- half past

When the long hand (hour hand) is pointing to the 6, the time is a "half past" time. The short hand (hour hand) above is pointing halfway between the 3 and the 4 so it is half past 3.

## total

The number of items altogether. The result once everything has been added.

## two-dimensional (2D) shapes

Flat shapes are two-dimensional.
They have length and width.

circle
1 curved side

triangle
3 sides
3 corners

square
4 equal sides
4 corners

rectangle
2 equal long sides and 2 equal short sides, like a stretched square

oval
1 curved side, like a squashed circle

pentagon
5 sides
5 corners

hexagon
6 sides
6 corners

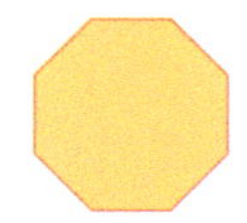

octagon
8 sides
8 corners

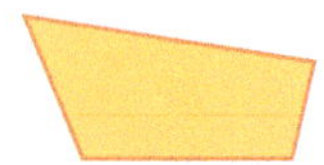

quadrilaterals
4 sides and 4 corners. Squares and rectangles are quadrilaterals.

## vertex (plural is vertices)

A corner of a shape or object.

## volume

Volume is the amount of space an object takes up.

# The mouse and the platypus

1. How many animals are in this picture?
2. What else can you count in this picture?
3. What are the mouse and the platypus doing?
4. The mouse is going to make a hat for its costume. Why should the mouse's hat have no ears?
5. Would it take longer for the mouse to make its hat or its tail?
6. How many noses can you see in this picture?
7. A snout is the nose and mouth of an animal. Would it take longer for the platypus to make the ears or the snout?
8. How are the mouse and the platypus different?
9. Make up your own question about this picture.
10. Which of these questions do you like best? Why do you like it?

 • *AUSTRALIAN SIGNPOST MATHS NSW 1* • ISBN 9780655709022

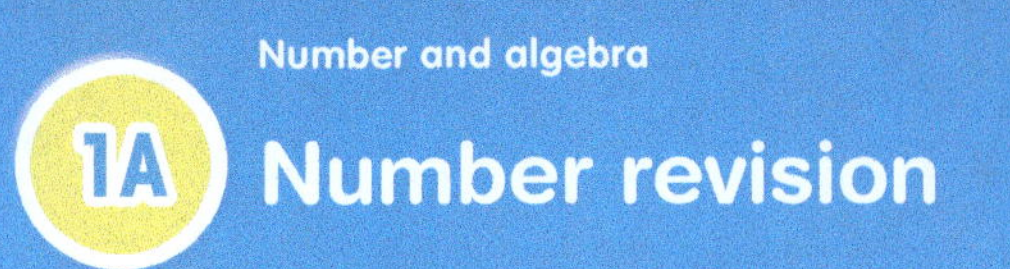

# 1A Number revision

1 Write the numeral and its name. Draw the number of balls.

| | | | | |
|---|---|---|---|---|
| 1 | | | one |  |
| 2 | | | | |
| 3 | | | | |
| 4 | | | | |
| 5 | | | | |

FUN SPOT

Match each word to a numeral on the number track.

one zero three two five four

This is a number track.

| | | | | | |
|---|---|---|---|---|---|
| | | | | | |
| 0 | 1 | 2 | 3 | 4 | 5 |

# 1B Number revision

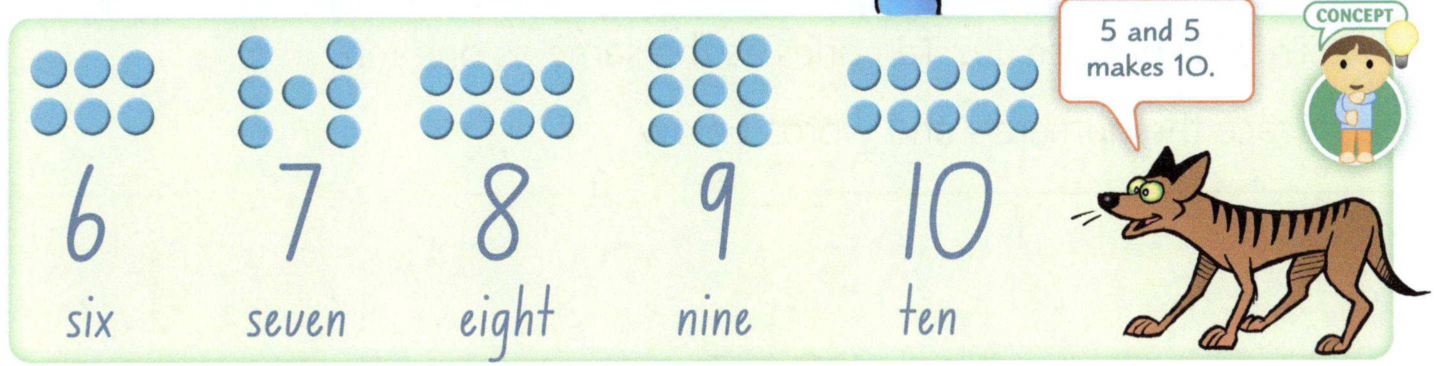


1 Write the numeral and its name. Draw the number of hats.

| 6 | | | six |  |
|---|---|---|---|---|
| 7 | | | | |
| 8 | | | | |
| 9 | | | | |
| 10 | | | | |

Match each word to a numeral on the number track.

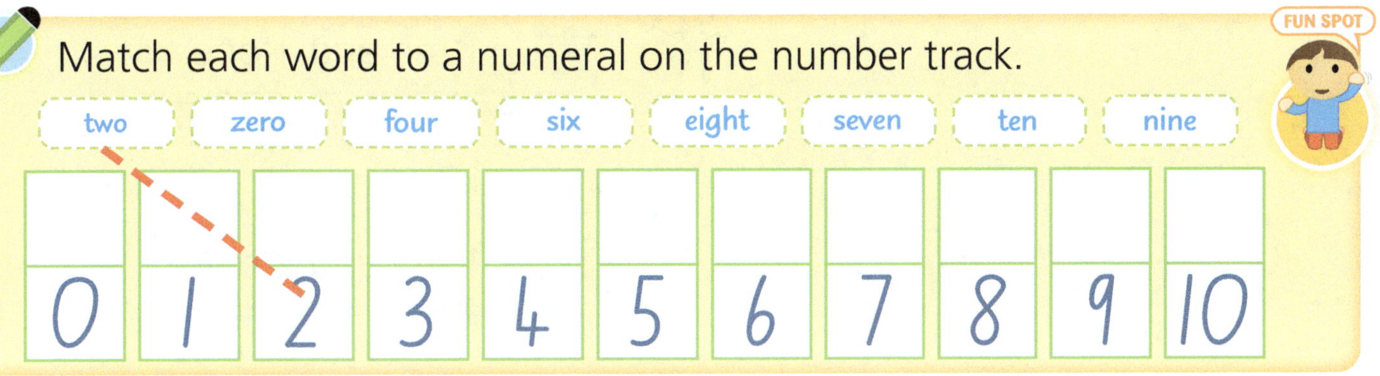


© PEARSON AUSTRALIA 2023 • *AUSTRALIAN SIGNPOST MATHS NSW 1* • ISBN 9780655709022

# 1C Numbers to 20

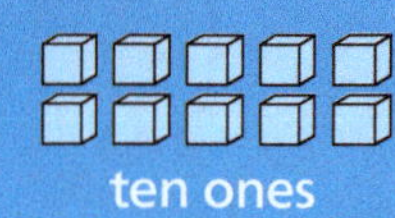

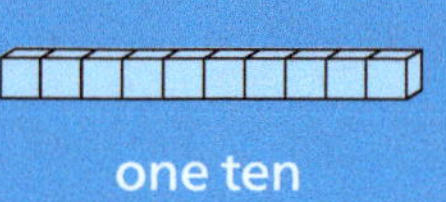

1. True (T) or False (F)? Ten ones as the same as one ten. ☐

2. Trace the numerals and words below.

3. Count and write the number of objects.

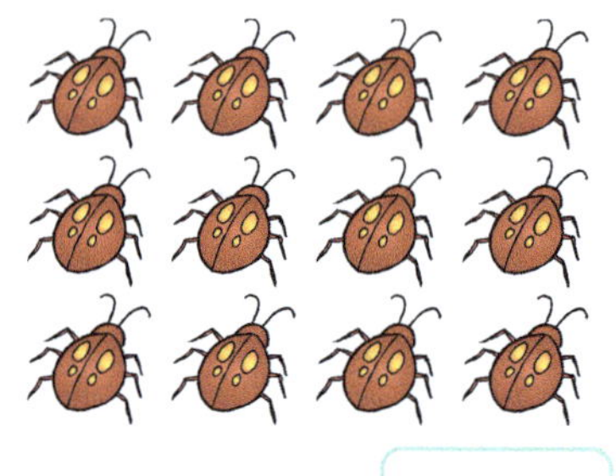

4. Count forwards and backwards. Colour every second number. Discuss.

| 1 | 2 | 3 | 4 | 5 | 6 | 7 | 8 | 9 | 10 |
|---|---|---|---|---|---|---|---|---|---|
| 11 | 12 | 13 | 14 | 15 | 16 | 17 | 18 | 19 | 20 |

5. Trace and write the numerals.

6. How many blocks?

1 ten and 0 ones ☐

1 ten and 1 one ☐

1 ten and 2 ones ☐



 • *AUSTRALIAN SIGNPOST MATHS NSW 1* • ISBN 9780655709022

# 1D Shapes and patterns

two shape (CT, CT)

three shapes (SCT, SCT)

1 Colour the shapes in the picture:

SCT means 'square, circle, triangle'.

red

yellow

green

blue

How many circles?

How many squares?

How many triangles?

How many rectangles?

two-shape pattern:
Code: SC, SC, SC ...

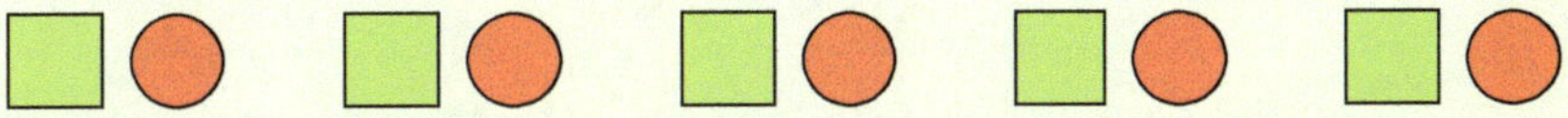

three-shape pattern:
Code: RST, RST ...

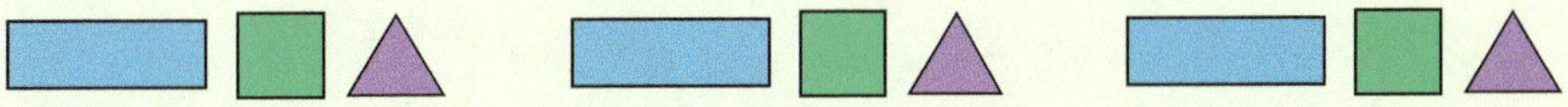

2 Draw a two-shape pattern and a three-shape pattern of your own.

 • *AUSTRALIAN SIGNPOST MATHS NSW 1* • ISBN 9780655709022

# 2A Adding two groups

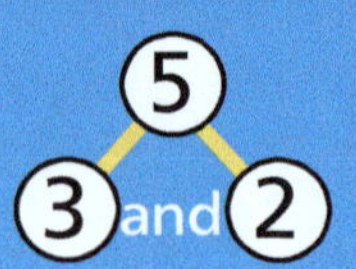

1 a  [4] and [ ] makes [ ].

b [ ] and [ ] makes [ ].

c [ ] and [ ] makes [ ].

d [ ] and [ ] makes [ ].

e [ ] and [ ] makes [ ].

2 Draw your own picture to complete the problem.

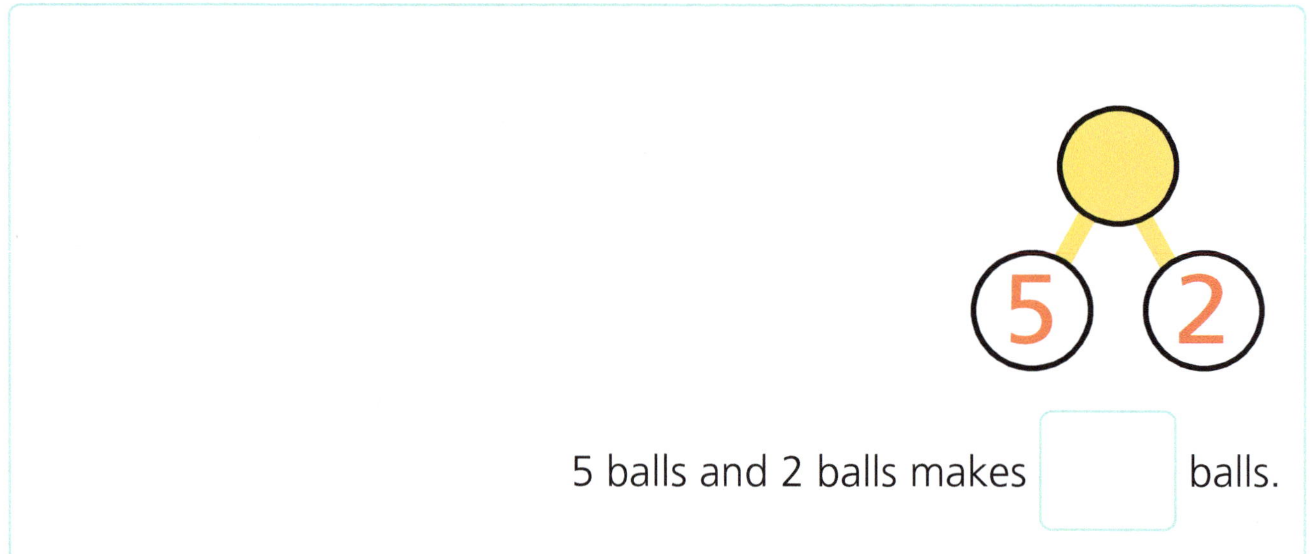


5 balls and 2 balls makes [ ] balls.

3 Write your own number sentence to solve the problem.

How many blocks?

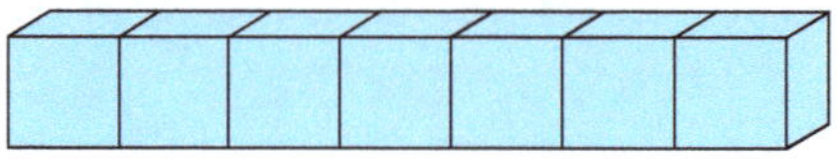

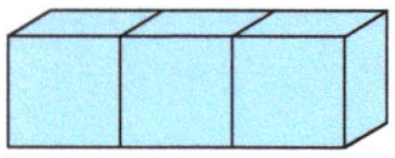

# Addition sentences

1 Complete the number sentences.

a   ☐ + ☐ = ☐

b   ☐ + ☐ = ☐

c   ☐ + ☐ = ☐

d   ☐ + ☐ = ☐

ACTIVITY

Make your own number sentence and number bond.

☐ + ☐ = ☐

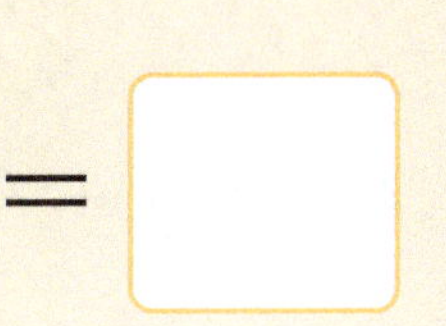

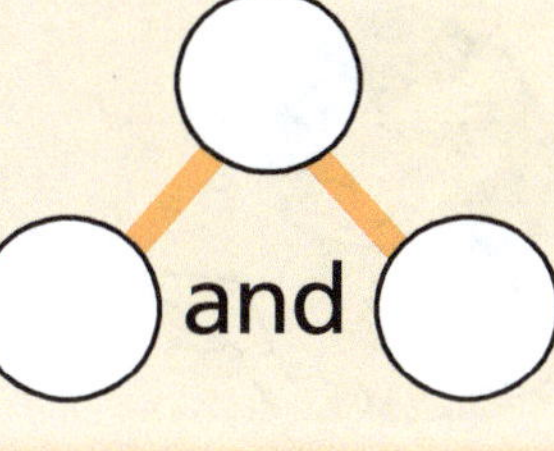

# 2C Combinations up to 10

1 Numbers can make patterns. Use the faces to find answers. Talk about patterns you can see.

1 and 8 makes ______.

2 and 7 makes ______.

3 and 6 makes ______.

4 and 5 makes ______.

5 and 4 makes ______.

6 and 3 makes ______.

7 and 2 makes ______.

8 and 1 makes ______.

Add each row.

| 10 | | Answer |
|---|---|---|
| 1 | 9 | |
| 2 | 8 | |
| 3 | 7 | |
| 4 | 6 | |
| 5 | 5 | |
| 6 | 4 | |
| 7 | 3 | |
| 8 | 2 | |
| 9 | 1 | |

INVESTIGATION

Use counters to make patterns of your own for 6 and 5.

4 = 1 + 3 →
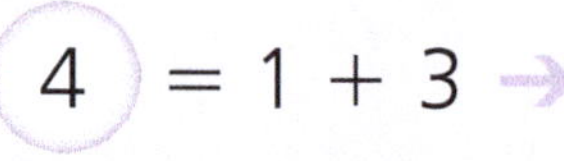
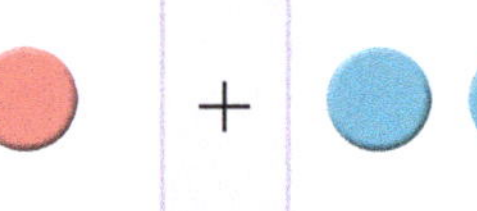

4 = 2 + 2 →

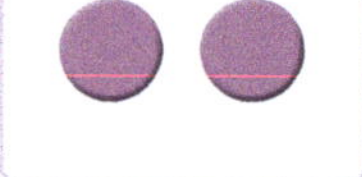

4 = 3 + 1 →

 ISBN 9780655709022

# Identifying objects

1 Colour the picture, then count all the objects like these.

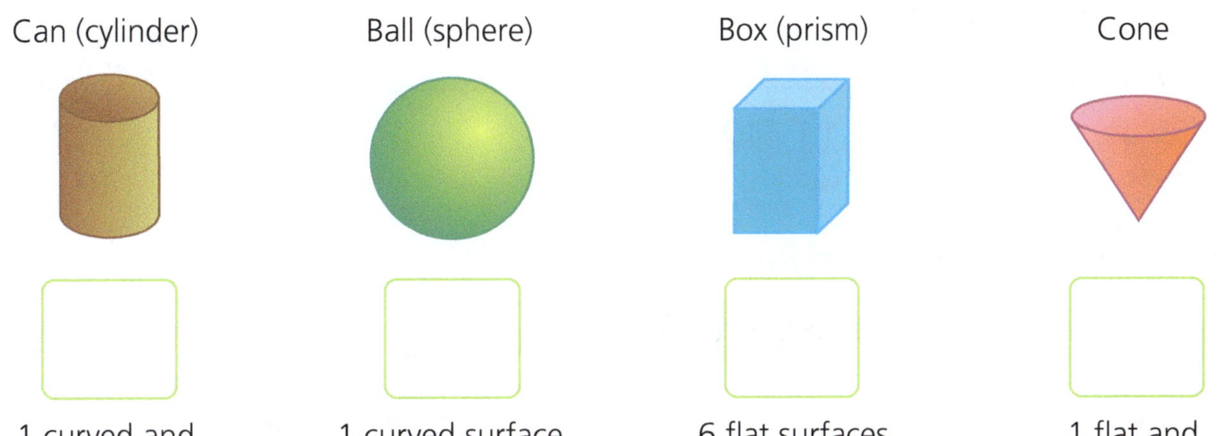

| Can (cylinder) | Ball (sphere) | Box (prism) | Cone |
|---|---|---|---|
| 1 curved and two flat surfaces | 1 curved surface | 6 flat surfaces | 1 flat and 1 curved surface |

 • *AUSTRALIAN SIGNPOST MATHS NSW 1* • ISBN 9780655709022

# 3A Numbers 11 to 20

CONCEPT

We can make larger numbers by counting on from 10.

...11, 12, 13, 14

1 Count the objects and complete.

10 and 3 is ☐.

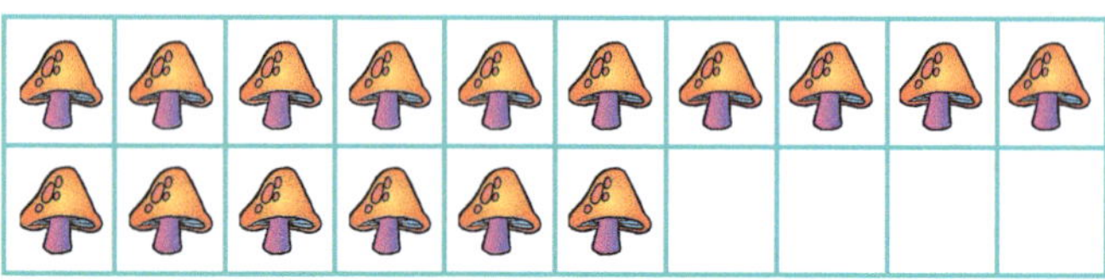

10 and 6 is ☐.

10 and 9 is ☐.

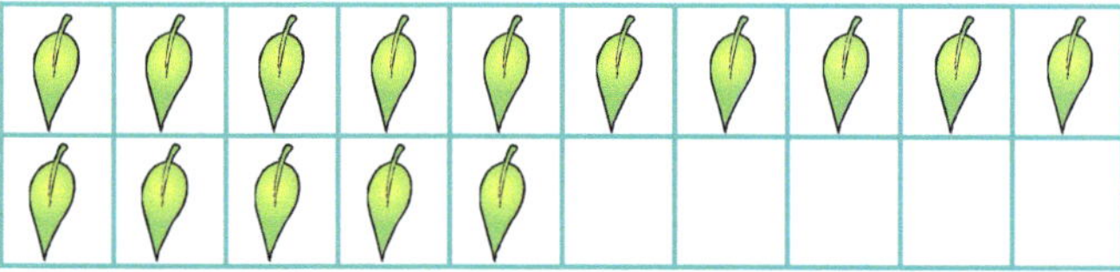

10 and 5 is ☐.

2 10 and 1 is ☐.

10 and 2 is ☐.

10 and 4 is ☐.

10 and 7 is ☐.

10 and 8 is ☐.

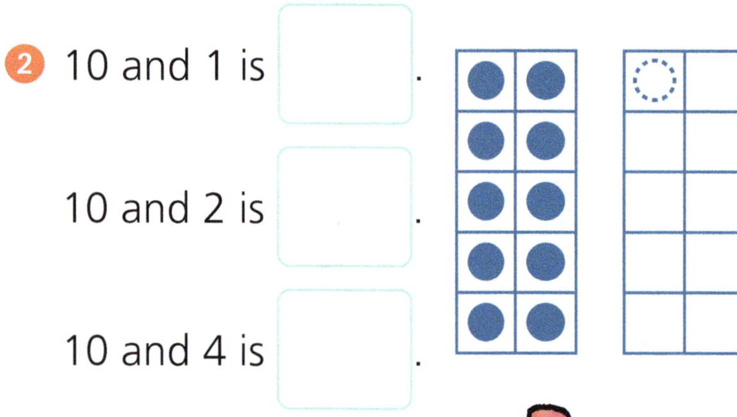

INVESTIGATION

Circle groups of 10.

☐ tens is ☐.



 • *AUSTRALIAN SIGNPOST MATHS NSW 1* • ISBN 9780655709022

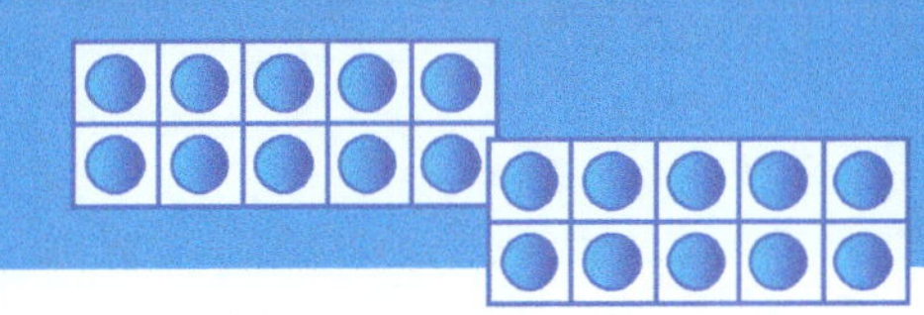

1 Write the missing numbers. Count forwards and backwards to 20.

| | | | | | | | | | |
|---|---|---|---|---|---|---|---|---|---|
| 1 | 2 | 3 | | | | 7 | | | |
| | 12 | | | 15 | | | 18 | | 20 |

2 Use place-value blocks to find:

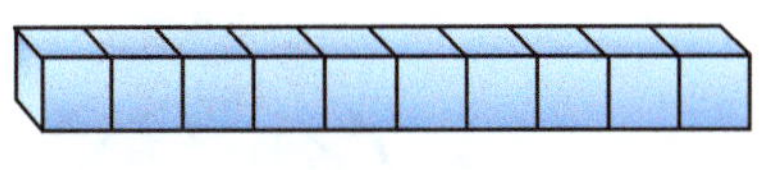
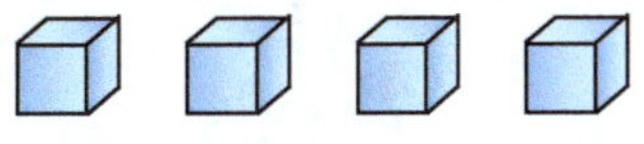
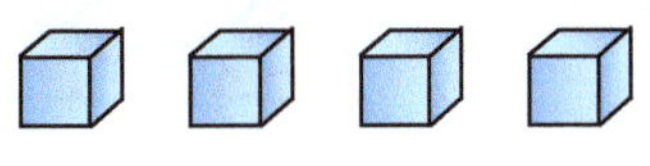

10 and 8 is ☐.
10 and 4 is ☐.
10 and 5 is ☐.
10 and 1 is ☐.
10 and 3 is ☐.
10 and 7 is ☐.
10 and 6 is ☐.
10 and 2 is ☐.

3 Write the numbers before (one less then) and after (one more than).

| | | | | | | | |
|---|---|---|---|---|---|---|---|
| a | | 20 | | b | | 13 | |
| c | | 14 | | d | | 17 | |
| e | | 18 | | f | | 19 | |

Two spiders. How many legs altogether? ☐

 • *AUSTRALIAN SIGNPOST MATHS NSW 1* • ISBN 9780655709022

# 3C Analog time

The minute hand points to 12.

## 1 Read each time. Complete the labels.

a 

b 

c 

d

☐ o'clock  o'clock

## 2 Show the time.

a 
7 o'clock

b 
5 o'clock

c 
2 o'clock

d 
9 o'clock

## 3 Match each picture with the best time.

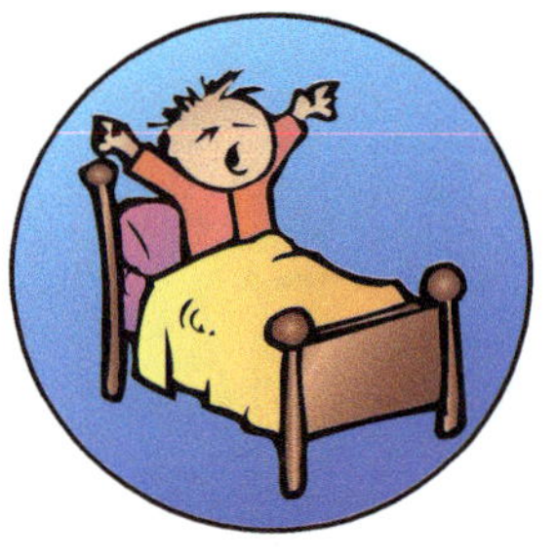

8 o'clock

10 o'clock

7 o'clock

4 o'clock

9 o'clock

12 o'clock

5 o'clock

6 o'clock

# Digital and analog time

o'clock times end in :00

1 Write the time shown.

2 Show the analog time.

a 3 o'clock

b 7 o'clock

c 1 o'clock

d 10 o'clock

e 11 o'clock

f 5 o'clock

g 9 o'clock

h 2 o'clock

# 4A Numbers to 20

1 Write the numerals 11 to 19 in order. Match each numeral to its name.

thirteen fourteen seventeen eighteen

| | | | | | | | | | 20 |
|---|---|---|---|---|---|---|---|---|---|

twelve fifteen eleven sixteen nineteen

2 a Trace and order these numbers from smallest to largest.

16 11 19 13

b one more than 16 one less than 20 one less than 18

3 10 and 3 is ___.

10 and 6 is ___.

10 and 8 is ___.

10 and 9 is ___.

4 Guess how many marbles are in each bag. Circle the largest group.

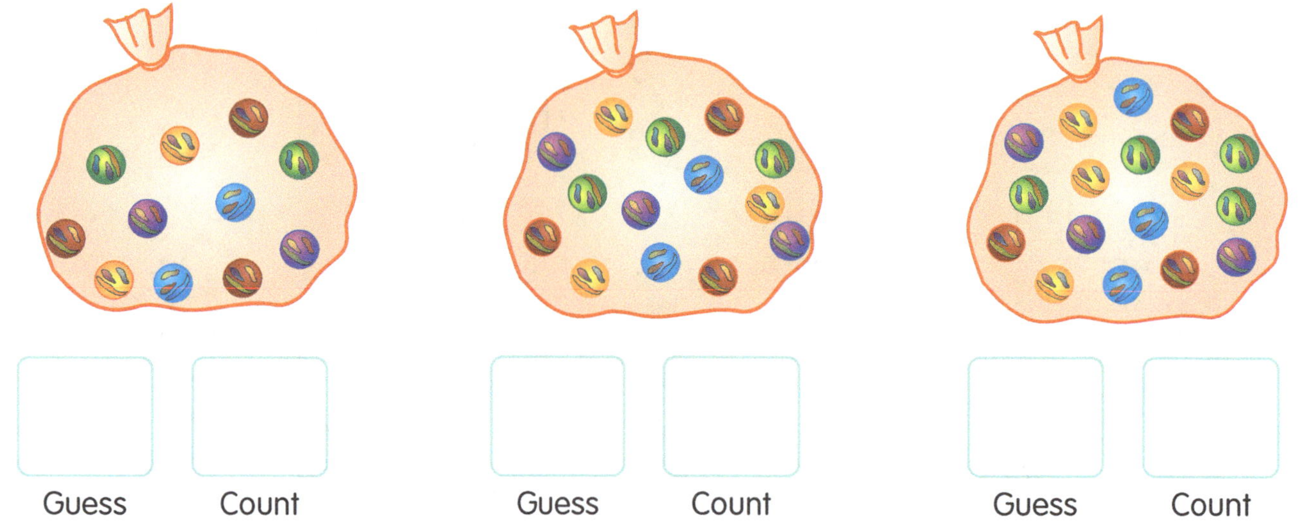

Guess Count Guess Count Guess Count

# 4B Friends of 10

1 Add dots so that each has a total of 10.

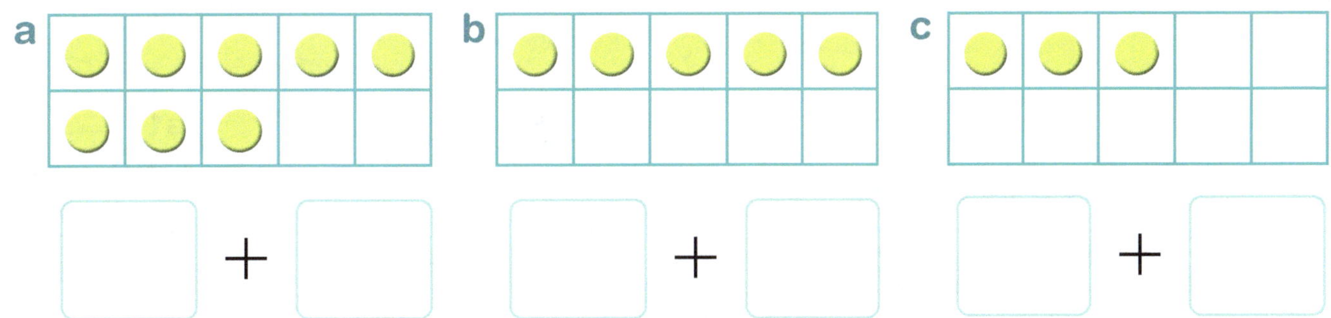


2 Use 10 counters. Find 9 ways we can add the counters to make 10.

3 Write True (T) or False (F).

a 3 + 7 = 9 + 1

b 2 + 8 = 8 + 2

- Match two sets of number cards 0 to 10 to make pairs of numbers that add up to 10. How many matches did you make?

# 4C Position language

- The triangle is on the left.
- The square is on the right.
- The circle is between the triangle and the square.

1. Use the picture to answer these questions. Choose the correct position word.

| Position words | |
|---|---|
| next to | towards |
| above | between |
| left | right |
| in front of | |

a The bucket is ______ the sandcastle.

b The cloud is ______ the water.

c The girl is on the ______ of the picture.

d The flag is on the ______ of the picture.

e The girl is walking ______ the flag.

f The sandcastle is ______ the bucket and the flag.

2. Circle the correct answer (from the boy's point of view):

a The ball is on the boy's left / right.

b The bird is on the boy's left / right.

# 4D Position language

1. Look at the picture and circle the correct words in each sentence.

   a. The caterpillar is crawling along / beneath the stick.
   b. The mouse is above / below the hawk.
   c. The house is between / inside the hills.
   d. The hills are far from / close to the tree.
   e. The car is in front of / behind the house.
   f. The ant is under / over the tree.
   g. The kookaburra is perched on / over the branch.
   h. The girl is to the right / left of the pram.
   i. The bat is hanging upside down / right side up.

2. Where would the girl go to take the apples into the house?

   → Talk about this.

3. In this picture, draw:

   a. a fork on the left of the plate
   b. a knife on the right of the plate
   c. a star in the centre of the window
   d. a book on a corner of the table
   e. a bottle on the edge of the table
   f. a picture above the clock

   How would you set this table for dinner?

 ISBN 9780655709022

# 5A Addition facts

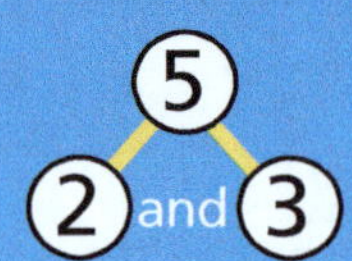

1 Complete. You can use two dice to practise addition.

a

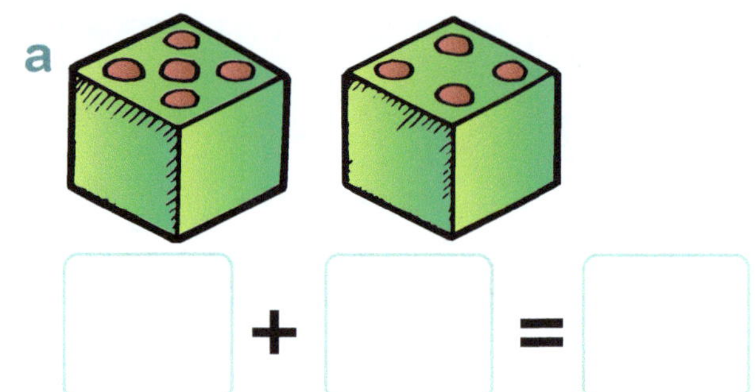

☐ + ☐ = ☐

b

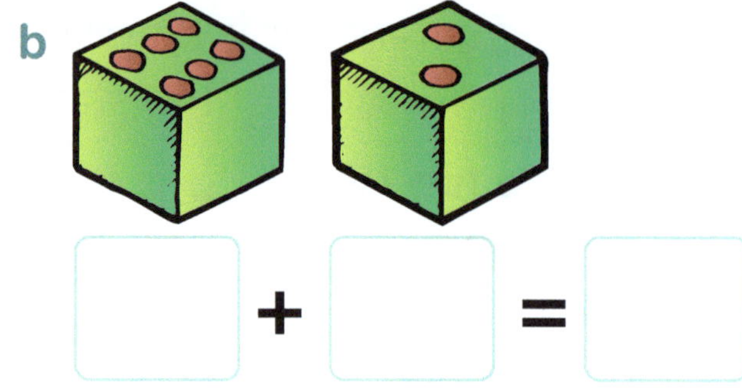

☐ + ☐ = ☐

2

a 6 + 2 = ☐

b 8 + 0 = ☐

c 3 + 7 = ☐

d 0 + 10 = ☐

e 4 + 5 = ☐

f 1 + 6 = ☐

3 Match:

| | | |
|---|---|---|
| 4 + 3 | 5 | 3 + 2 |
| 2 + 3 | 6 | 3 + 4 |
| 5 + 1 | 7 | 1 + 5 |
| 8 + 2 | 8 | 7 + 2 |
| 2 + 7 | 9 | 3 + 5 |
| 5 + 3 | 10 | 2 + 8 |

4 4 dogs, 3 cats, 2 mice. How many animals?

☐ + ☐ + ☐ = ☐

Learn addition facts to 10.



© PEARSON AUSTRALIA 2023 • *AUSTRALIAN SIGNPOST MATHS NSW 1* • ISBN 9780655709022

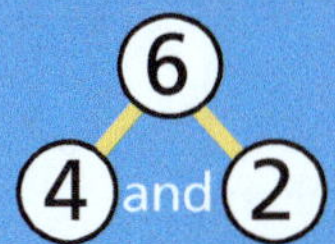

CONCEPT

4 + 2 = 6

We can find a different sum by moving the dotted lines.

1

☐ + 6 = 7

2 + ☐ = 7

3 + 4 = ☐

4 + ☐ = 7

☐ + 2 = 7

6 + ☐ = 7

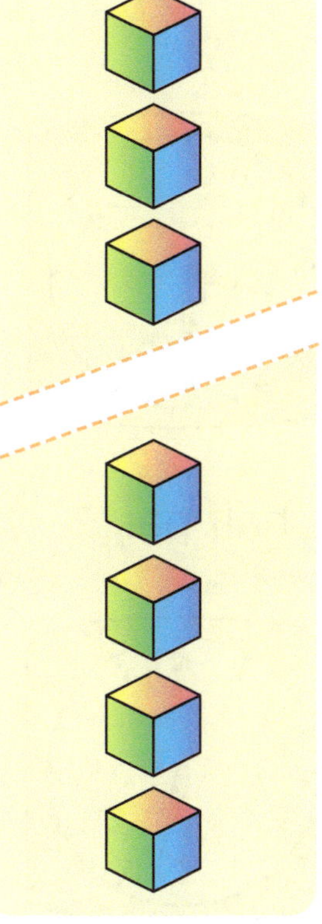

3 + 4

2 The numbers in each row add up to 6.

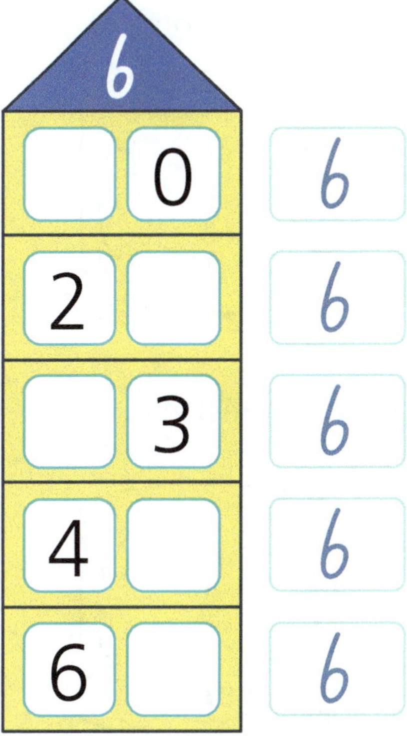


INVESTIGATION

- Using counters, make up your own partitioning patterns for 10, 9, 8 and 5.

1 + 2 = 3 →  +  =

2 + 1 = 3 → + = 

# 5C Half past

The minute hand is halfway around the clock face.

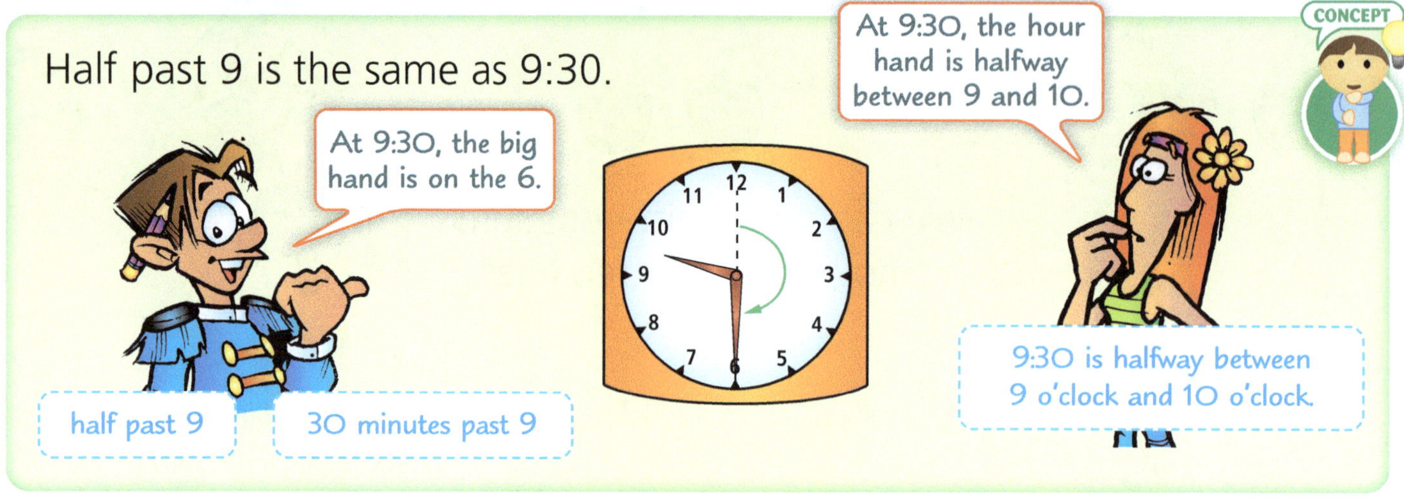


1 Write the times shown.

a half past ☐

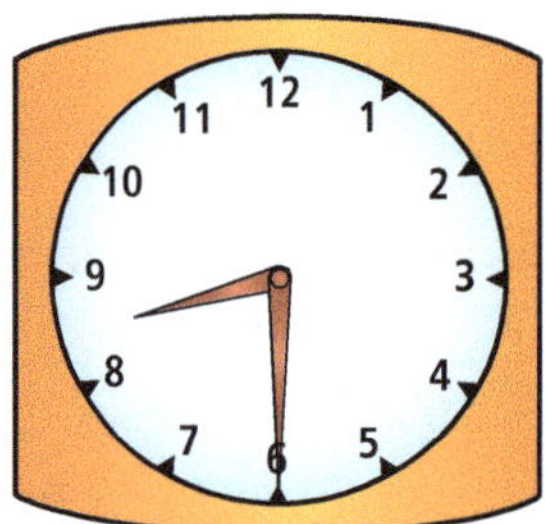

b half past ☐

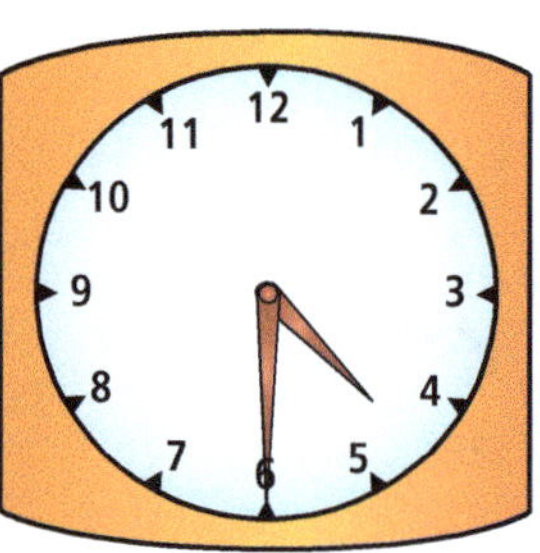

c half past ☐

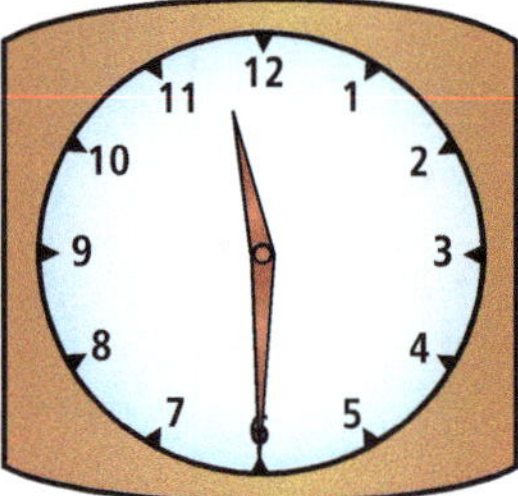

d half past ☐

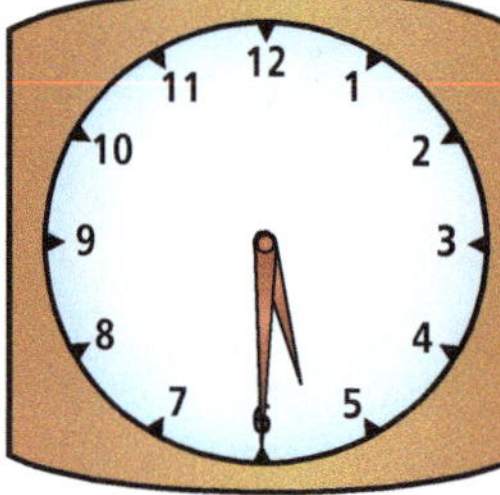

e half past ☐

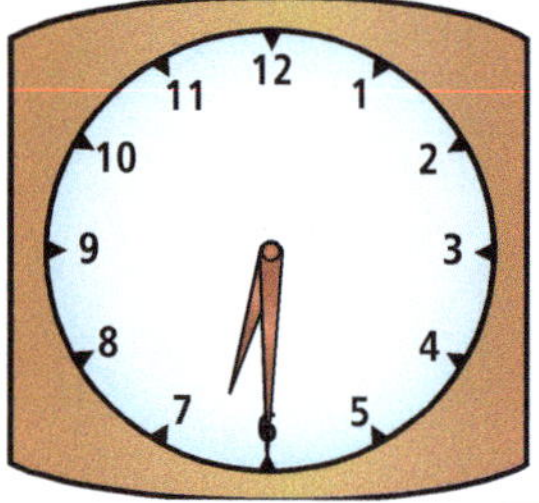

f half past ☐

2 Show these times.

a half past 3

b 10 thirty

c 30 minutes past 1

# Half past

30 minutes past 2,
half past 2,
two thirty

half past 2

On digital clocks, **half past** times always have **30** as the last two digits.

60 minutes = 1 hour

30 minutes = half an hour

1. Read the time. Complete the label.

a

half past ☐

b 11:30

half past ☐

c

☐ thirty

d

30 minutes past ☐

e 1:30

30 minutes past ☐

f

☐ thirty

2. Write the digital time for each.

a half past 3 ☐

b half past 5 ☐

3. a How many minutes are in an hour? 

b How many minutes from 10:00 till 11:00? 

c How many minutes are in half an hour? 

d How many minutes from 7:00 till 7:30? ☐

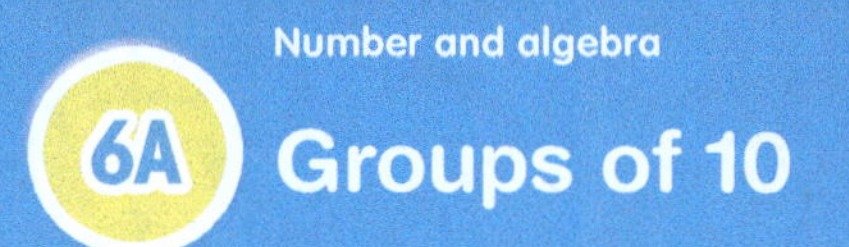

# 6A Groups of 10

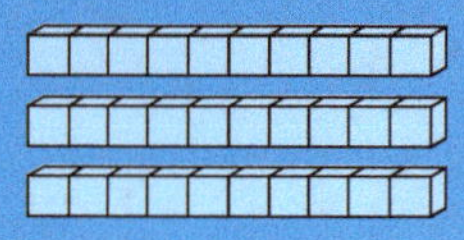

CONCEPT

| 10 | 20 | 30 | 40 | 50 | 60 | 70 | 80 | 90 | 100 |
|---|---|---|---|---|---|---|---|---|---|
| ten | twenty | thirty | forty | fifty | sixty | seventy | eighty | ninety | one hundred |

Practise counting by tens.

This is 8 groups of ten.
There are 80 pencils.

1 Count the groups of ten.

a  ☐ tens

b 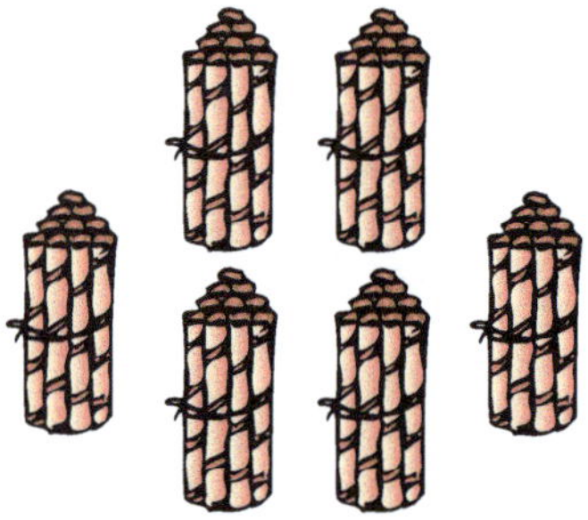 ☐ tens

c  ☐ tens

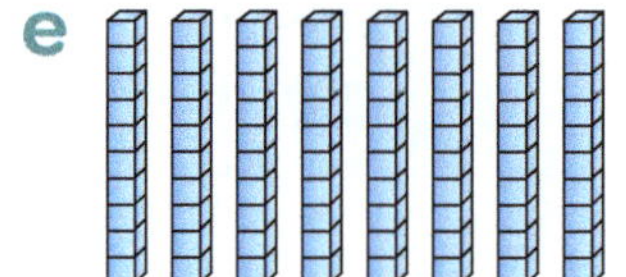

d  ☐ tens

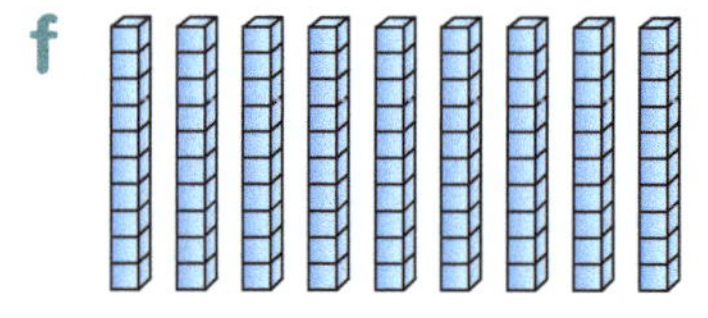

e ☐ tens

f ☐ tens

2 Circle groups of ten.

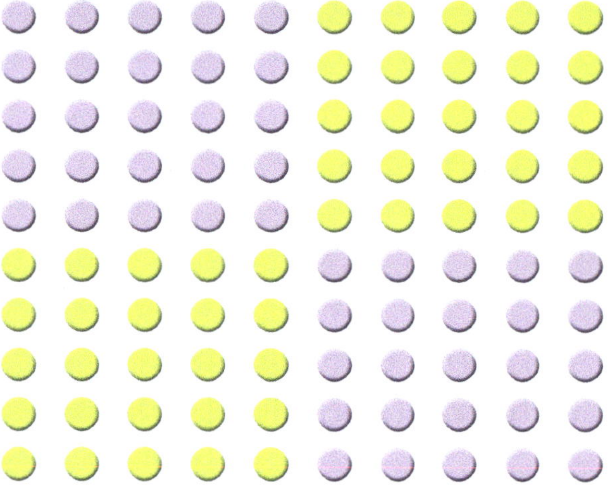

☐ tens

Talk about your answer.

3 Estimate then count.

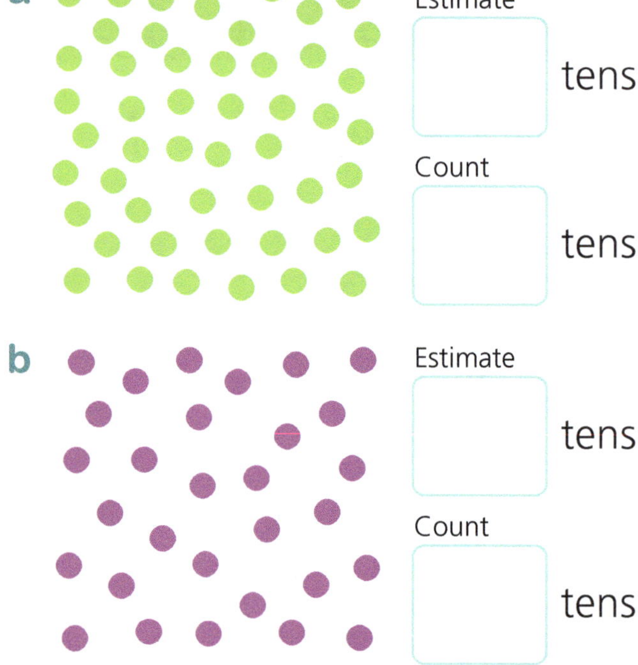

a
Estimate ☐ tens
Count ☐ tens

b
Estimate ☐ tens
Count ☐ tens



 ISBN 9780655709022

# 6B Counting by tens

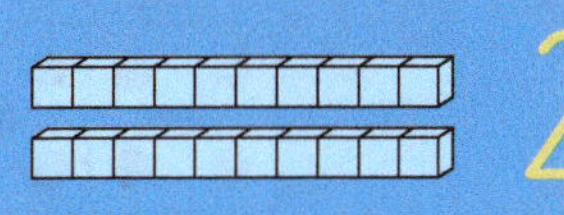

20

CONCEPT

| 0 | 10 | 20 | 30 | 40 | 50 | 60 | 70 | 80 | 90 | 100 |
|---|---|---|---|---|---|---|---|---|---|---|

ten twenty thirty forty fifty sixty
seventy eighty ninety one hundred

Start 10 20 30 40 50 60 70 80 90 100

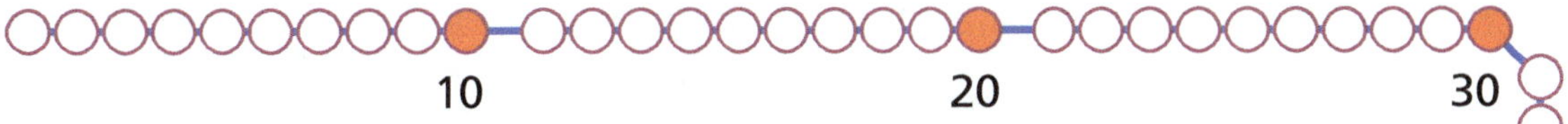

1 Use the beads to count by tens to 100 and then count from 100 to 10.

2 Write the numbers shown.

a

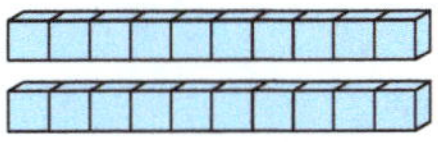

b

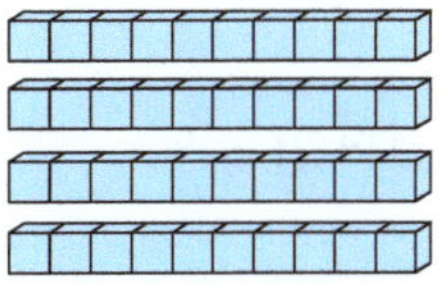

c

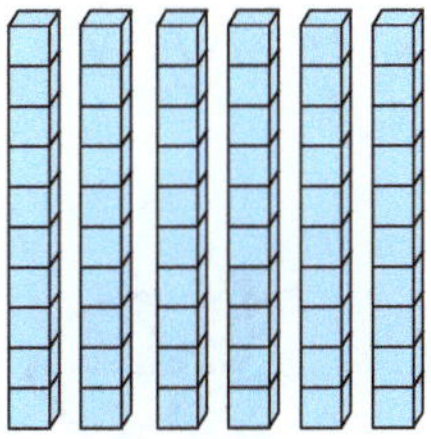

d

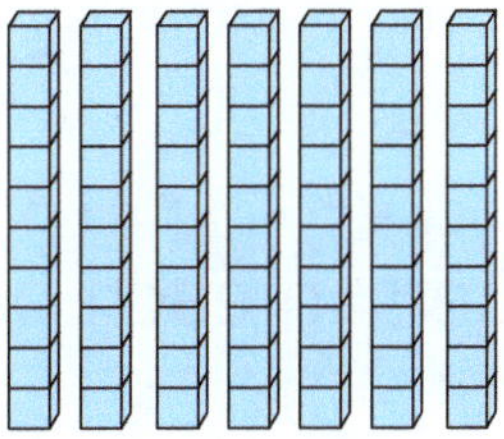

e

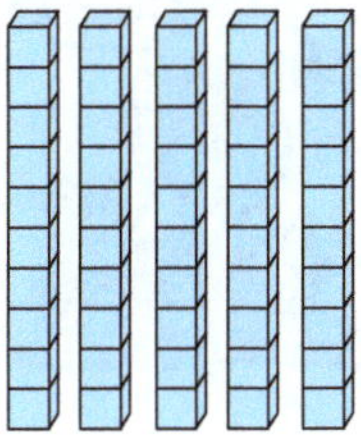

f

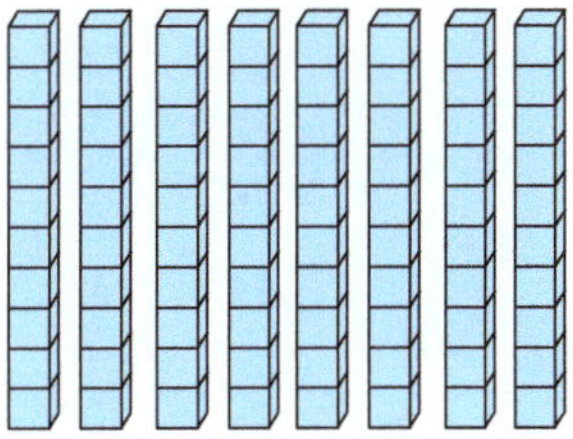

Ninety is 9 tens.

Forty is 4 tens.

Seventy is 7 tens.

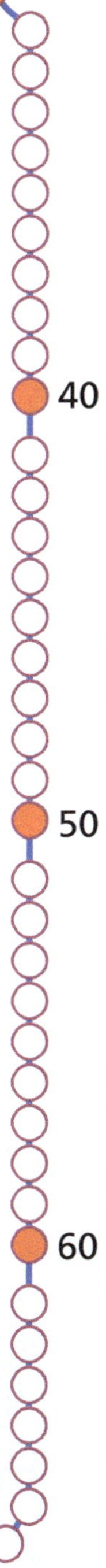

3 Write the tens number that comes before and after.

a ☐ 20 ☐

b ☐ 30 ☐

c ☐ 40 ☐

d ☐ 50 ☐

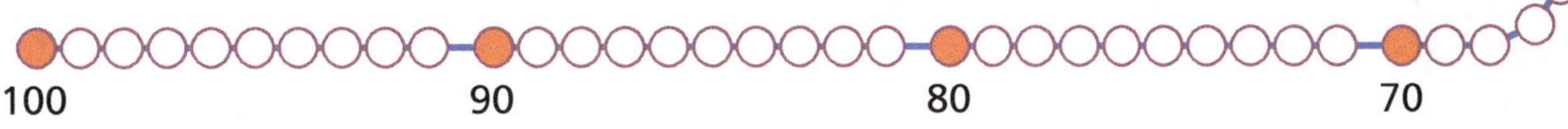

 • *AUSTRALIAN SIGNPOST MATHS NSW 1* • ISBN 9780655709022

# 6C Counting by tens

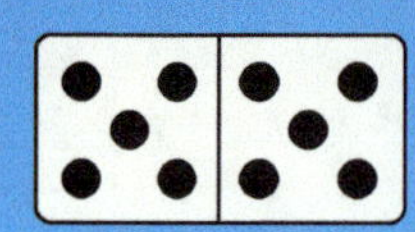

CONCEPT

| 10 | 20 | 30 | 40 | 50 |
|---|---|---|---|---|
| ten | twenty | thirty | forty | fifty |
| 60 | 70 | 80 | 90 | 100 |
| sixty | seventy | eighty | ninety | one hundred |

1 a Count forwards by tens to 100.

b Count backwards by tens from 100.

2 Write these numbers as numerals.

a twenty ☐ b eighty ☐ c ninety ☐ d forty ☐

3 Write the next four numbers in each pattern.

a 10, 20, 30, ☐, ☐, ☐, ☐

b 90, 80, 70, ☐, ☐, ☐, ☐

FUN SPOT

4 Begin at 10 and join the dots to count forwards by tens.

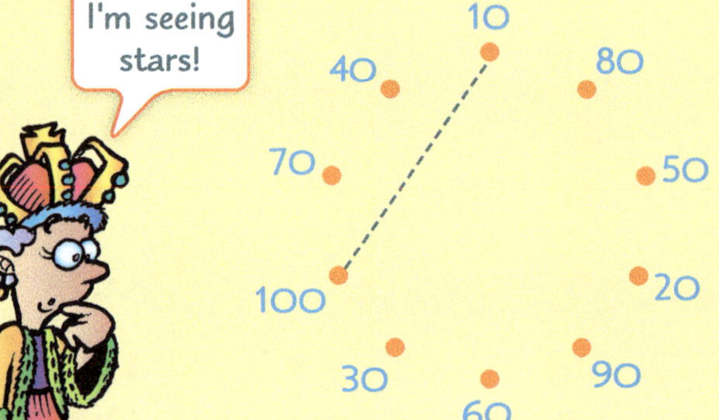


5 How much money?

☐ cents


 ISBN 9780655709022

# Data displays

1 a How many balls did we win?

b How many bears did we win?

c Which prize did we win most often?

d How many prizes did we win?

2 a Which room had most shoes?

b Which room had least shoes?

c How many shoes were in Room 3?

d How many shoes altogether?

3 a For how many days did Greg draw pictures?

b How many days were sunny?

c How many days were not sunny?

d Write a question of your own.

Greg's weather chart

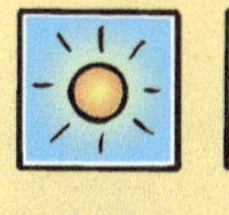

 • *AUSTRALIAN SIGNPOST MATHS NSW 1* • ISBN 9780655709022

# 7A Subtraction

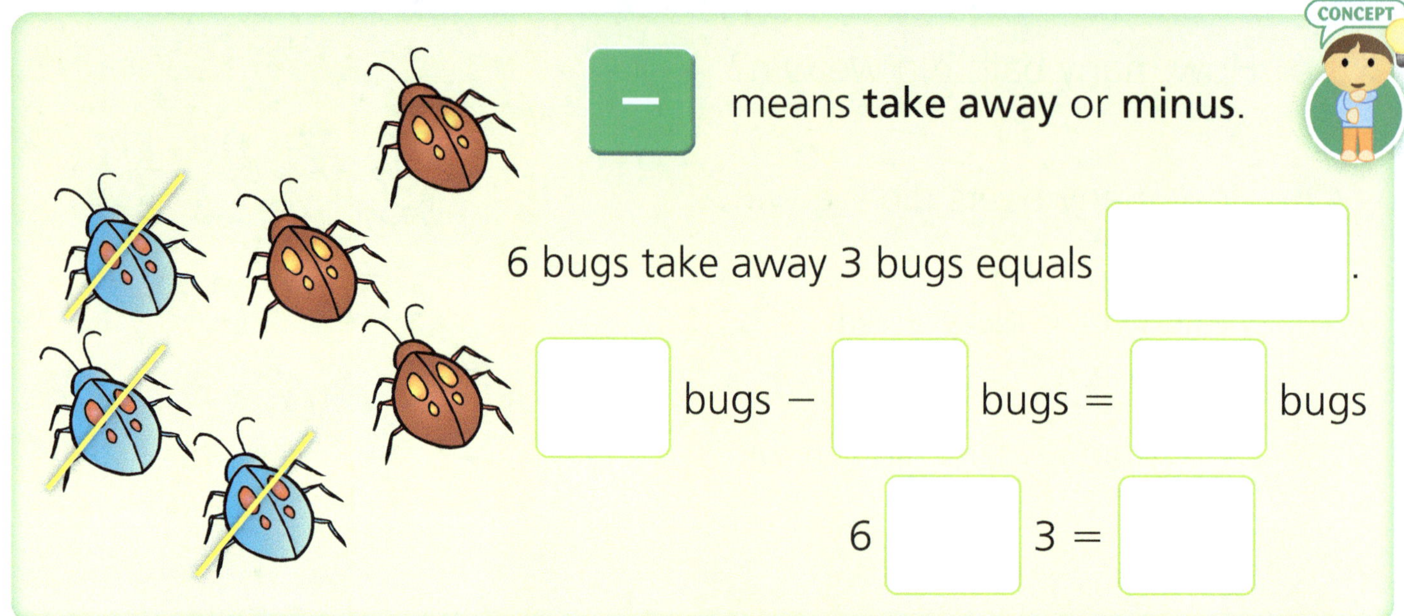


− means **take away** or **minus**.

6 bugs take away 3 bugs equals ☐.

☐ bugs − ☐ bugs = ☐ bugs

6 ☐ 3 = ☐

1

11 − 4 = ☐

2

10 − 5 = ☐

3

15 − 10 = ☐

4

16 − 0 = ☐

5

18 − 6 = ☐

6

20 − 10 = ☐



 • *AUSTRALIAN SIGNPOST MATHS NSW 1* • ISBN 9780655709022

– means take away or minus.
= means equals.

*Take away* is the same as *subtraction* or *minus*.

8 – 2

Cross out 2 dogs and complete the story.

8 take away 2 equals ☐.

1     4 take away 1 equals ☐. 

2      5 take away 3 equals ☐. 

3      6 take away 4 equals ☐. 

4   5 take away 5 equals ☐. 

5  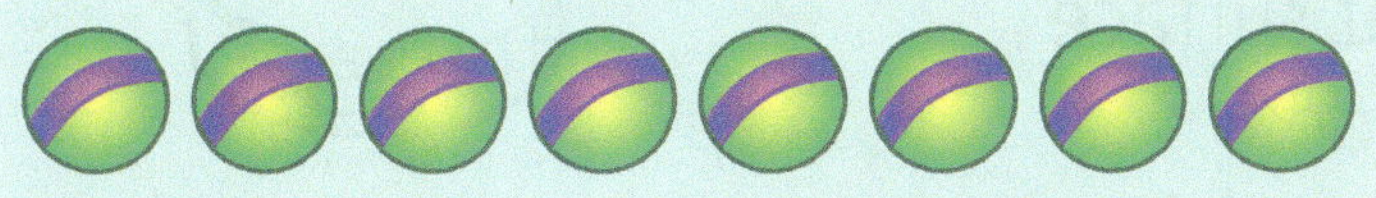  8 – 6 = ☐

6   9 – 3 = ☐ 

7   10 – 5 = ☐

 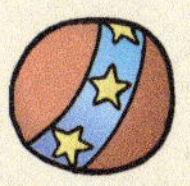 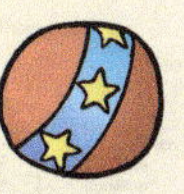 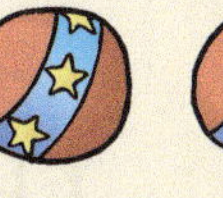  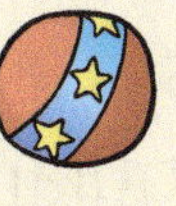

Cross out some balls and record your number sentence.

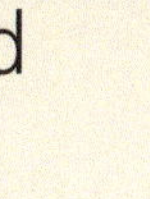  ☐ – ☐ = ☐ 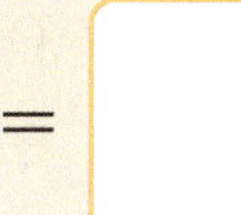

Measurement and space

# 7C 3D objects

Three dimensional

Two dimensional

1 Colour the pictures that match the objects on the left. Discuss the choices.

Sphere

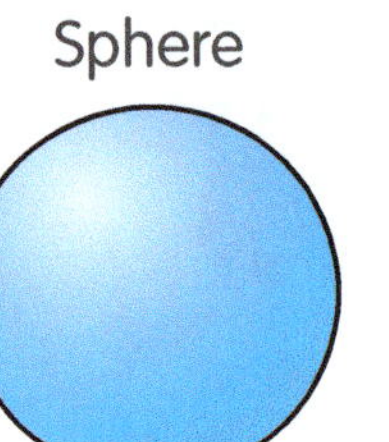

**Ball-shaped object**
A *sphere* has 1 curved surface.
It can roll.

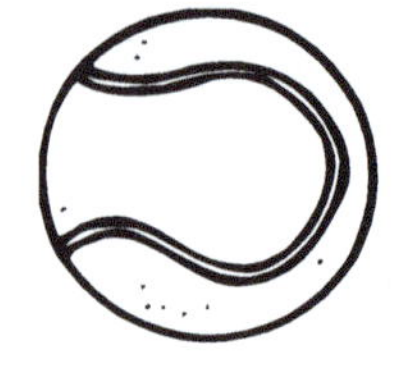

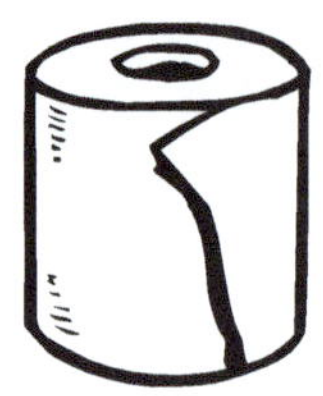

Cylinder

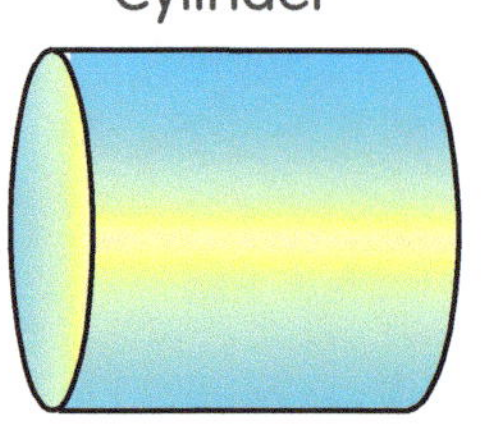

**Can-shaped object**
A *cylinder* has 1 curved surface and 2 flat surfaces.
It can roll and slide.

Cube

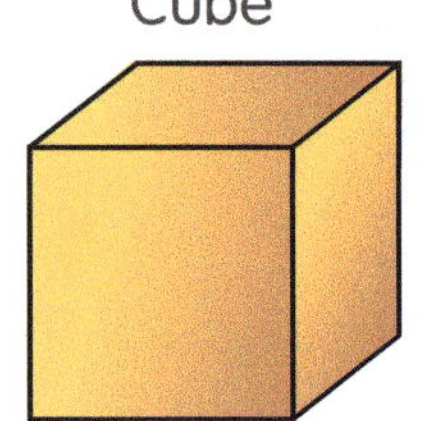

**Box-shaped object**
A *cube* has 6 flat surfaces.
It can slide. All 6 surfaces are squares.

Cone

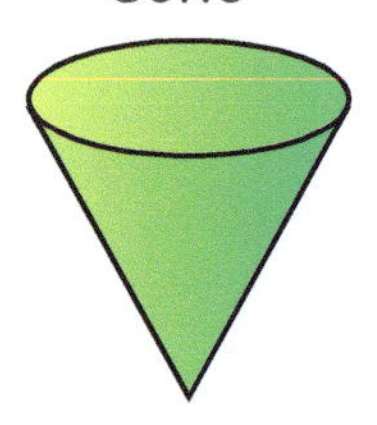

**Cone-shaped object**
A *cone* has 1 curved surface and 1 flat surface.
It can roll and slide.

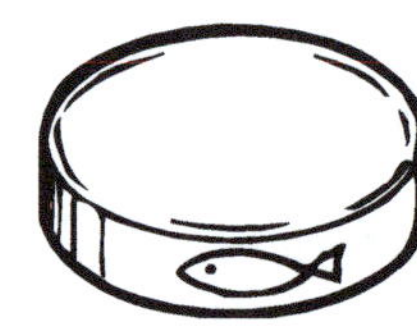

Prism

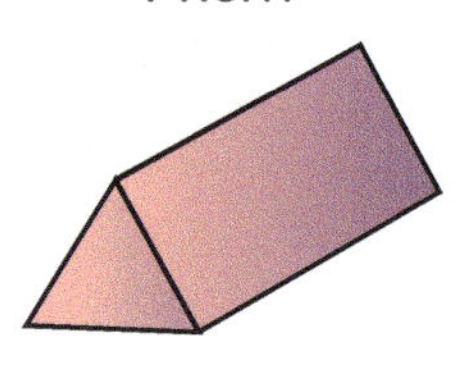

**Box-shaped object**
A *prism* has flat surfaces.
It has 2 identical ends.
The other surfaces are rectangles. It can slide.

Rectangular prism

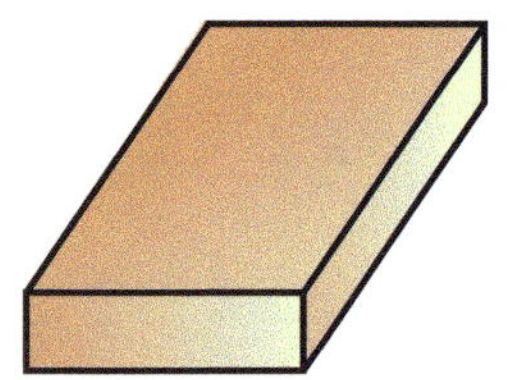

**Box-shaped object**
A *rectangular prism* is a prism that has rectangular ends.
All surfaces are rectangles.

# Objects in our world

1 Match each photo with one of the objects in the middle.

2 Draw a simple two-dimensional shape (circle or square) that is in each object. Use plasticine or playdough to make these 3D models.

# 8A Odd and even numbers

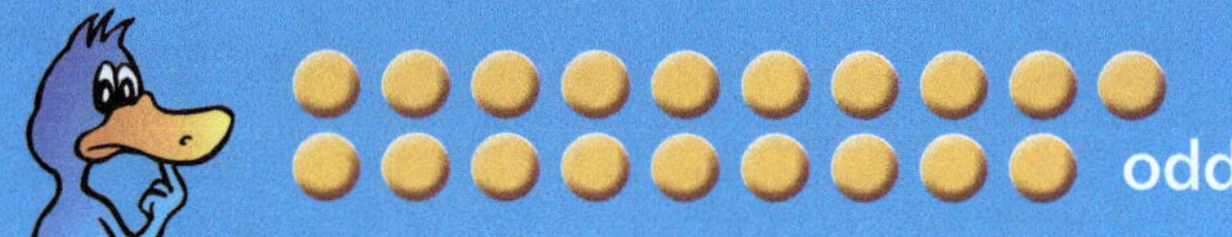

CONCEPT

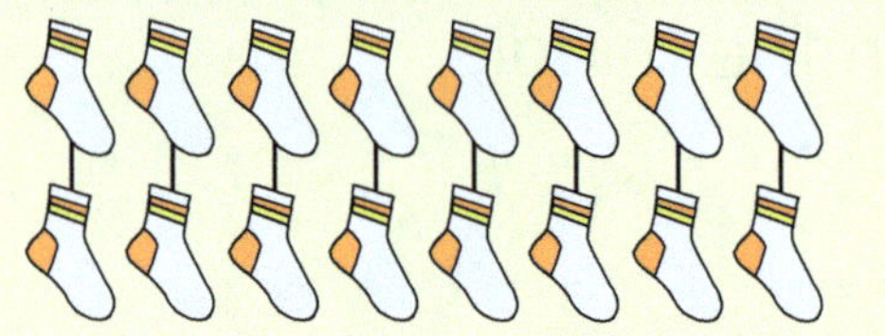

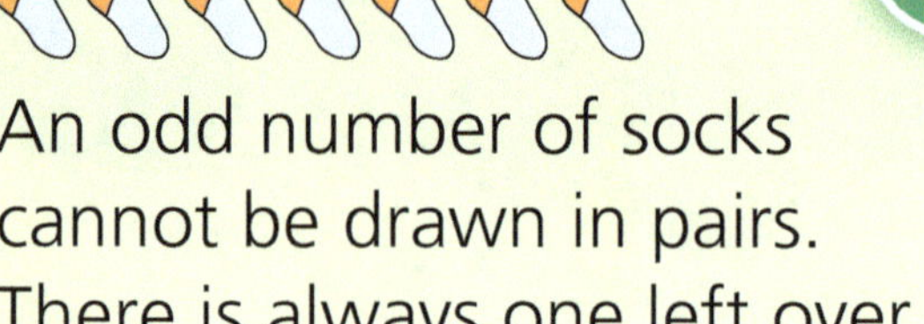

An even number of socks can be drawn in pairs.

An odd number of socks cannot be drawn in pairs. There is always one left over.

Even numbers end in 0, 2, 4, 6 or 8.
16 is an even number.

Odd numbers end in 1, 3, 5, 7 or 9.
15 is an odd number.

1. Under each group, write **odd** or **even** and then write the number.

a 

b 

c 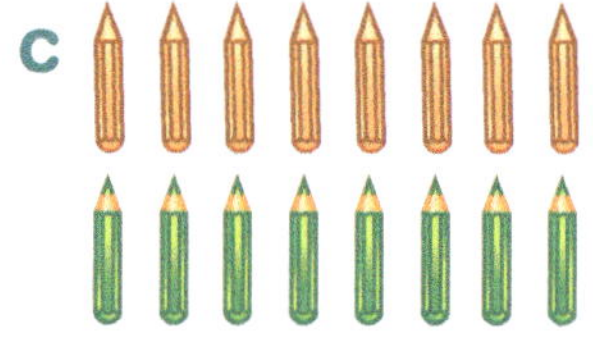

d 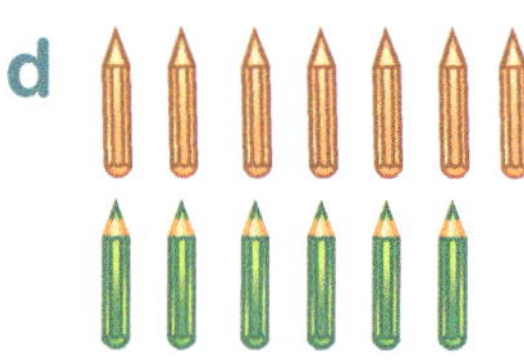

e 

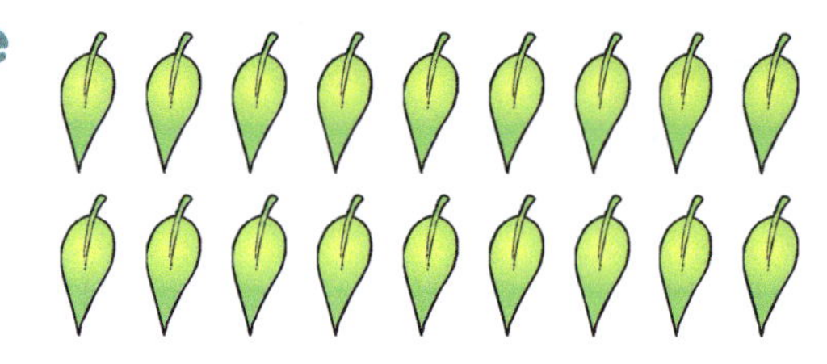

f 

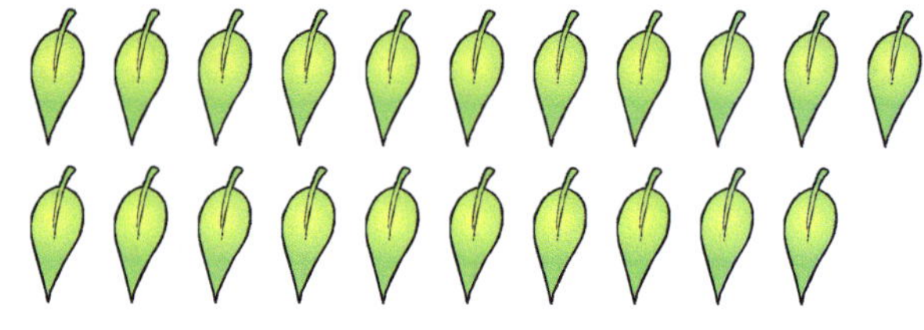

ACTIVITY

| Write some even numbers here. | Write some odd numbers here. |
| --- | --- |
| | |



 • *AUSTRALIAN SIGNPOST MATHS NSW 1* • ISBN 9780655709022

# 8B Addition to 20

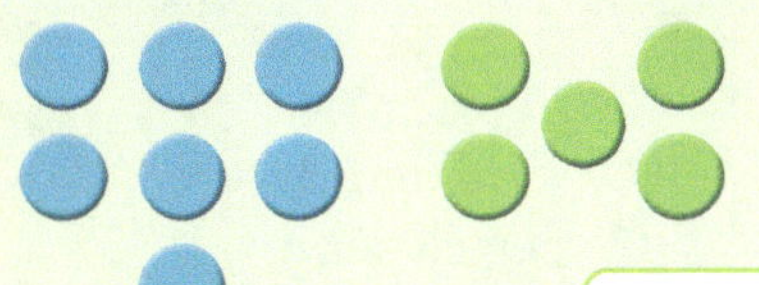

 means **add**, **and** or **plus**.

 means **makes** or **equals**.

$7 + 5 =$ ☐

1 Complete the number sentences.

Adding zero does not change the number.

**a**

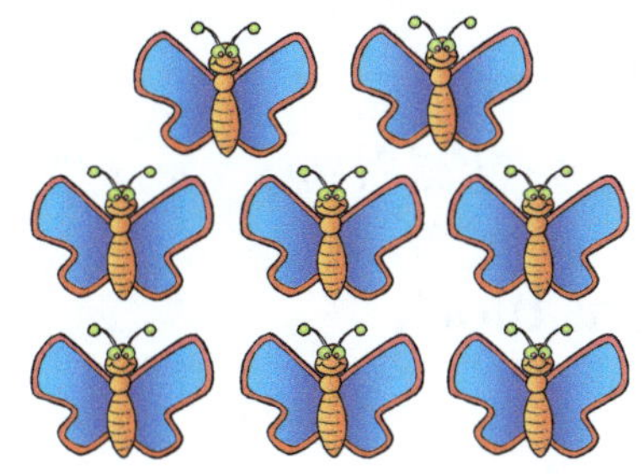 and 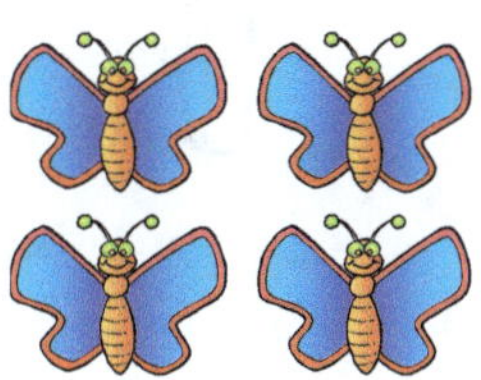

$8 + 4 =$ ☐

**b**

 and 

$9 + 7 =$ ☐

**c**

 and 

$10 + 10 =$ ☐

Draw pictures to make up your own number stories. Write a number sentence to match.

☐ + ☐ = ☐

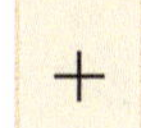

# 8C Units of length

We need a lot more little units.

CONCEPT

No gaps. No overlaps.

ACTIVITY

1 Use objects of the same size to measure the length of your desk.

| Object | Length of desk | |
|---|---|---|
| This book | | books |
| A pen | | pens |
| A tens block | | blocks |

2 Use a shoe to measure the length of each object.

| | | |
|---|---|---|
| Desk | | shoes |
| Window | | shoes |
| Your arm | | shoes |

- Which is longest?

- Which is shortest?

INVESTIGATION

Count steps to measure distance.

- From your seat to the door: ___ steps
- Along a path: ___ steps
- ___ ___ steps
- Would we use more pencils (P) or steps (S) to measure a distance?

# Informal units of length

1 Use different units to measure length.

| Length | Tally | Measurement unit |
|---|---|---|
| Length of pencil | \|\|\|\| | 4 toothpicks |
| Height of desk | | hand spans |
| Width of book | | paperclips |
| Width of door | | straws |
| Length of room | | books |

What do we do with the bit left over?

- over 4
- less than 5
- 4 and a bit

2 Estimate (guess) and then measure these lengths using craft sticks.

a

Guess
Measure

b

Guess
Measure

c

Guess
Measure

d

Guess
Measure

e
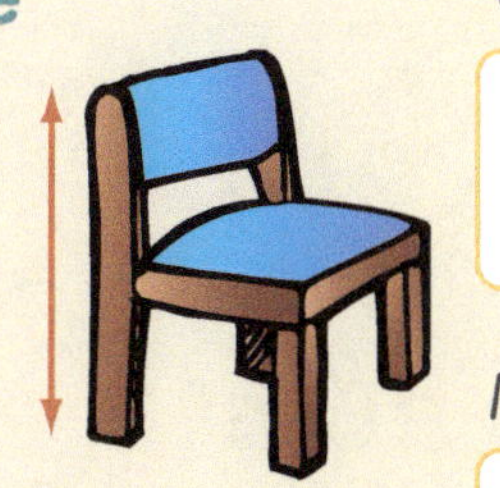
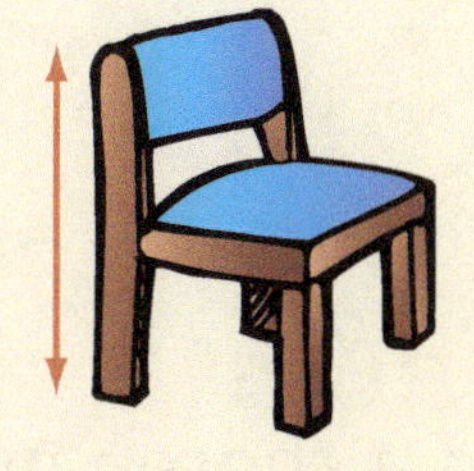

Guess
Measure

f

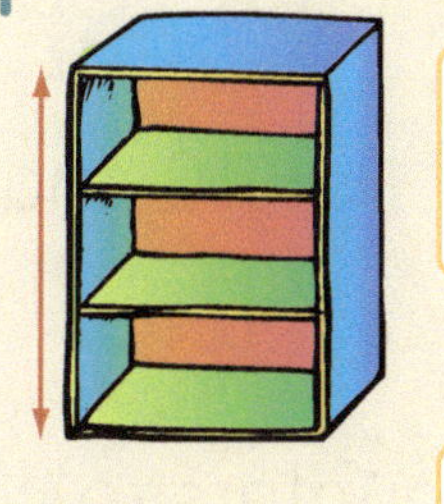
Guess
Measure

 • *AUSTRALIAN SIGNPOST MATHS NSW 1* • ISBN 9780655709022

# Counting on

3 ... 4, 5, 6

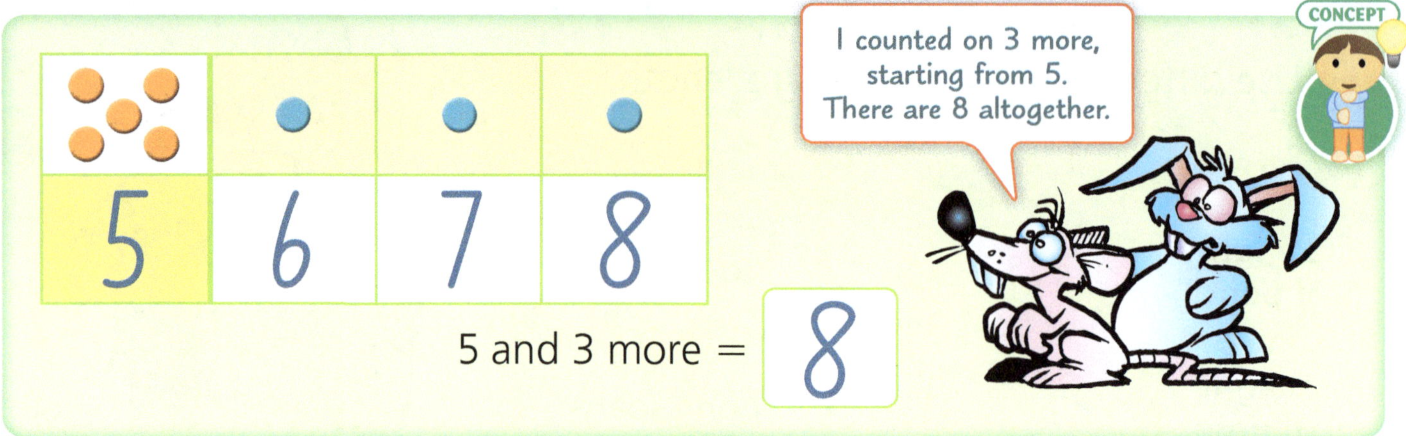


1 Count on to find how many altogether.

a

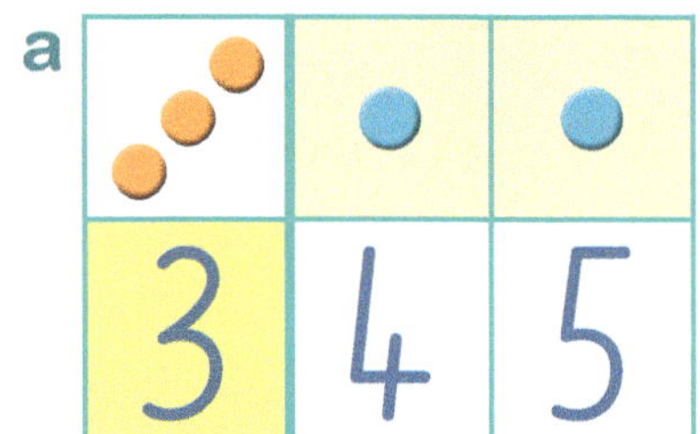


3 and 2 more = ☐

b

6 and 2 more = ☐

c

6 and 4 more = ☐

d

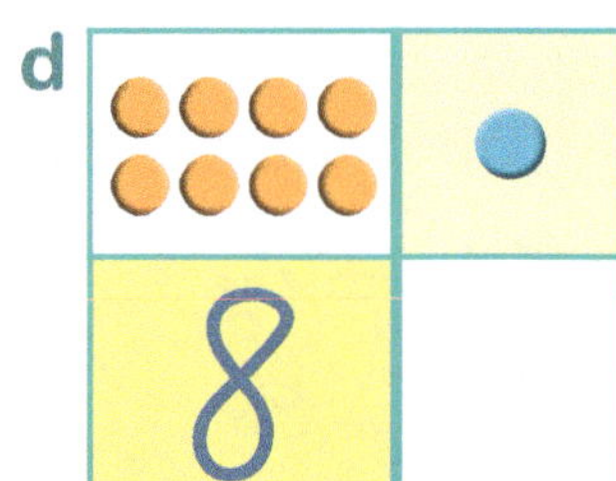


8 and 1 more = ☐

e

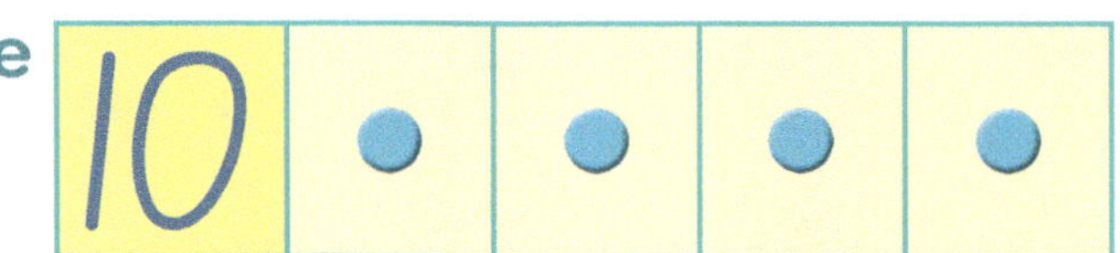


10 and 4 more = ☐

f

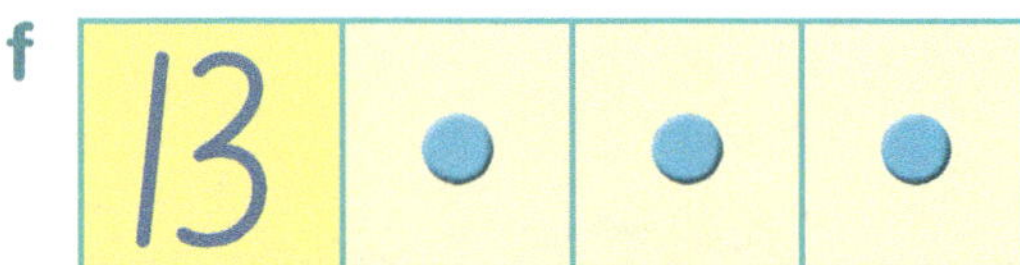


13 and 3 more = ☐

Use counters to count on from a chosen number.
Discuss and record your number sentences.

 • *AUSTRALIAN SIGNPOST MATHS NSW 1* • ISBN 9780655709022

# 9B Counting on

You can start with 6 and then use your fingers to count on 3 more.

1 Use fingers to count on.

a 5 + 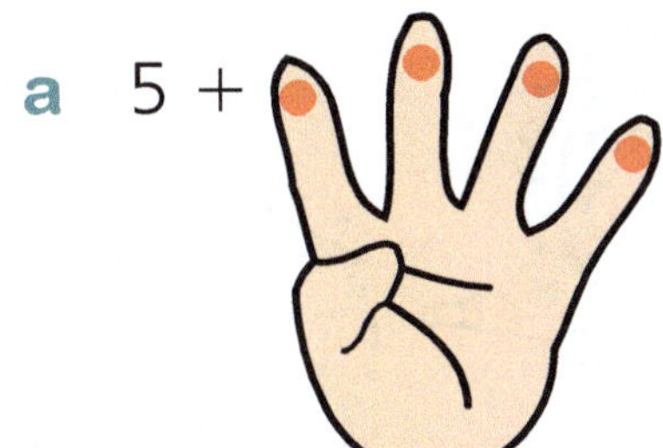

5 + 4 = ☐

b 8 + 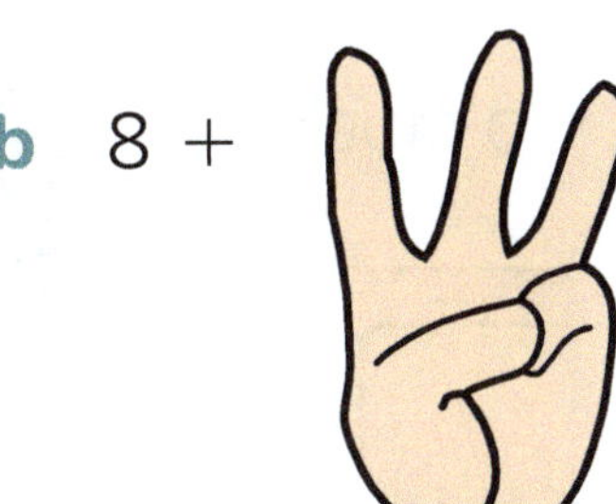

8 + 3 = ☐

c 9 + 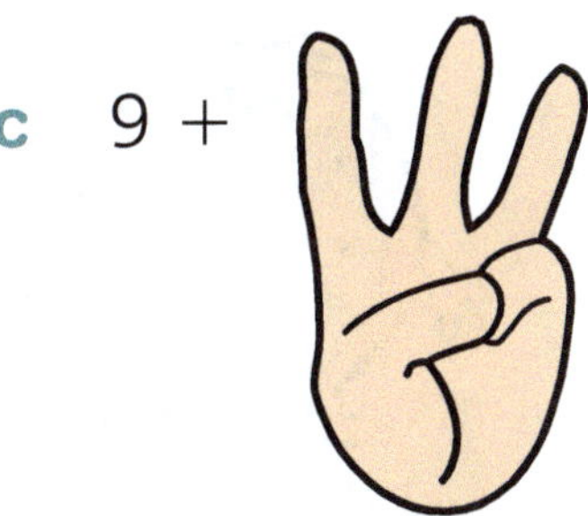

9 + 3 = ☐

d 9 +

9 + 2 = ☐

e 13 + 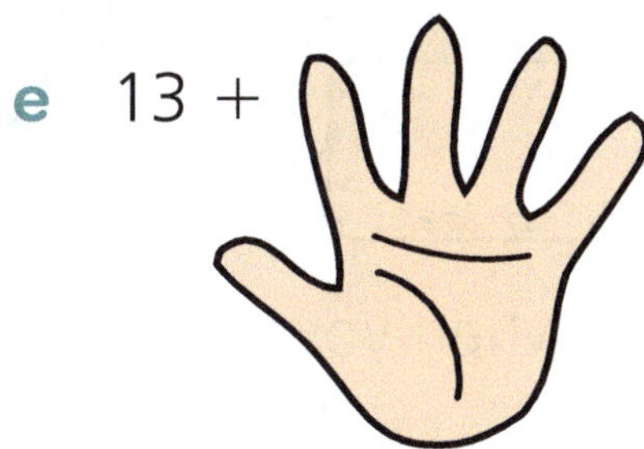

13 + 5 = ☐

f 11 + 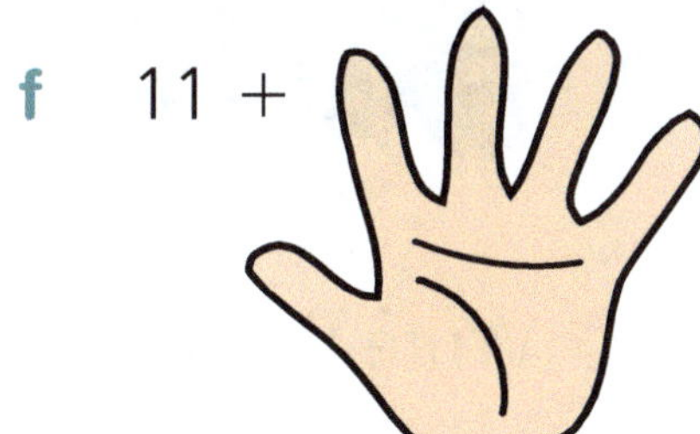

11 + 5 = ☐

Use your own fingers to count on.

a 7 + 4 = ☐

b 14 + 4 = ☐

c 9 + 3 = ☐

d 17 + 2 = ☐

e 16 + 4 = ☐

Make up more questions of your own.

# 9C Analog and digital time

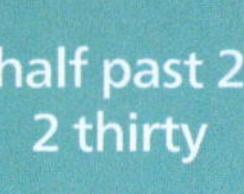

1 Read each time. Complete the labels.

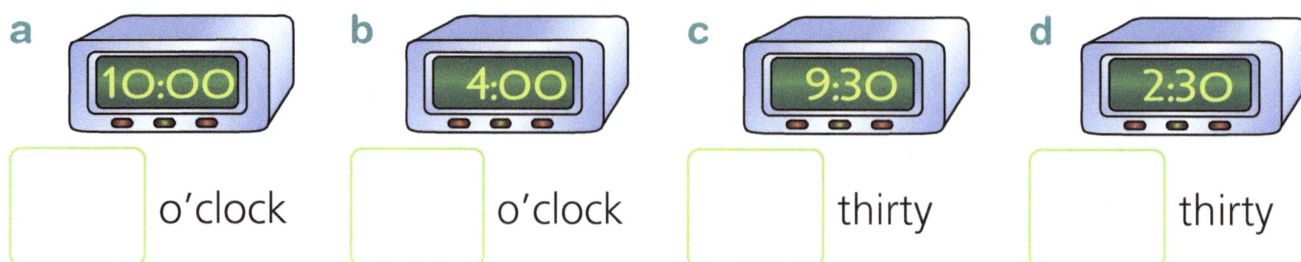


a ☐ o'clock   b ☐ o'clock   c ☐ thirty   d ☐ thirty

2 Write the time, then show it on the digital clock.

a ☐ o'clock

b ☐ o'clock

c ☐ thirty

d ☐ thirty

3 Write the analog time when you:

a have dinner ☐

b have breakfast ☐

c get up ☐

d have recess ☐

Write the digital time.

e The bell for the end of school rings at ☐.

f The bell for the start of school rings at ☐.

4 Write the times you wrote in **c** to **f** above, in order, from earliest to latest.

☐



 • *AUSTRALIAN SIGNPOST MATHS NSW 1* • ISBN 9780655709022

# 9D Digital and analog time

half past 10
10 thirty

half past 7

seven thirty

30 minutes past 7

The hour hand is halfway between the 7 and the 8.

1 Read and write each time.

a 

half past   thirty

 minutes past 

b 

half past ☐ ☐ thirty

☐ minutes past ☐

There are 30 minutes in half an hour.
The minute hand is halfway around the clock.

2 Draw the time on each clock.

a half past 2

b half past 4

c five thirty

d half past 9

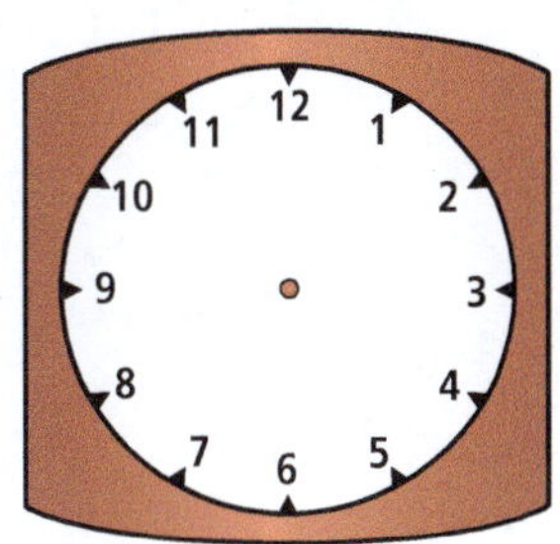

e half past 11

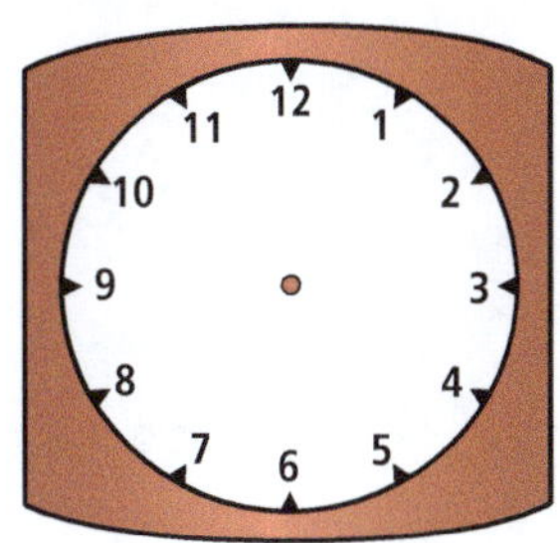

f thirty minutes past 10

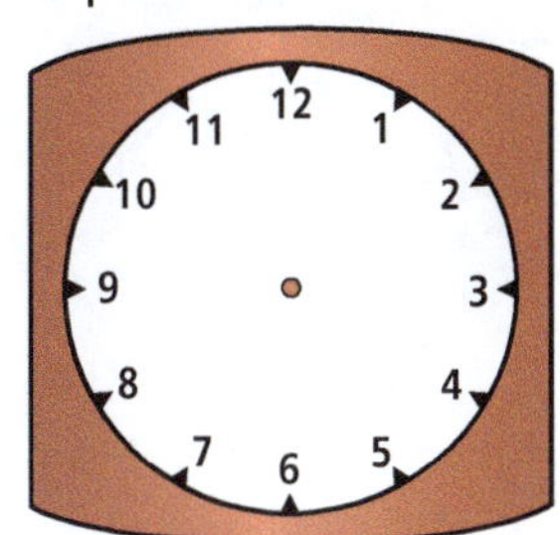

# 10A Addition to 20

Write the first number then count on.

INVESTIGATION

1 Write number sentences about the picture.

| | | | | |
|---|---|---|---|---|
| | + | | = | |

| | | | | |
|---|---|---|---|---|
| | + | | = | |



 ISBN 9780655709022

Start 10 20 30 40 50 60 70 80 90 100

1 Write the number modelled.

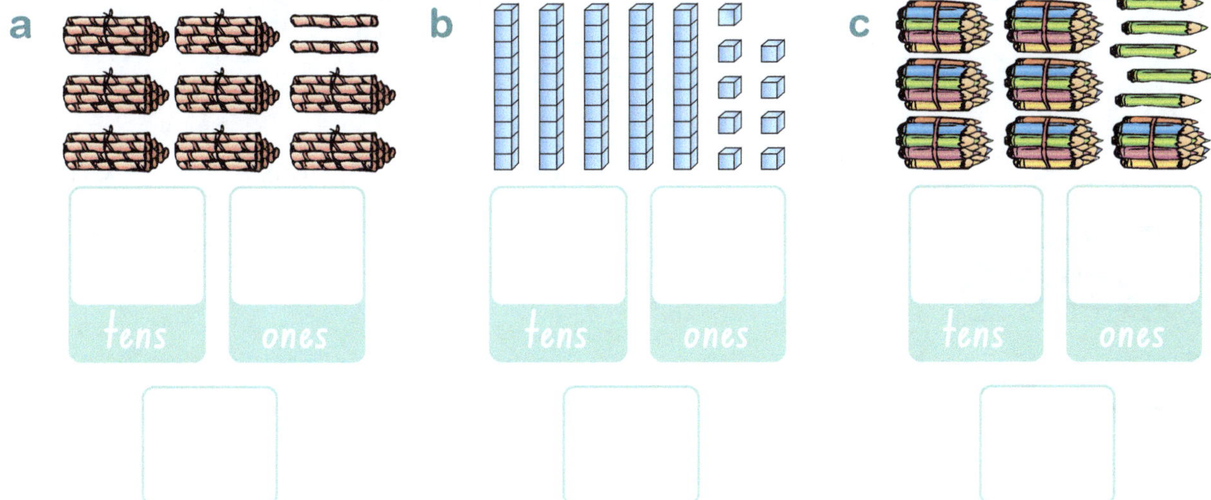


2 From Question 1, write the number that is:

a the smallest

b the largest

Starting from the top, every 10th bead around this page is coloured. Circle the beads at these numbers.

a 13 b 29 c 45 d 67 e 80 f 98 g 120

For each number say how many tens and how many ones.

# 10C Informal units of length

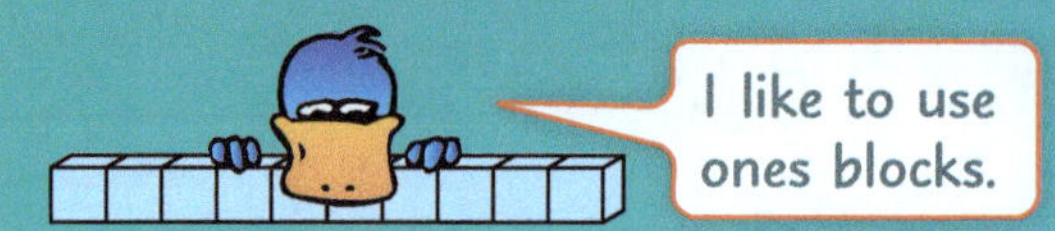

1 Use pencils 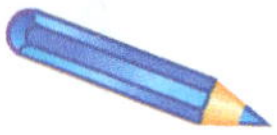 to measure the length:

a ☐ pencils

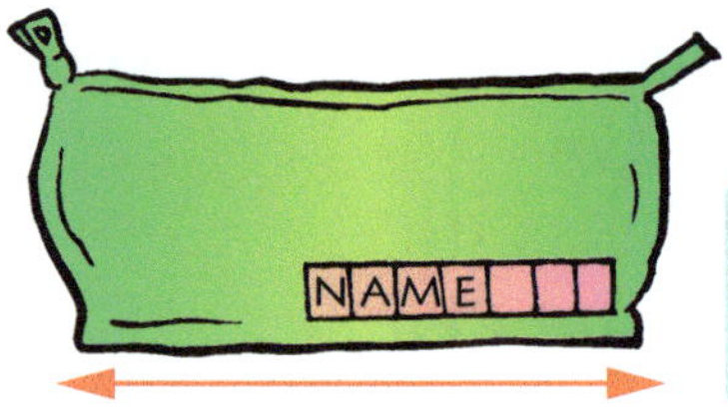

b ☐ pencils

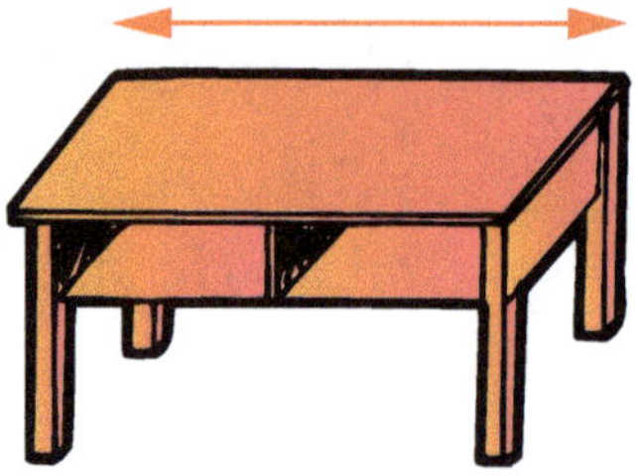

2 a ☐ pencils (guess)

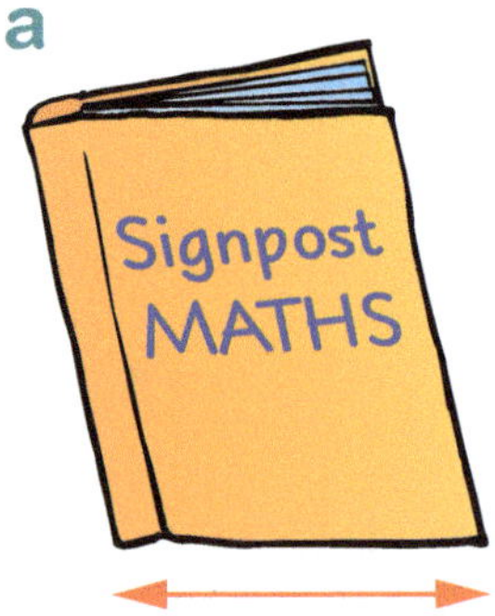

☐ pencils

b ☐ pencils (guess)

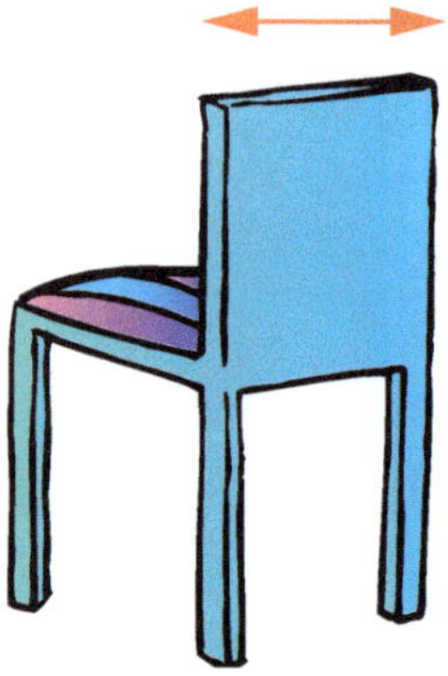

☐ pencils

3

| Unit of length | Length of desk | | Width of desk | |
|---|---|---|---|---|
| | Guess | Check | Guess | Check |
| 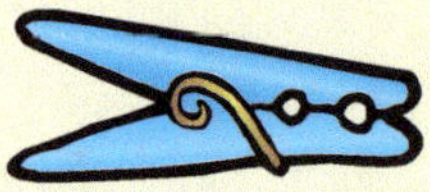 (peg) | | | | |
| 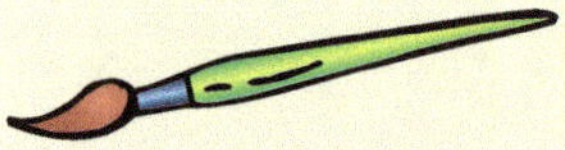 (brush) | | | | |

Why do we need more pegs than brushes?

INVESTIGATION

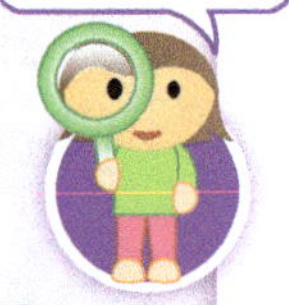

- How would you record this length of string? Tick two ways. Discuss your answers.

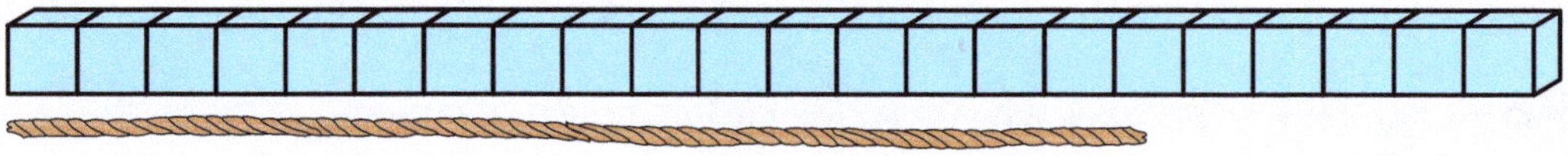

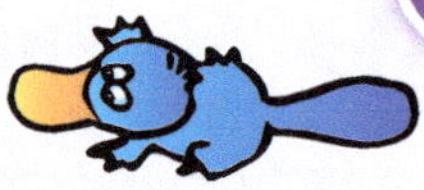

more than 16 blocks ☐ sixteen and a half blocks ☐ less than 17 blocks ☐



 ISBN 9780655709022

# Measuring length

1 Estimate the longer line in each pair. Use a piece of string to check. Circle the longer line.

a
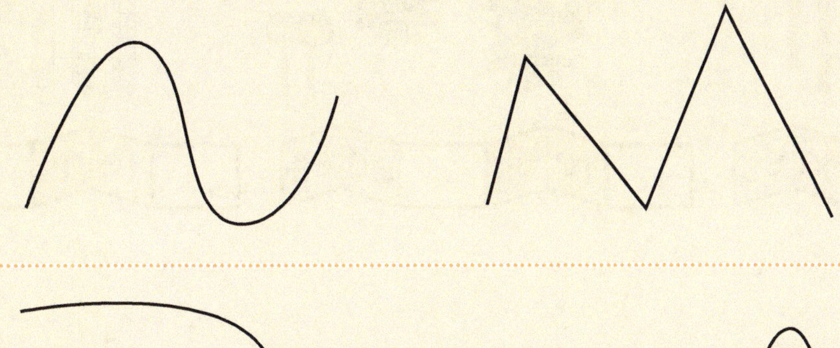

b
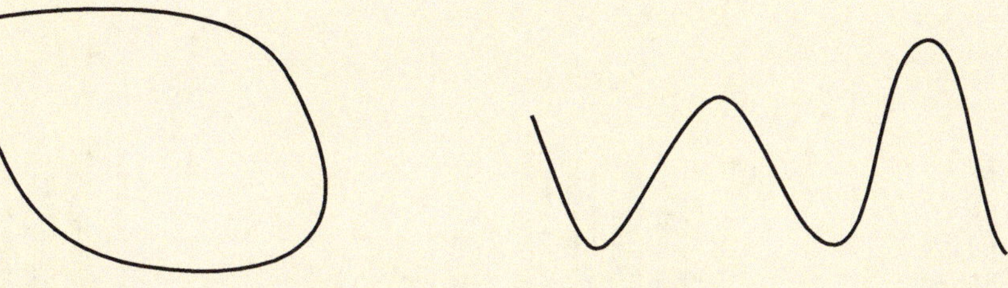

2 Measure and record the lengths of these objects. Place the objects side-by-side and end-to-end to check your answers. Tick the longer object for each pair.

a

| | | | |
|---|---|---|---|
| Book | | blocks | ✓ |
| Paper | | blocks | ✓ |

b

| | | | |
|---|---|---|---|
| Pencil | | finger widths | ✓ |
| Your hand | | finger widths | ✓ |

c

| | | | |
|---|---|---|---|
| Scissors | | blocks | ✓ |
| Felt pen | | blocks | ✓ |

d

| | | | |
|---|---|---|---|
| Ruler | | hand spans | ✓ |
| Book | | hand spans | ✓ |

3 Discuss different ways of comparing lengths: using string, placing objects side-by-side and using concrete materials.

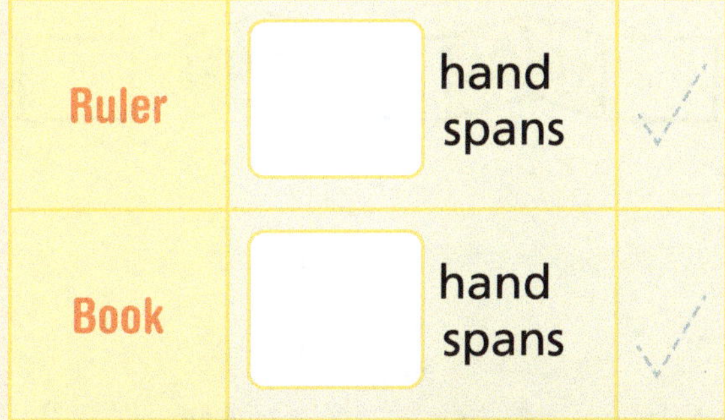
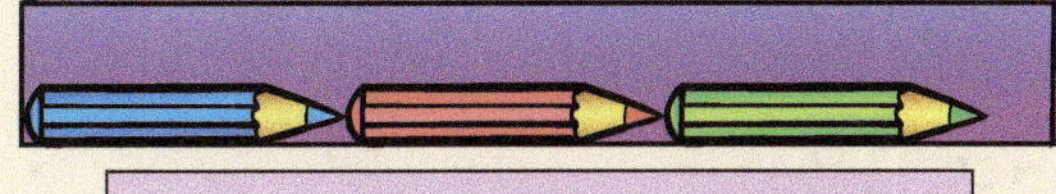

# 11A Numbers to 100

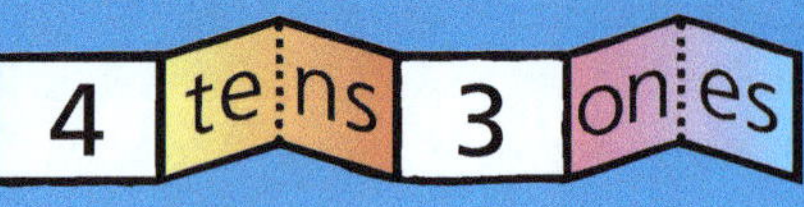

1 Complete each numeral expander and label.

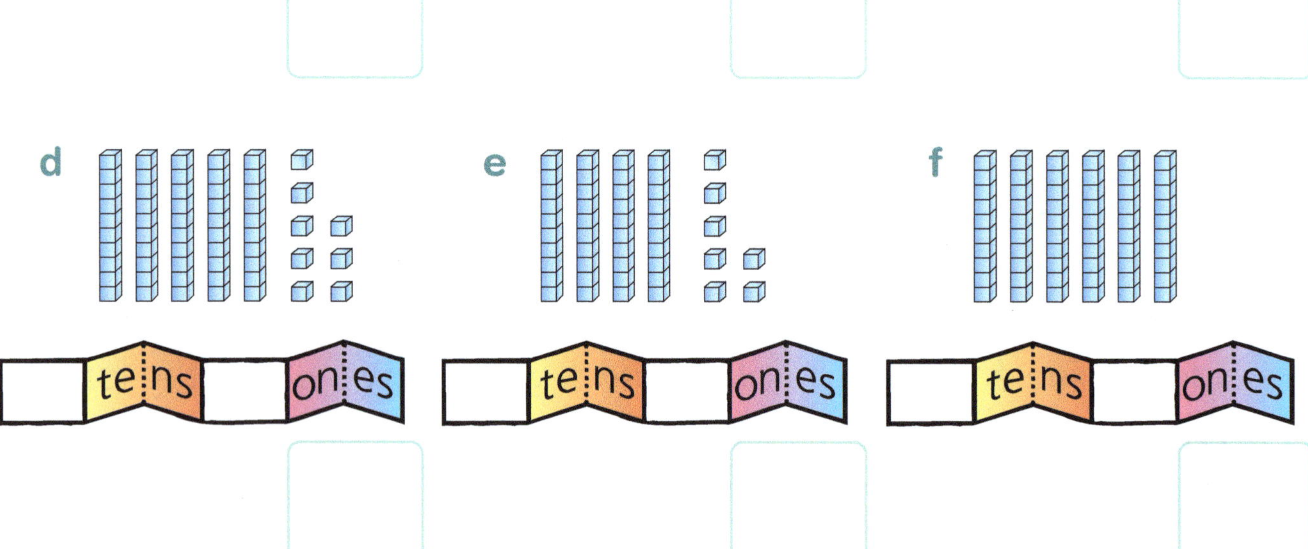


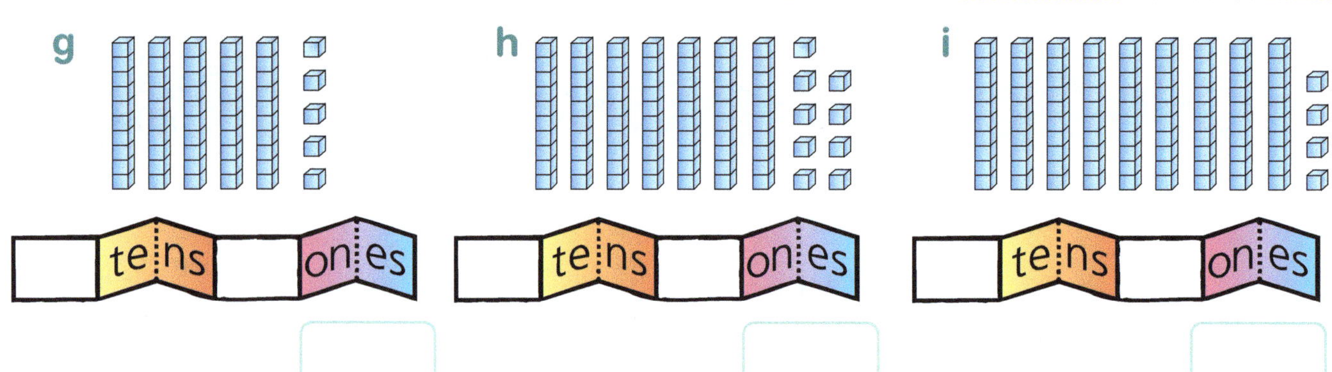


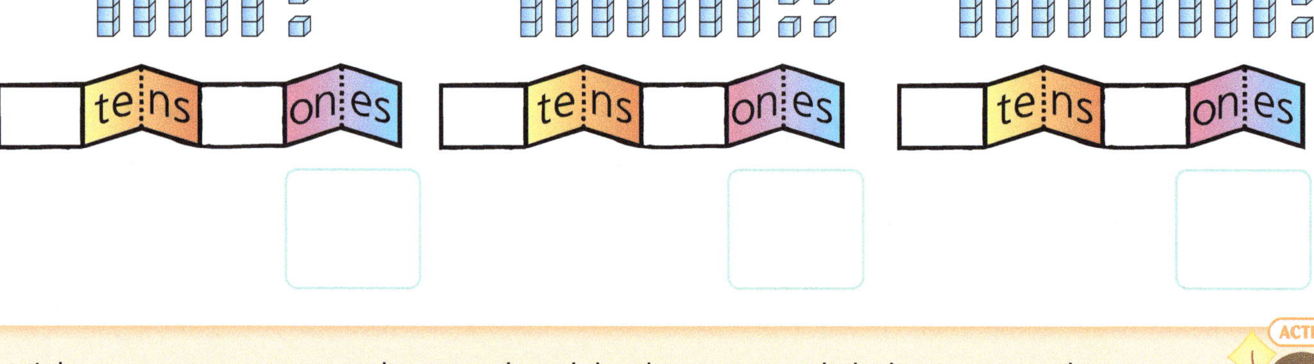


ACTIVITY

With a partner, use place-value blocks to model these numbers. Talk about your answers.

- 18
- 27
- 40
- 31
- 64
- 83
- 50
- 79
- 99
- 90



 • *AUSTRALIAN SIGNPOST MATHS NSW 1* • ISBN 9780655709022

# 11B Subtraction to 20

10 – 3
10 ... 9, 8, 7

1 Count back to complete each number sentence.

a

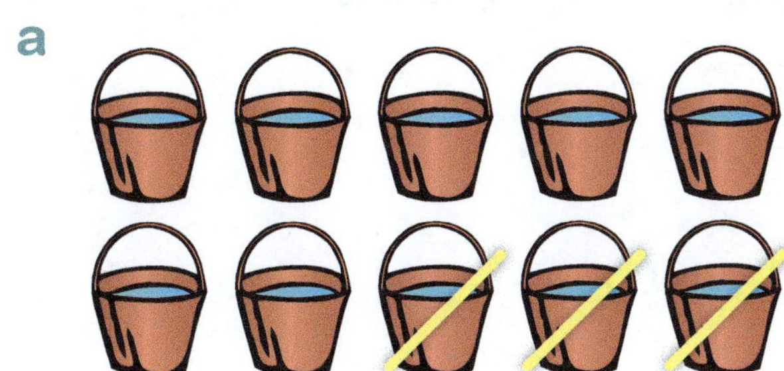

10 − 3 = ☐

b

11 − 6 = ☐

c

16 − 4 = ☐

d

15 − 9 = ☐

e

19 − 8 = ☐

f

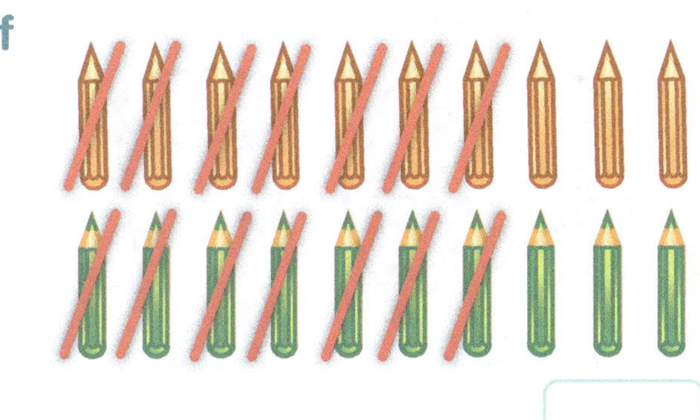

20 − 14 = ☐

2 a Count back 2.

11, ☐, ☐

14, ☐, ☐

b Count back 4.

17, ☐, ☐, ☐, ☐

20, ☐, ☐, ☐, ☐

 • *AUSTRALIAN SIGNPOST MATHS NSW 1* • ISBN 9780655709022

# 11C Comparing capacities

To find which holds more, pour the contents of one into the other.

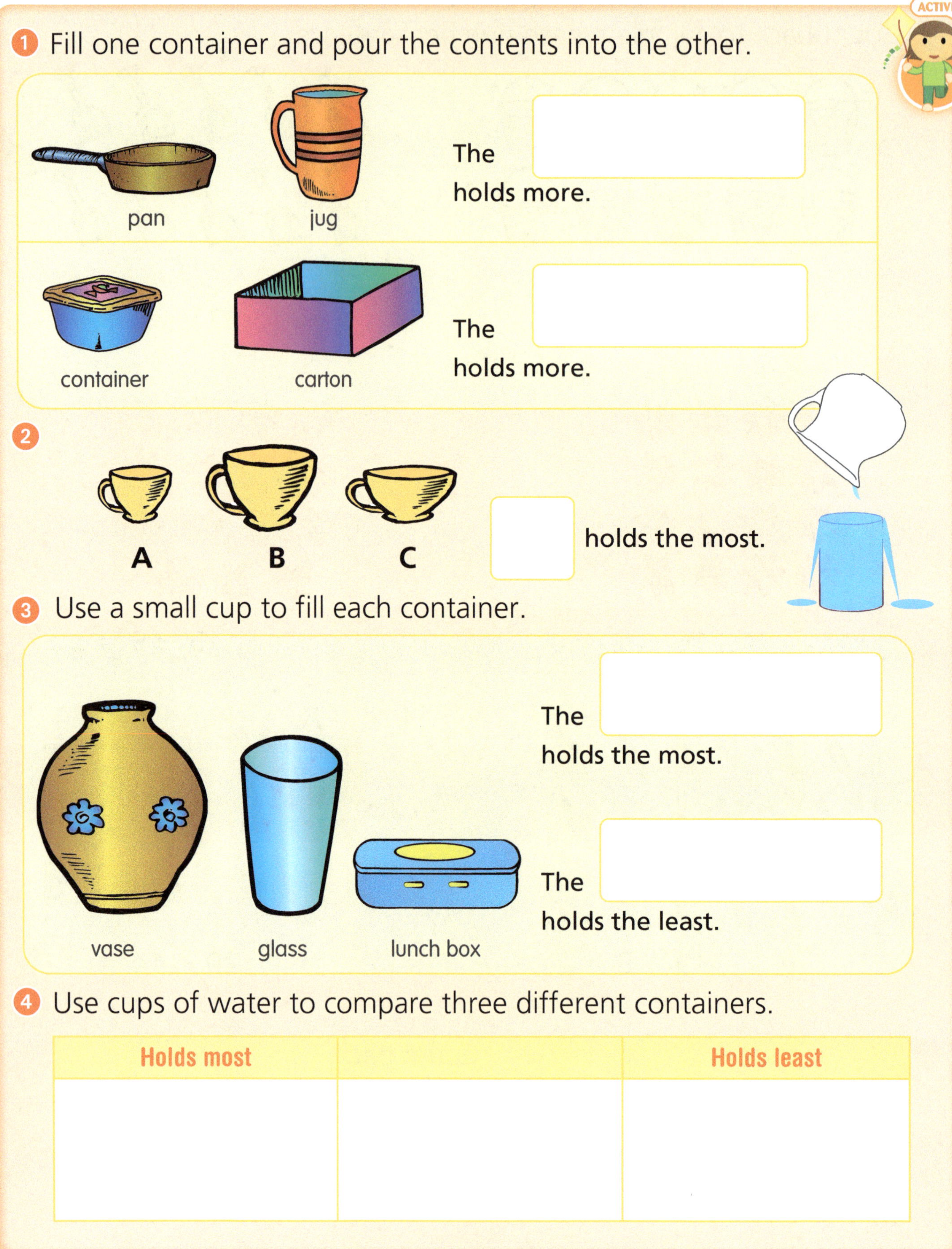


1 Fill one container and pour the contents into the other.

The ______ holds more.

The ______ holds more.

2 ______ holds the most.

3 Use a small cup to fill each container.

The ______ holds the most.

The ______ holds the least.

4 Use cups of water to compare three different containers.

| Holds most | | Holds least |
|---|---|---|
| | | |



 • *AUSTRALIAN SIGNPOST MATHS NSW 1* • ISBN 9780655709022

# Informal units of capacity

INVESTIGATION

1 Estimate then measure how many units fill the containers.

| | Cups of water | | Bottles of water | |
|---|---|---|---|---|
| pan | Guess | Check | Guess | Check |
| ice-cream container | Guess | Check | Guess | Check |
| jug | Guess | Check | Guess | Check |
| bucket | Guess | Check | Guess | Check |

2 Which holds more?

a the pan or the bucket?

b the jug or the pan?

3 Which unit was better to use in each case, cups or bottles?

a pan cups bottles

b ice-cream container cups bottles

c jug cups bottles

d bucket cups bottles

Discuss your answers.

4 Why are more cups than bottles needed to fill each container?

# 12A Addition sentences

+ means and, add or plus.
= means makes or is equal to.

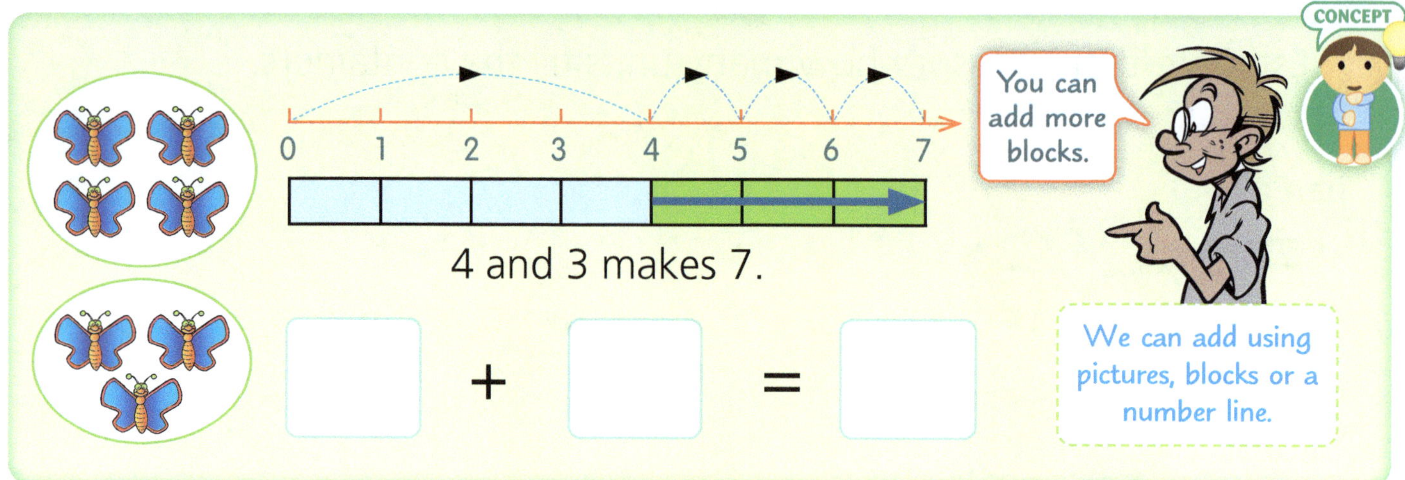


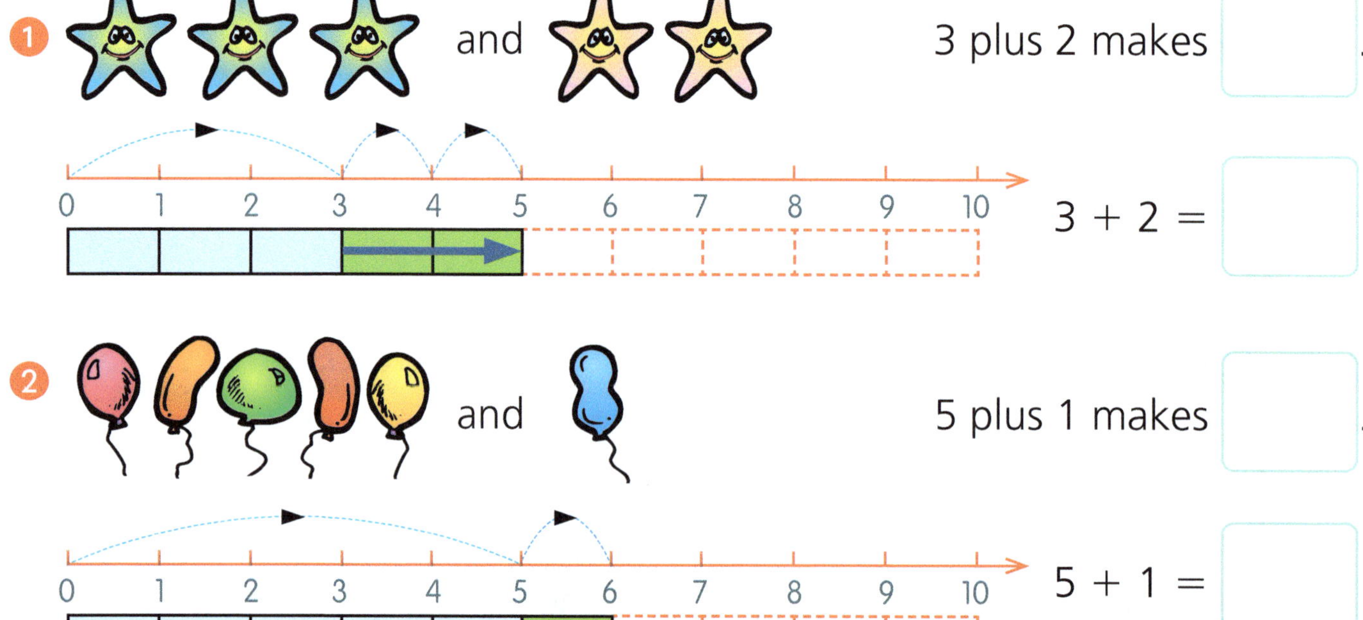


1 and 3 plus 2 makes ☐.

3 + 2 = ☐

2 and 5 plus 1 makes ☐.

5 + 1 = ☐

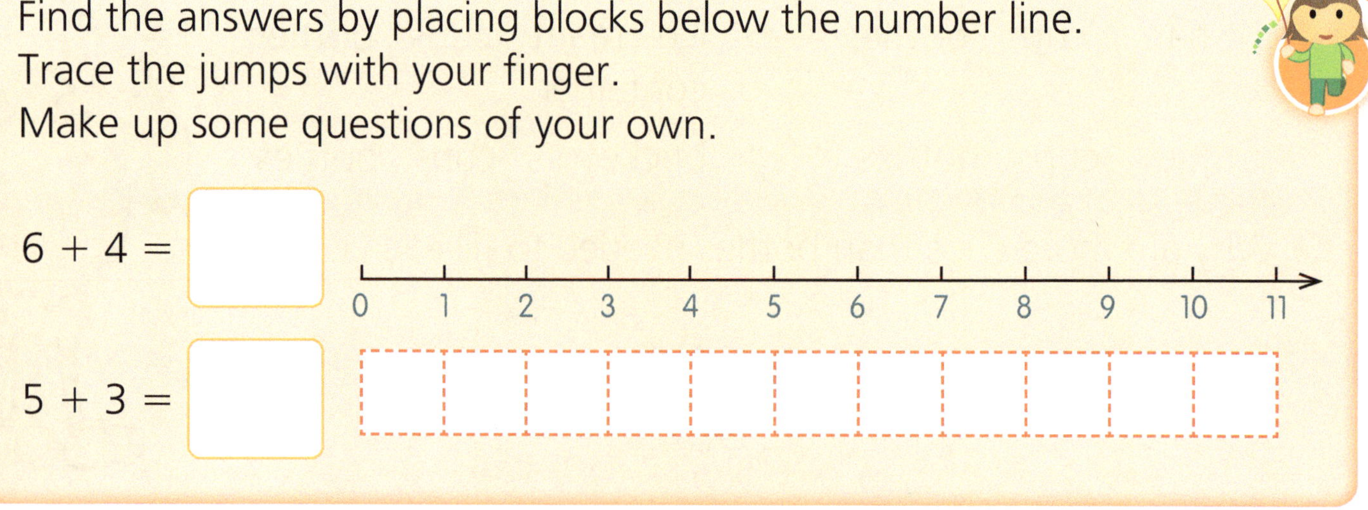


Find the answers by placing blocks below the number line.
Trace the jumps with your finger.
Make up some questions of your own.

6 + 4 = ☐

5 + 3 = ☐

2 + 6 is the same as 6 + 2

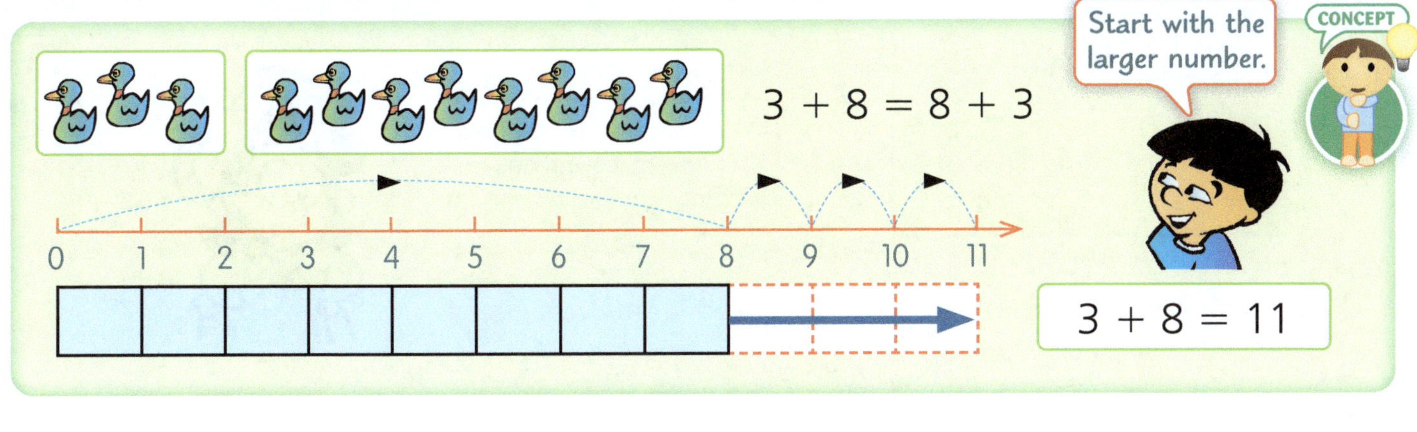


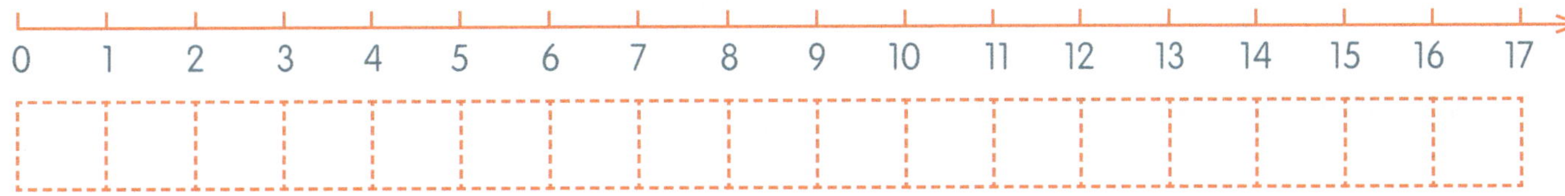


1 Use the number line above to answer these questions.

**a** 2 and 5 makes ☐.　　**b** 5 and 4 makes ☐.

**c** 9 + 3 = ☐　　**d** 6 + 5 = ☐　　**e** 7 + 3 = ☐

**f** 8 + 3 = ☐　　**g** 5 + 5 = ☐　　**h** 6 + 6 = ☐

**i** 7 + 4 = ☐　　**j** 8 + 7 = ☐　　**k** 5 + 4 = ☐

**l** 6 + 3 = ☐　　**m** 2 + 7 = ☐　　**n** 1 + 8 = ☐

**o** 5 + 6 = ☐　　**p** 4 + 6 = ☐　　**q** 8 + 9 = ☐

**r** 9 + 7 = ☐　　**s** 6 + 9 = ☐　　**t** 7 + 7 = ☐

# 12C Addition by counting on

**1** Use the dots to count on.

a $8 + 1 =$ ☐ b $9 + 2 =$ ☐ c $17 + 1 =$ ☐

d $12 + 2 =$ ☐ e $18 + 1 =$ ☐ f $15 + 2 =$ ☐

g $9 + 3 =$ ☐ h $8 + 2 =$ ☐ i $11 + 4 =$ ☐

j $14 + 2 =$ ☐ k $17 + 3 =$ ☐ l $19 + 1 =$ ☐

**2** Use the number line to find the answers.

0 1 2 3 4 5 6 7 8 9 10 11 12 13 14 15 16 17 18 19 20 21

a $8 + 4 =$ ☐ b $9 + 5 =$ ☐

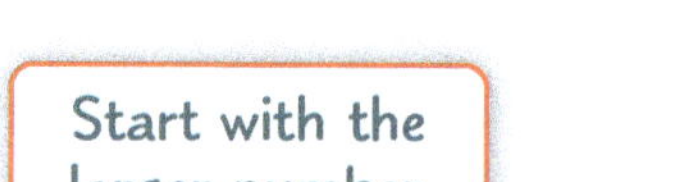


c $16 + 3 =$ ☐ d $7 + 6 =$ ☐

e $12 + 4 =$ ☐ f $17 + 4 =$ ☐

# Comparing capacities

1 How many times can one jug fill each container?

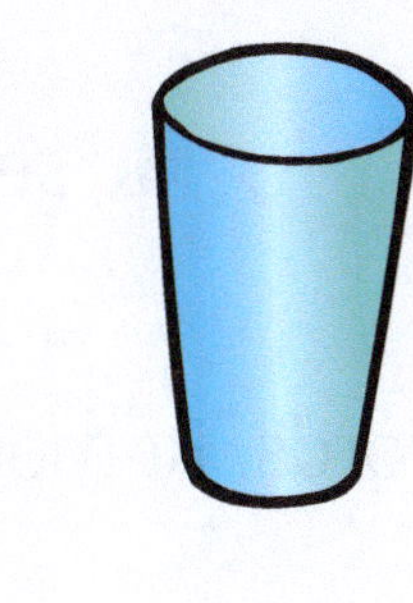
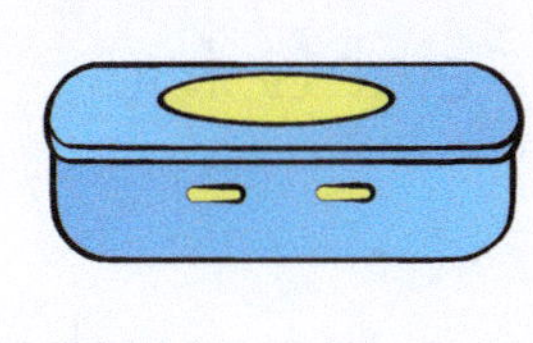

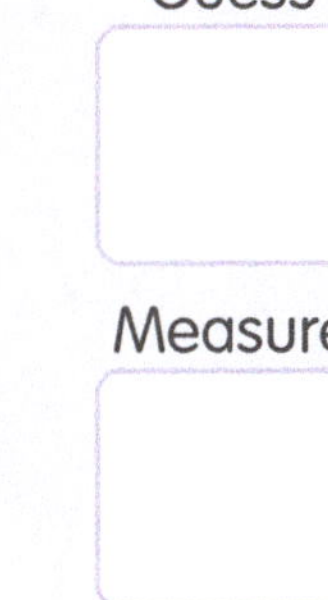
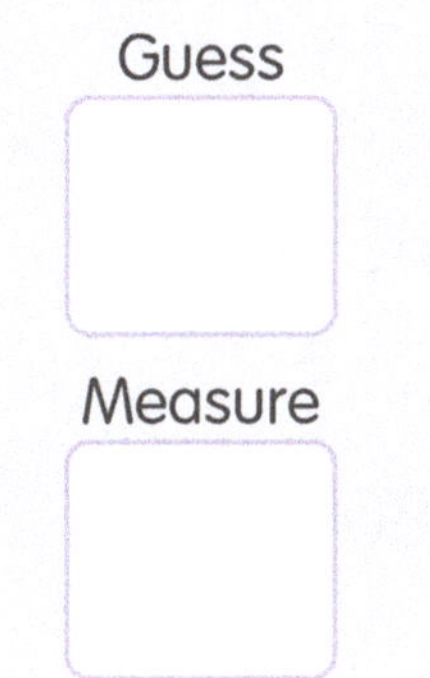

| | A bottle | B glass | C lunch box |
|---|---|---|---|
| Guess | | | |
| Measure | | | |

Which container (A, B or C):

a holds the most? ☐

b holds the least? ☐

2 How many cups fill each container?

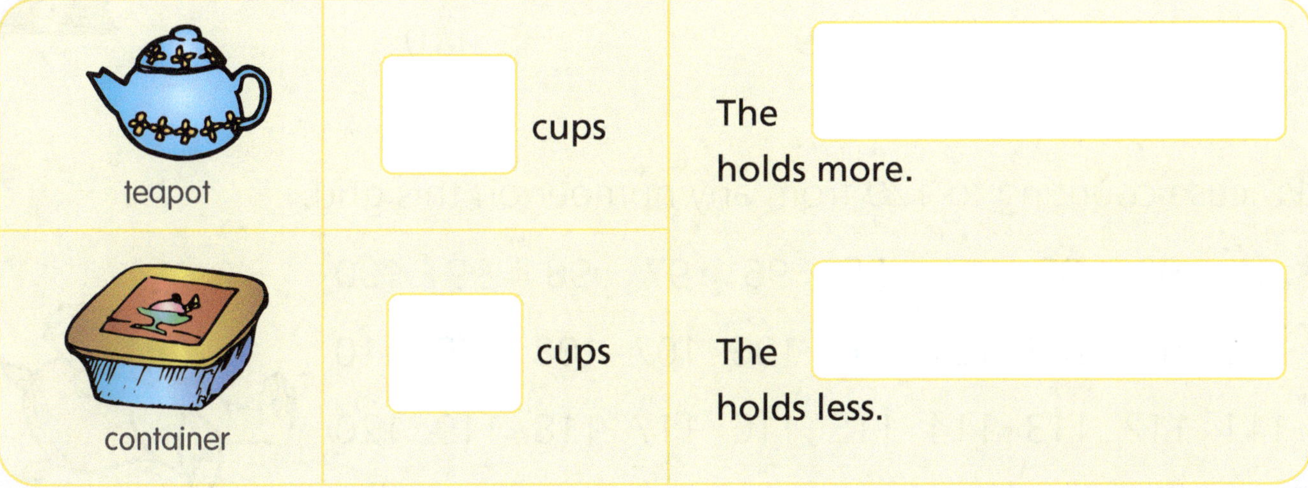

| | | |
|---|---|---|
| teapot | ☐ cups | The ☐ holds more. |
| container | ☐ cups | The ☐ holds less. |

 • *AUSTRALIAN SIGNPOST MATHS NSW 1* • ISBN 9780655709022

# 13A Numbers to 120

| one hundred and seven | 107 |
|---|---|
| one hundred and seventeen | 117 |
| one hundred and ten | 110 |

**1** Write the numeral.

a sixty-one    b twenty-two 

c eighty-four    d seventy-nine 

twenty two
thirty three
forty four
fifty five
sixty six
seventy seven
eighty eight
ninety nine
one hundred

**2** Write the number in words. Remember to use a hyphen.

a 65

b 43

c 80

d 27

e 96

**3** Write the number that is 1 more than:

a 33   b 59    c 110

ACTIVITY

Practise counting to 120 from any number on this grid.

| 91 | 92 | 93 | 94 | 95 | 96 | 97 | 98 | 99 | 100 |
|---|---|---|---|---|---|---|---|---|---|
| 101 | 102 | 103 | 104 | 105 | 106 | 107 | 108 | 109 | 110 |
| 111 | 112 | 113 | 114 | 115 | 116 | 117 | 118 | 119 | 120 |

Practise counting backwards from 120 to 91.

# 13B Numbers to 120

| one hundred and nine | 109 |
|---|---|
| one hundred and nineteen | 119 |
| one hundred and twenty | 120 |

1 Use numerals to write these numbers.

a sixteen 

b one hundred and sixteen 

c sixty-six 

d one hundred and seven 

e one hundred 

f one hundred and seventeen 

2 Write words for these numbers.

a 21

b 101

c 116

Don't forget to use a hyphen for twenty-one.

3

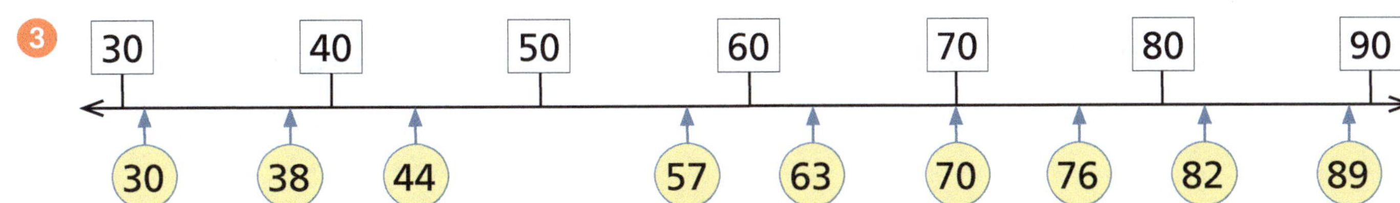


Look at the number line and write the nearest ten to:

a 63 

b 31 

c 82

d 38 

e 70 

f 89 

g 44 

h 57 

i 76 

# 13C The hexagon

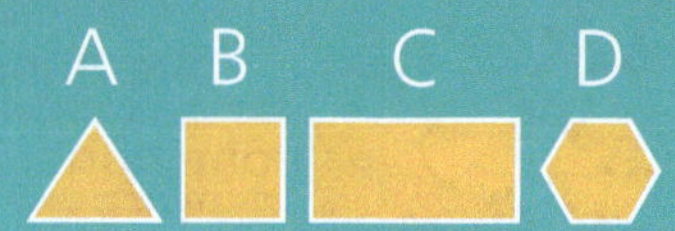


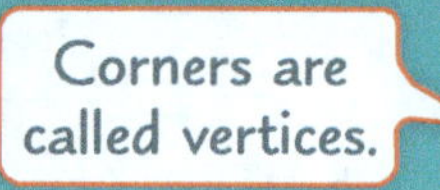

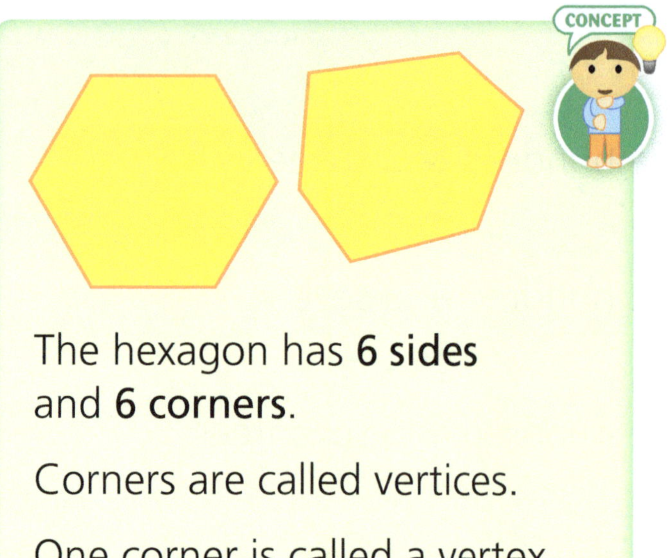

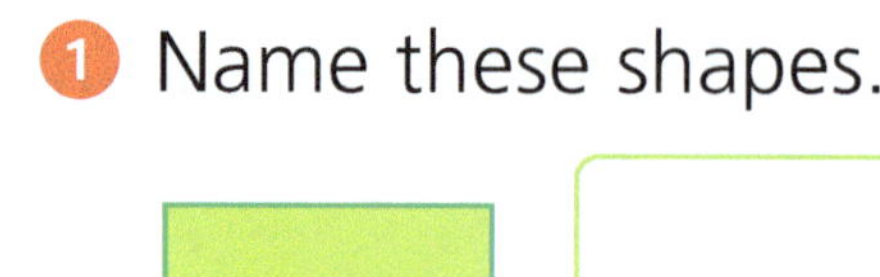

The hexagon has **6 sides** and **6 corners**.

Corners are called vertices.

One corner is called a vertex.

1. Name these shapes.

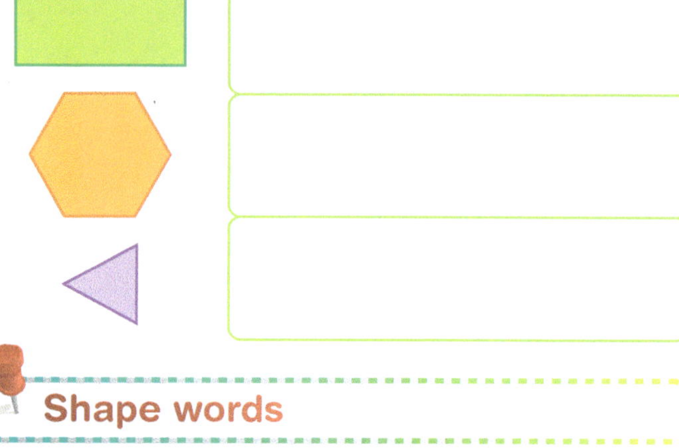

**Shape words**

circle triangle square rectangle hexagon

2. Trace each shape. Write its name.

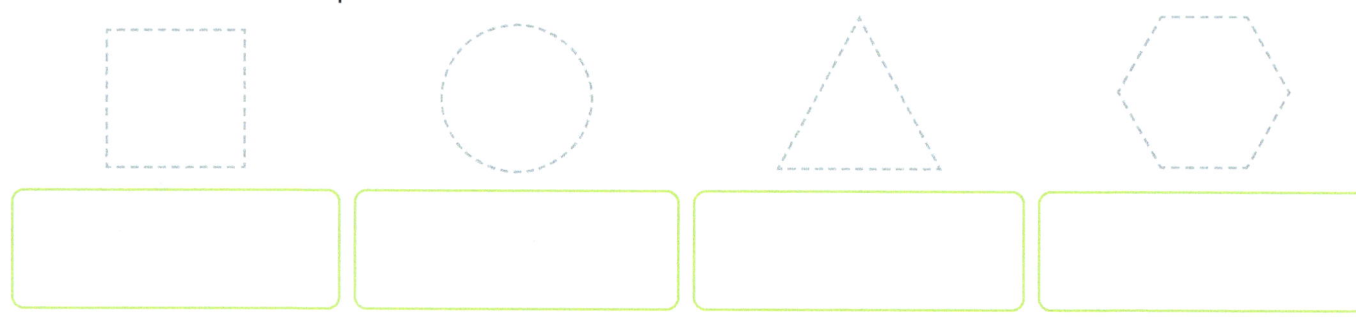

3. Colour the hexagons red.

4. Draw a hexagon.

All of these are hexagons.

5. A hexagon has ☐ sides and ☐ vertices.



 ISBN 9780655709022

# Picture graphs

1

**Straight or curly hair**

Straight hair

Curly hair

a How many people had straight hair?

b How many people had curly hair?

c How many people are shown altogether?

d How many more people had straight hair than curly hair?

2

**Favourite school day for Class 1M**

Monday

Tuesday

Wednesday

Thursday

Friday

a Which day was chosen least?

b How many of the class chose Monday?

c How many people chose a day?

d What is your favourite day?

# 14A Subtraction

– means take away or minus.
= means leaves or is equal to.

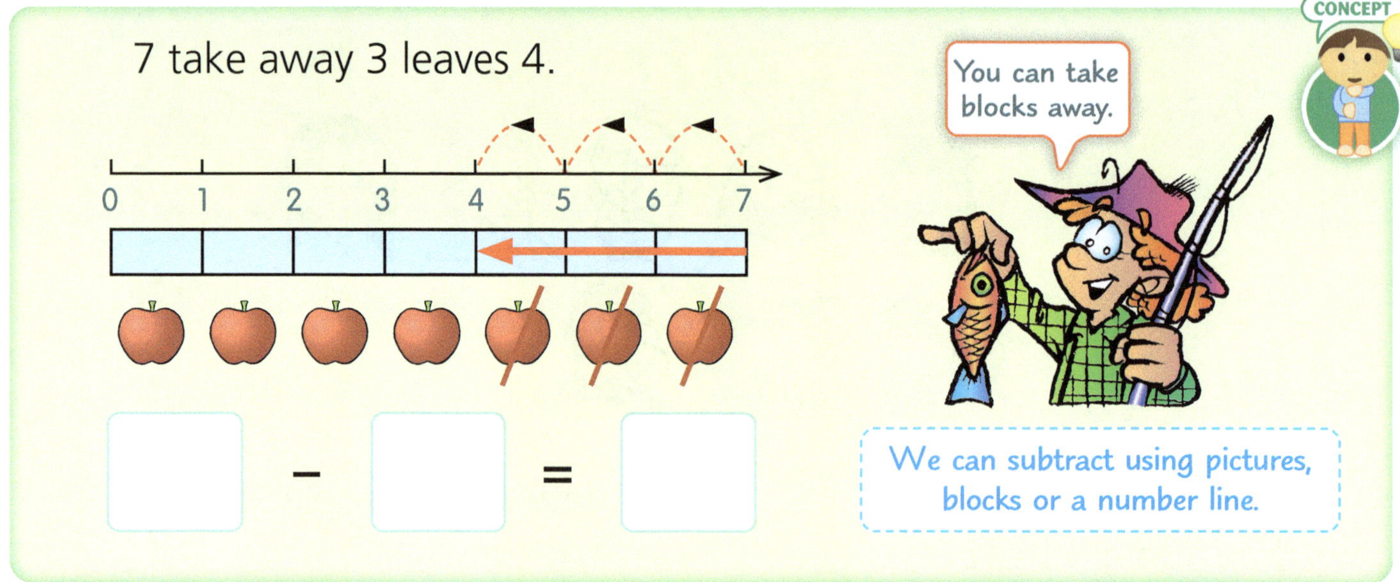


☐ – ☐ = ☐

1 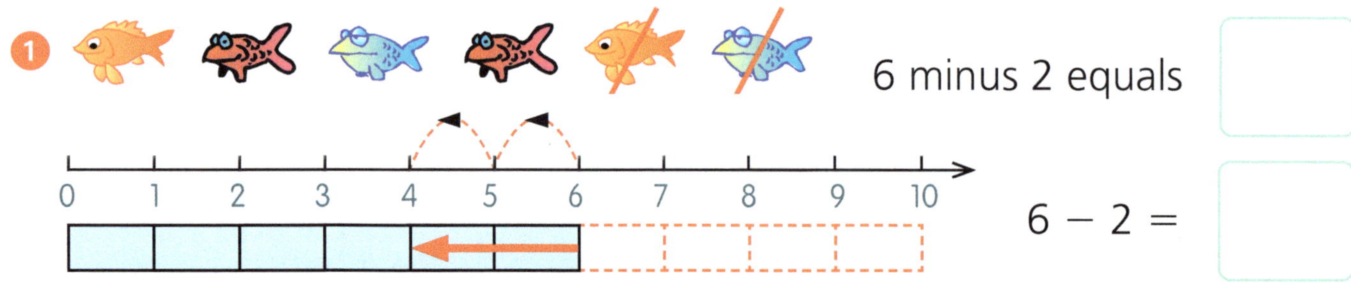


6 minus 2 equals ☐.

6 – 2 = ☐

2 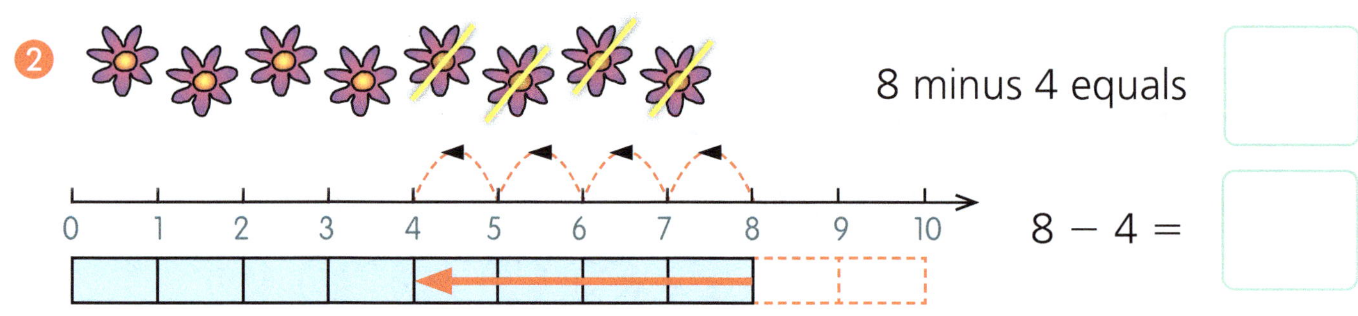


8 minus 4 equals ☐.

8 – 4 = ☐

ACTIVITY

Find the answers by taking away blocks placed below the number line. Trace the jumps with your finger. Make up some questions of your own.

9 – 7 = ☐

10 – 4 = ☐

0 1 2 3 4 5 6 7 8 9 10 11

# Subtraction

If 5 + 4 = 9 then 9 – 4 = 5

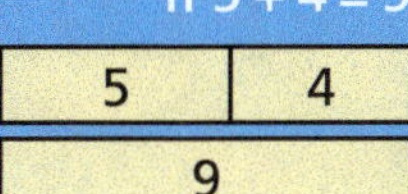

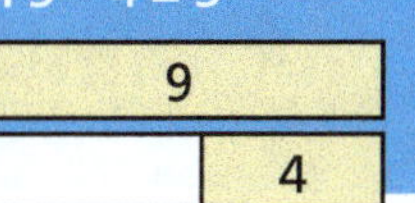

CONCEPT

9 take away 4 leaves 5. 9 – 4 = 5. 9 minus 4 is equal to 5.

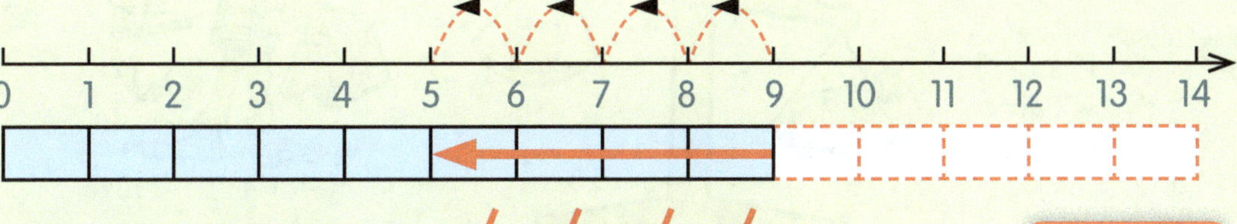

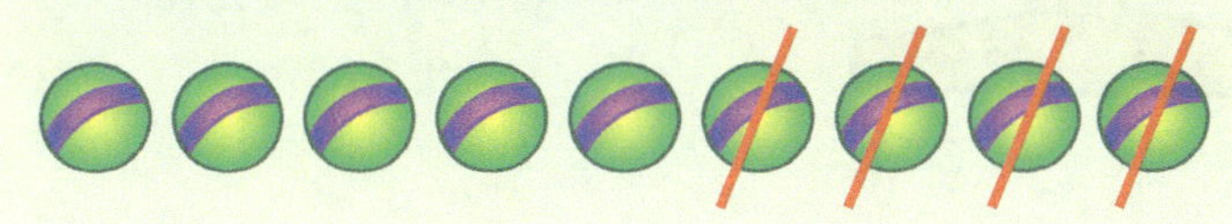

0 1 2 3 4 5 6 7 8 9 10 11 12 13 14

1. Use the number line above to answer these questions.

a 7 minus 4 equals ☐.  b 6 minus 3 equals ☐.

c 8 – 1 = ☐  d 6 – 5 = ☐  e 7 – 2 = ☐

f 9 – 5 = ☐  g 5 – 5 = ☐  h 8 – 5 = ☐

i 9 – 6 = ☐  j 8 – 3 = ☐  k 9 – 3 = ☐

l 10 – 3 = ☐  m 11 – 4 = ☐  n 7 – 5 = ☐

o 12 – 4 = ☐  p 13 – 6 = ☐  q 9 – 7 = ☐

# 14C Comparing the mass of objects

The heavier one goes down.

1 Circle the lighter object. Colour the heavier object. Trace the words.

Predict the heavier object by hefting. Use a balance scale to check. Circle the heavier object. Explain how you used the balance scales.

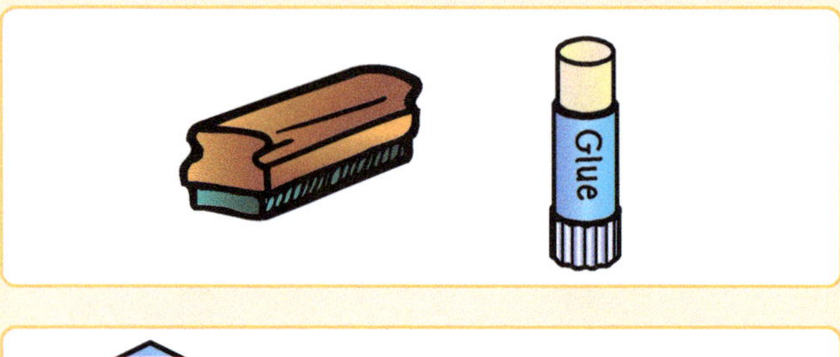

CONCEPT

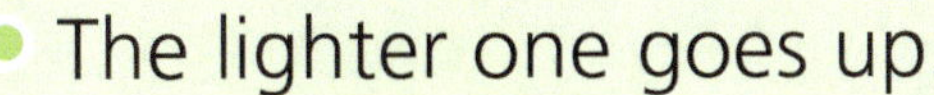

- The lighter one goes up.

The bottle is heavier.

- The scales are balanced.

**1** Cross out the heavier object. Circle objects that are balanced.

ACTIVITY

Use balance scales to compare these objects.
Circle the heavier object.

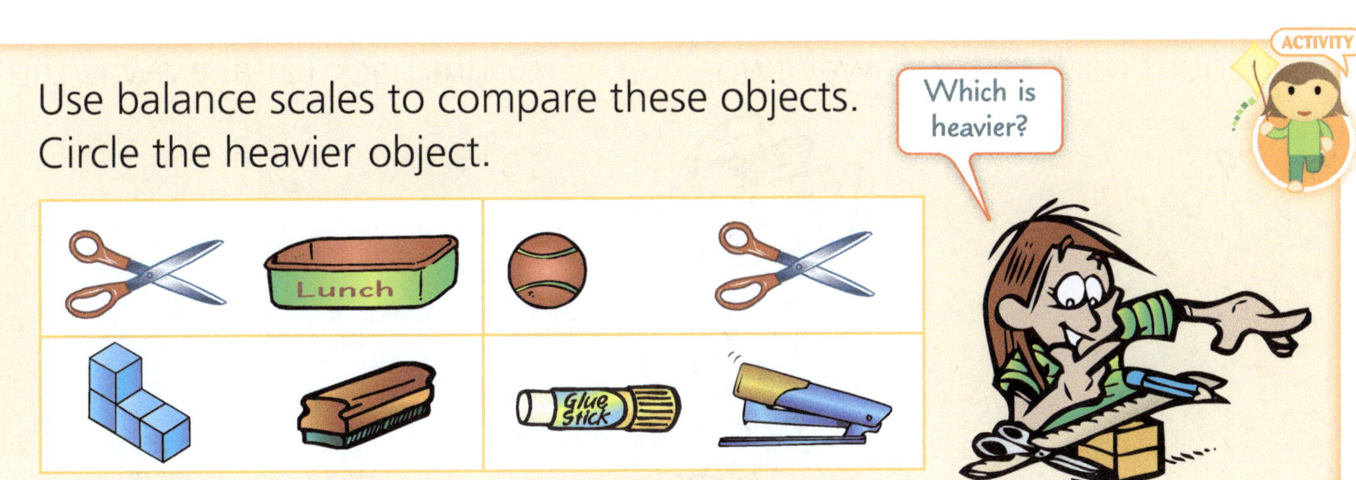

10 – 4
10 ... 9, 8, 7, 6

CONCEPT

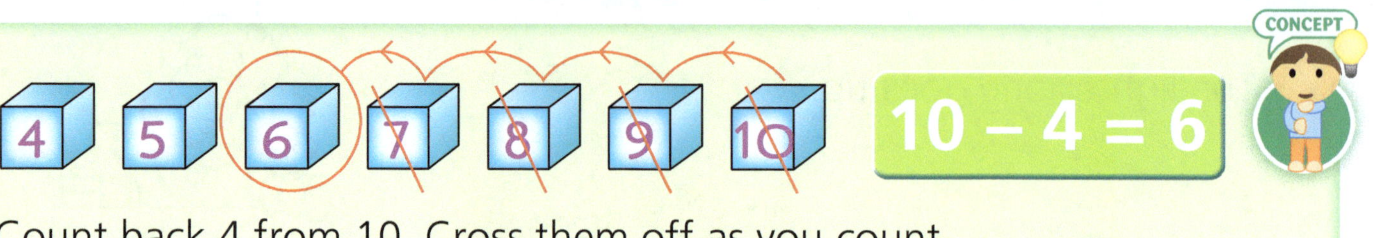


Count back 4 from 10. Cross them off as you count.

1. Count back to complete.

a

8 take away 1 leaves ☐.

b

11 take away 2 leaves ☐.

c

10 take away 3 leaves ☐.

d

8 take away 3 leaves ☐.

2. Count back to take away two.

| | | |
|---|---|---|
| 7 | ☐ | ☐ |
| 10 | ☐ | ☐ |
| 12 | ☐ | ☐ |

3. Count back to take away three.

| | | | |
|---|---|---|---|
| 15 | ☐ | ☐ | ☐ |
| 18 | ☐ | ☐ | ☐ |
| 20 | ☐ | ☐ | ☐ |



 ISBN 9780655709022

# 15B Counting back

We can use part of the line.

14 – 4 = 10

Start at 14.
Jump back 4.

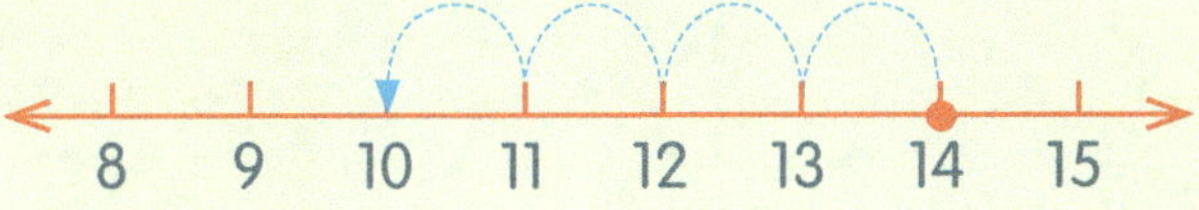

1 Use these number lines to count back.

a

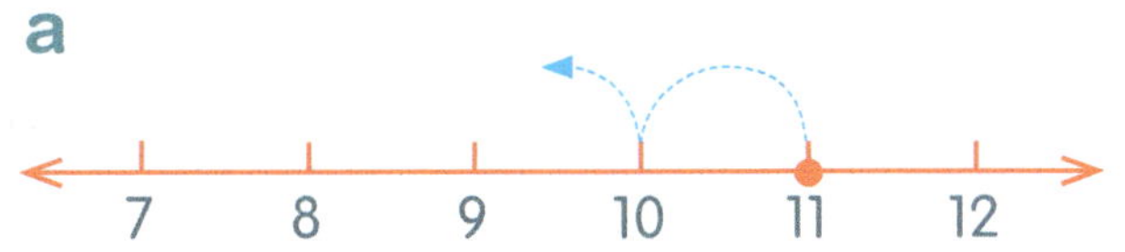


11 – 4 = ☐

b

15 – 5 = ☐

c

12 – 3 = ☐

d

16 – 6 = ☐

e

17 – 2 = ☐

f

19 – 4 = ☐

Use this number line to create your own subtraction sentences.

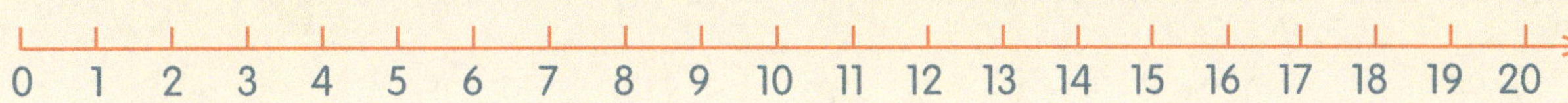

11 – 6 ... 10, 9, 8, 7, 6, 5

CONCEPT

Count back 6 from 11. $11 - 6 = 5$ Tally ||||||

0 1 2 3 4 5 6 7 8 9 10 11 12 13

1 Use the number line to complete each number sentence.

a $6 - 3 =$ ☐ b $13 - 6 =$ ☐ c $9 - 5 =$ ☐

d $14 - 9 =$ ☐ e $16 - 8 =$ ☐ f $15 - 9 =$ ☐

g $17 - 0 =$ ☐ h $20 - 5 =$ ☐ i $19 - 7 =$ ☐

2 a Ruby had $15. [15]
She spent $4. [4]
How much does she have left?

$ ☐

b Matt had 18 worms.
10 worms died.
How many worms are left?

3 Colour the words that mean –.

add | plus | difference between

take away | less than | subtract | minus

# Data displays

Everybody brought their pets to school.

1 Look at the picture and complete this table.

| Pets brought to school | | | |
|---|---|---|---|
| Birds | Cats | Dogs | Rabbits |
| | | | |

2 Draw a data display of the pets.

| Pets brought to school | | | | | |
|---|---|---|---|---|---|
| Birds | | | | | |
| Cats | | | | | |
| Dogs | | | | | |
| Rabbits | | | | | |

3 Write about this data display.

INVESTIGATION

What pets do people in your class have? Find out and fill in this graph.

| Birds | | | | | | | | | |
|---|---|---|---|---|---|---|---|---|---|
| Cats | | | | | | | | | |
| Dogs | | | | | | | | | |
| Fish | | | | | | | | | |
| Rabbits | | | | | | | | | |
| Other | | | | | | | | | |

# 16A Doubles

CONCEPT

When we add two numbers or groups that are the same, they are called **doubles**.

- Some doubles are: 1 + 1 2 + 2 3 + 3
- We say "Double 1", "Double 2", "Double 3".

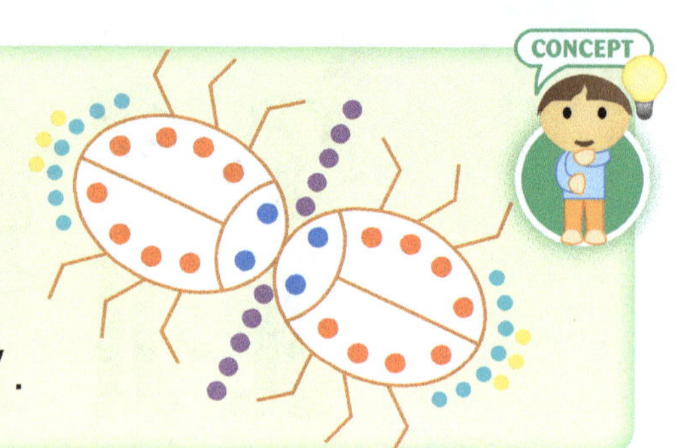

1 Use these pictures to complete the doubles.

a

| 2 | 2 |
|---|---|
| ? | |

2 horns and 2 horns

2 + ☐ = ☐

Double ☐ = ☐

b

| 4 | 4 |
|---|---|
| ? | |

4 legs and 4 legs

4 + ☐ = ☐

Double ☐ = ☐

c

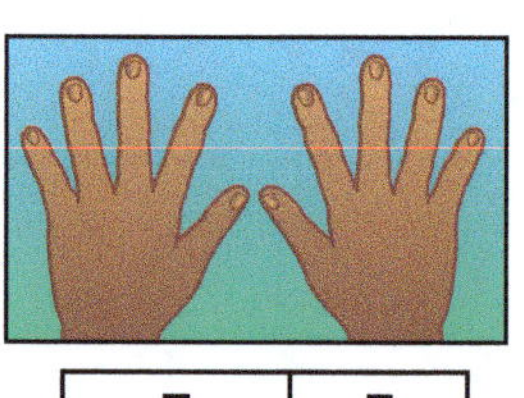

| 5 | 5 |
|---|---|
| ? | |

5 fingers and 5 fingers

☐ + ☐ = ☐

Double ☐ = ☐

INVESTIGATION

Circle all the doubles you can find on the bugs at the top.

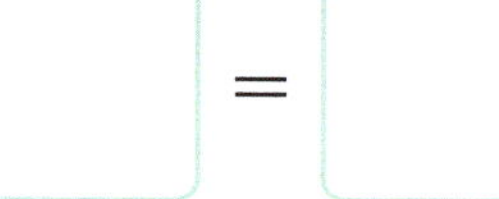

☐ + ☐ = ☐ ☐ + ☐ = ☐

☐ + ☐ = ☐ ☐ + ☐ = ☐

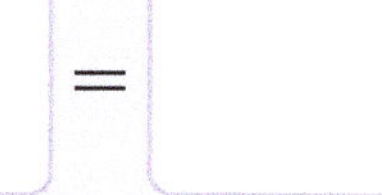

1 + 1 = 2 2 + 2 = 4 3 + 3 = 6 4 + 4 = 8 5 + 5 = 10

6 + 6 = 12 7 + 7 = 14 8 + 8 = 16 9 + 9 = 18 10 + 10 = 20

# Doubling and near doubling

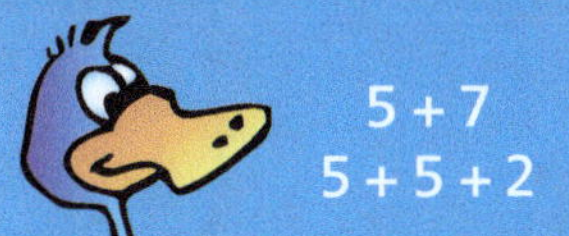

When you **double** a number, the answer will be **even**.

1. Complete each number sentence.

a double 3 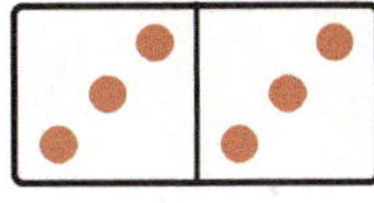

☐ + ☐ = ☐

b double 4 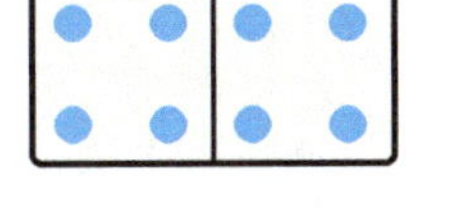

☐ + ☐ = ☐

c double 7 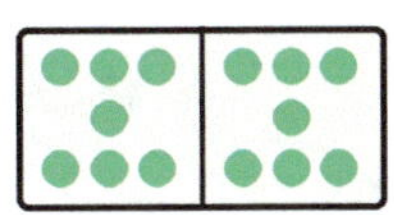

☐ + ☐ = ☐

d double 9 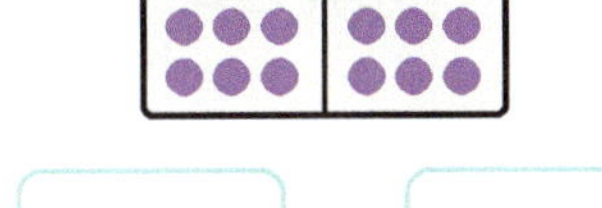

☐ + ☐ = ☐

2. a 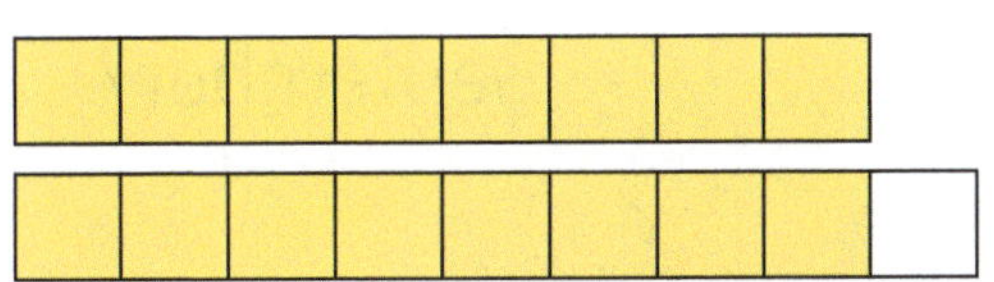

8 + 9 is double 8 plus 1.

8 + 8 + 1 = ☐

b 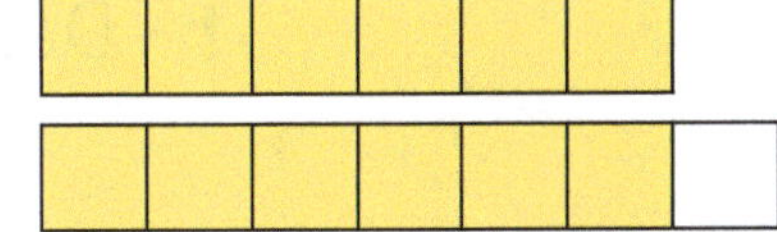

6 + 7 is double 6 plus 1.

6 + 6 + 1 = ☐

c 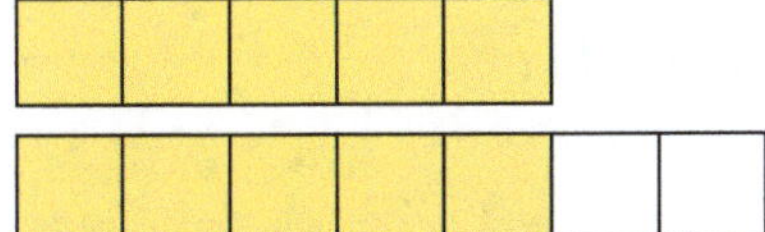

5 + 7 is double ☐ plus ☐.

☐ + ☐ + ☐ = ☐

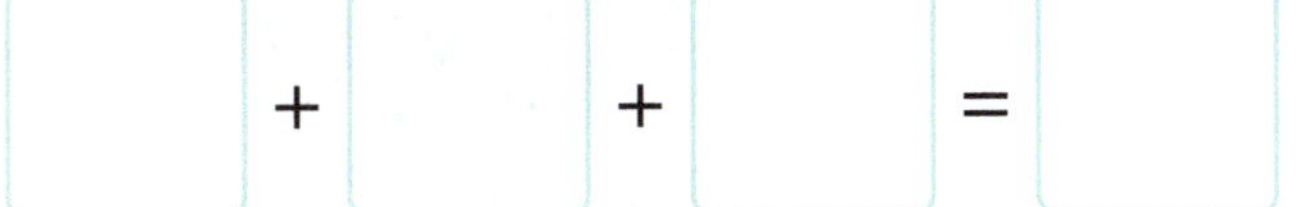

d 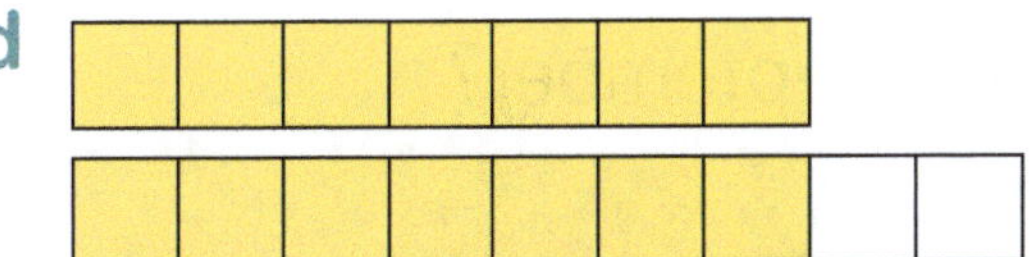

7 + 9 is double ☐ plus ☐.

☐ + ☐ + ☐ = ☐

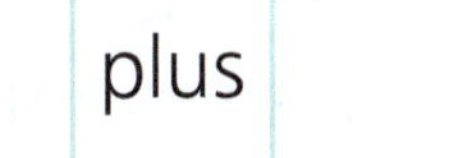

  ISBN 9780655709022

# 16C Months of the year

CONCEPT

The months of the year repeat in this order:

January, February, March, April, May, June, July, August, September, October, November, December

1 Which month comes after:

a February?

b August?

c October?

d December?

2 How many months are between January and:

a May?

b October?

c August?

d July?

e March?

f June?

g April?

h December?

i September?

3 Which month comes before:

a January?

b June?

c September?

d March?

ACTIVITY

Use the internet to find the months in which these events occur.

a Chinese New Year

b Valentine's Day

c Mother's Day

d Father's Day

# 16D Months and seasons

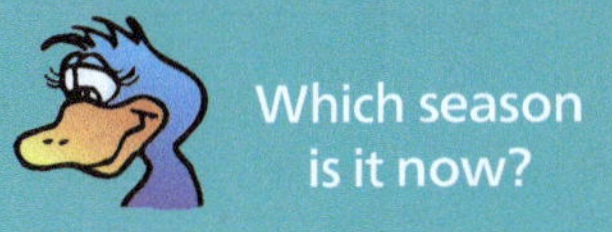

1 Write the months in their correct order within a calendar year.

| | | | |
|---|---|---|---|
| March | July | November | January |
| August | June | December | February |
| May | September | April | October |

| | | | |
|---|---|---|---|
| 1 | | 2 | |
| 3 | | 4 | |
| 5 | | 6 | |
| 7 | | 8 | |
| 9 | | 10 | |
| 11 | | 12 | |

Colour the summer months yellow. Colour the winter months blue.

# Patterns

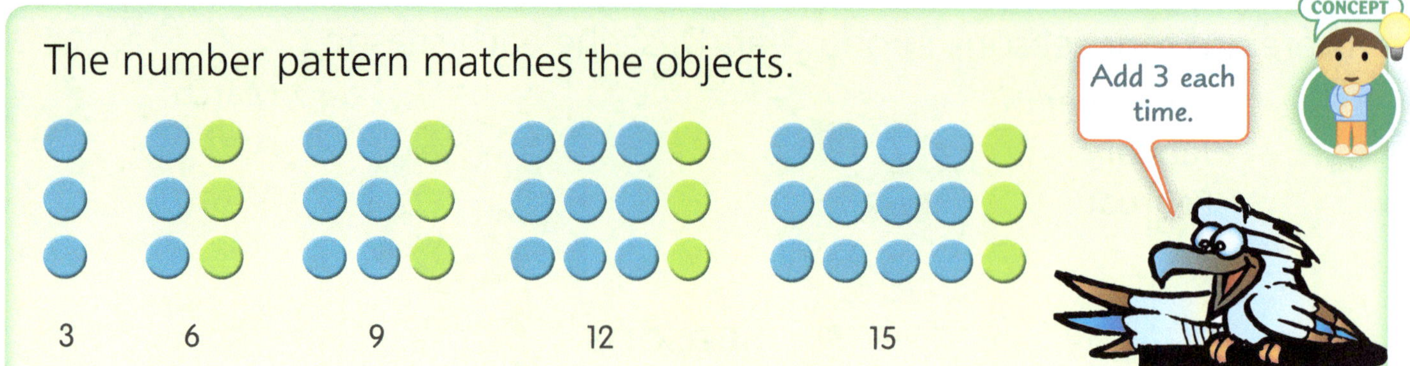


1 Complete each number pattern.

a

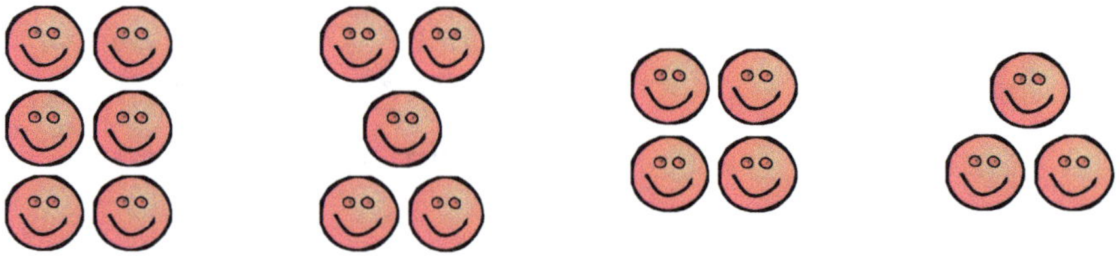

☐, ☐, ☐, ☐,

Subtract ☐ is the rule.

b

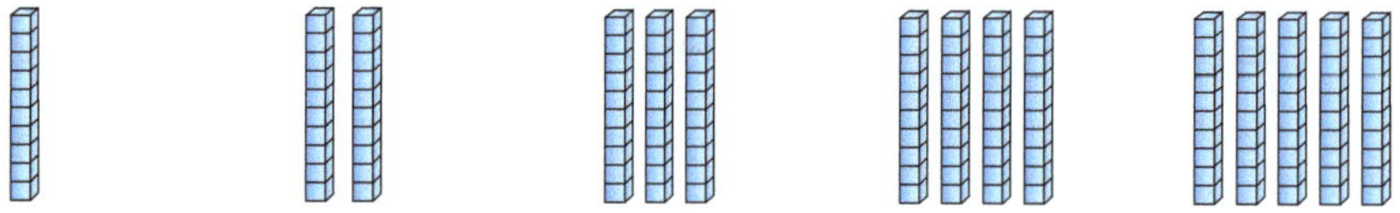

☐, ☐, ☐, ☐, ☐

Add ☐ is the rule.

c

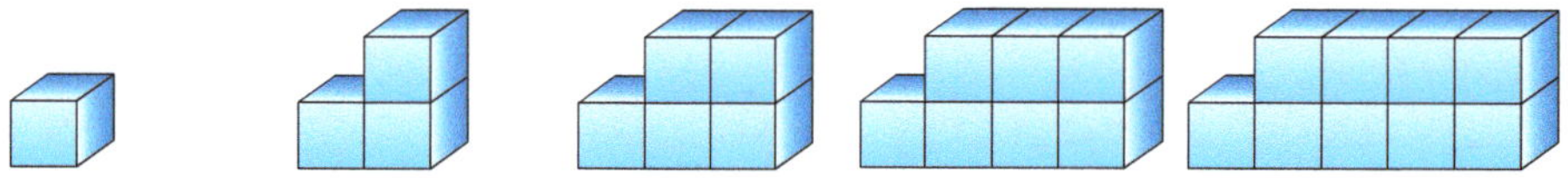

☐, ☐, ☐, ☐, ☐

Add ☐ is the rule.

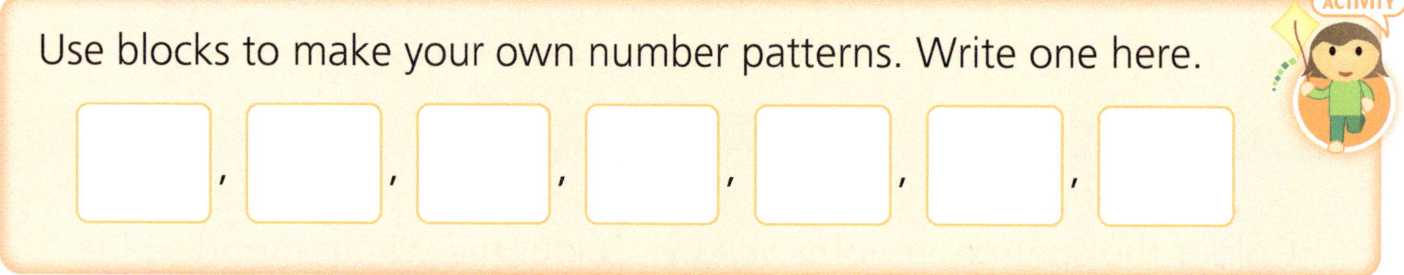

# Combinations for numbers

There are many ways to name the number nine.

one less than 10
three groups of 3
double 4 and one more

one more than 8
5 combined with 4
4 groups of 2 plus 1

1. Write the number 10 in different ways.

2. The numbers at the bottom add to give 9.

a

b

c

number bonds

3. Complete the number bond houses.

4. Circle true or false.

a $1 + 8 = 2 + 7$

true false

b $3 + 6 = 4 + 5$

true false

c $6 + 3 = 3 + 6$

true false

© PEARSON AUSTRALIA 2023 • *AUSTRALIAN SIGNPOST MATHS NSW 1* • ISBN 9780655709022

# 17C Object hunt

1 Draw an everyday object to match each 3D object below.

sphere

It is a ball-shaped object that has 1 curved surface. It can roll. It does not stack.

cube

It is a box-shaped object that has 6 flat square surfaces. It can slide and it stacks easily.

cylinder

It is a can-shaped object that has 2 flat circular surfaces and 1 curved surface. It can roll and it can slide. It stacks easily.

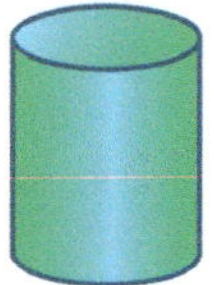

cone

It is a cone-shaped object that has 1 flat circular surface and 1 curved surface. It can roll and it can slide. It does not stack.

ACTIVITY

Use plasticine to make a model of each object.

prism

sphere

cylinder

cone

# Recognising 3D objects

1 Match each picture with a 3D object in the centre.

2 a Name two shapes that are the faces of each 3D object.

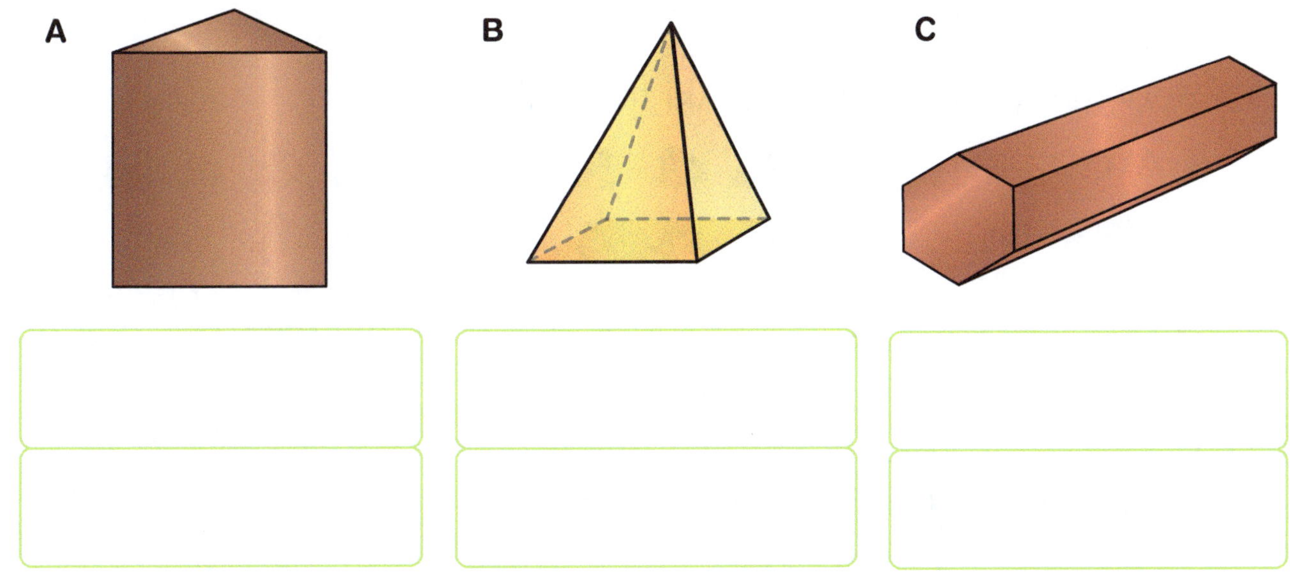


b How many faces? (A face is a flat surface with straight edges.)

A

B

C

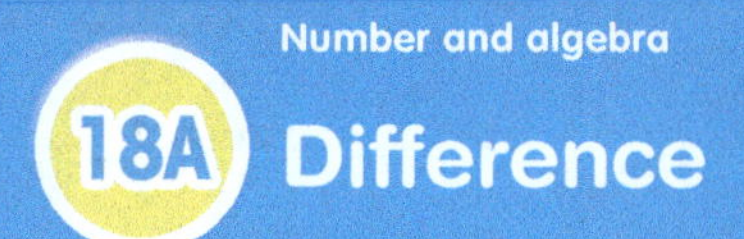

# 18A Difference

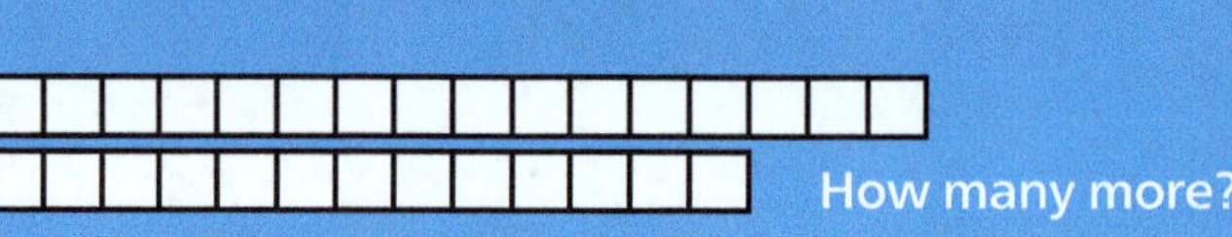

 can mean the **difference between**.

You can find the difference by counting on.
There are 4 more green counters.

1 Jane has ☐ ducks. 

Alex has ☐ ducks.      

☐ has ☐ more ducks than ☐.

2 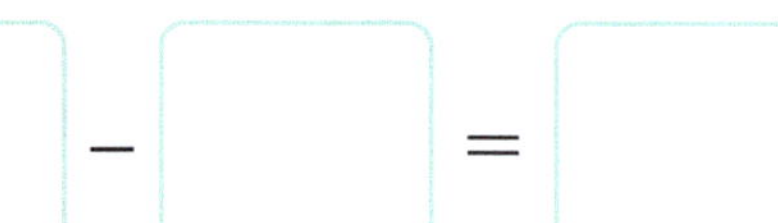

☐ – ☐ = ☐

There are ☐ more  than ☐. The difference is ☐.

3 How many more caps has Aki than Ella?

- Aki's caps:      
- Ella's caps:     

☐ – ☐ = ☐ Aki has ☐ more caps.

4 How many more  dots than  crosses?

Dots ● ● ● ● ● ● ● ● ● ● ● ● ● ● ● ● ●

Crosses X X X X X X X X X X X X X X

☐ – ☐ = ☐

 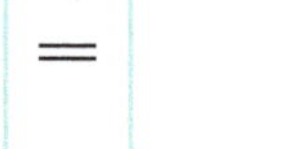

Use ones blocks to make examples of your own.



 • *AUSTRALIAN SIGNPOST MATHS NSW 1* • ISBN 9780655709022

# 18B Difference between groups

10 – 7

− also means the **difference between**.
Find the difference by counting on.
There are 3 more green counters.

1 

___ − ___ = ___

There are ___ more  than . The difference is ___.

2 

___ − ___ = ___

There are ___ more  than . The difference is ___.

3 

There are ___ more  than . The difference is ___.

4 

There are ___ more  than . The difference is ___.

Make 2 lines of counters that have a difference of 4.
Write a number sentence to match.

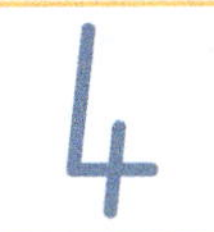 4 =  – 

# 18C The pentagon and octagon

A pentagon has 5 sides and 5 vertices (corners).

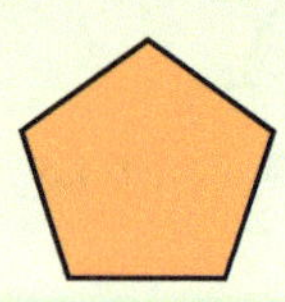
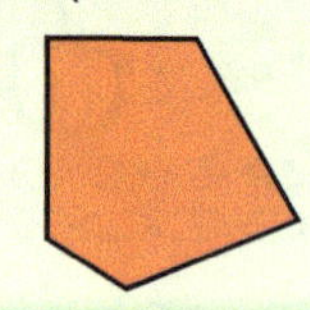

An octagon has 8 sides and 8 vertices (corners).

1 Trace around each shape. Write its name.

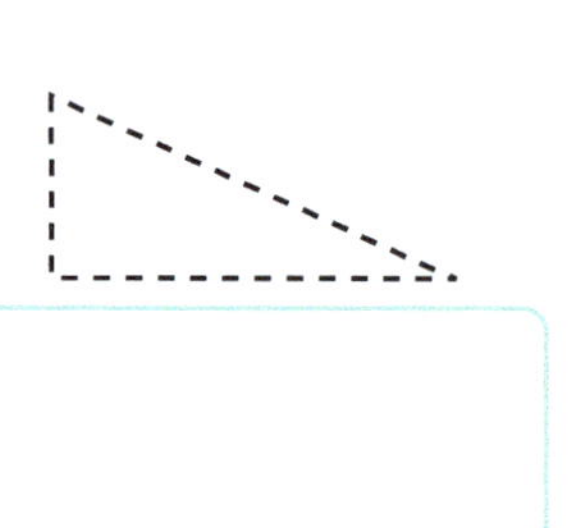

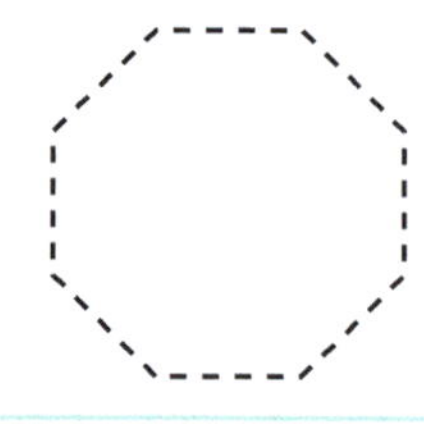

2 Colour the pentagons red and the octagons blue.

3 What am I?

a I have 5 sides and 5 vertices.

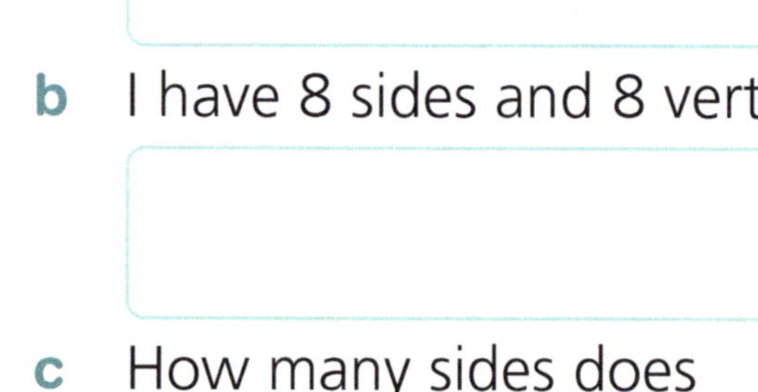

b I have 8 sides and 8 vertices.

c How many sides does a hexagon have?

4 Draw a pentagon.

5 Draw an octagon.

# Comparing areas

Area is the amount of surface on a shape.

1 Compare the top areas of these objects. List them from smallest to largest.

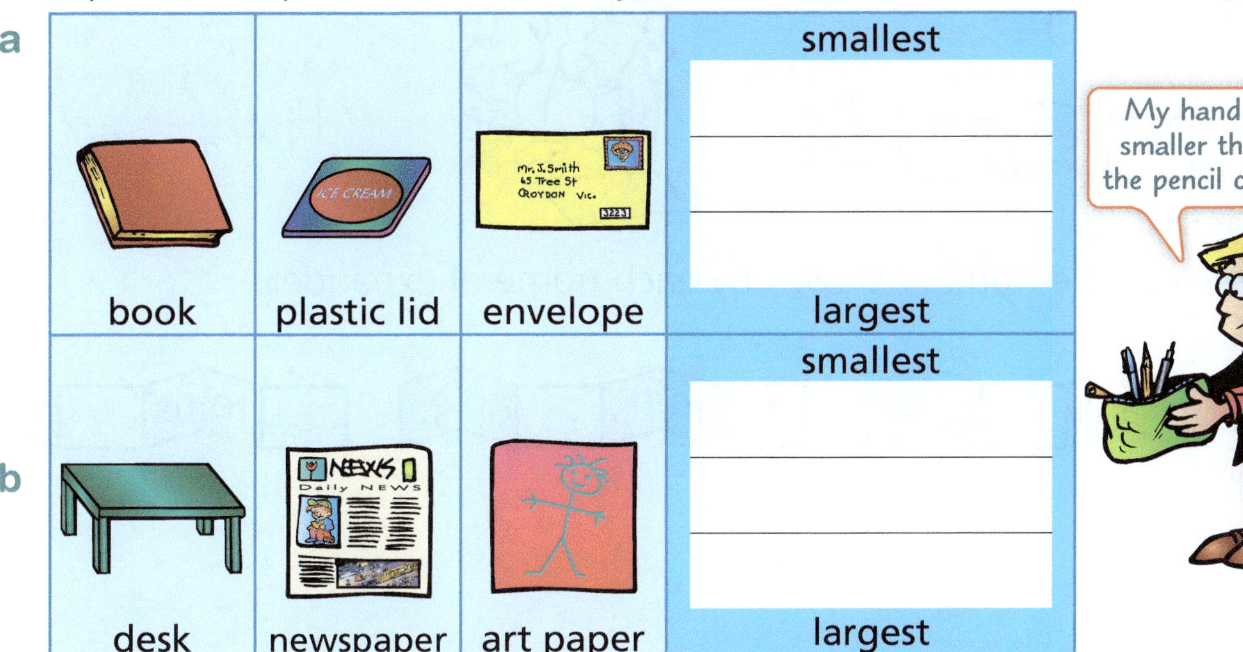


My hand is smaller than the pencil case.

2 Compare these objects. Circle the object with the smaller area.

a clock and book
b pencil case and hand
c towel and table
d newspaper and window
e art paper and window
f towel and cupboard door
g matchbox and book
h sheet of cardboard and window

3 Find objects in the classroom to complete the table. Check by covering. Draw the object.

| | Smaller area | About the same area | Larger area |
|---|---|---|---|
| newspaper | | | |
| book | | | |

The book has a smaller area than the newspaper.

4 Compare the area of two surfaces by cutting paper to cover one surface, then placing the cut paper on top of the other surface.

 • *AUSTRALIAN SIGNPOST MATHS NSW 1* • ISBN 9780655709022

# 19A Place value

79 70 + 9

1. Write the number shown by each numeral expander.

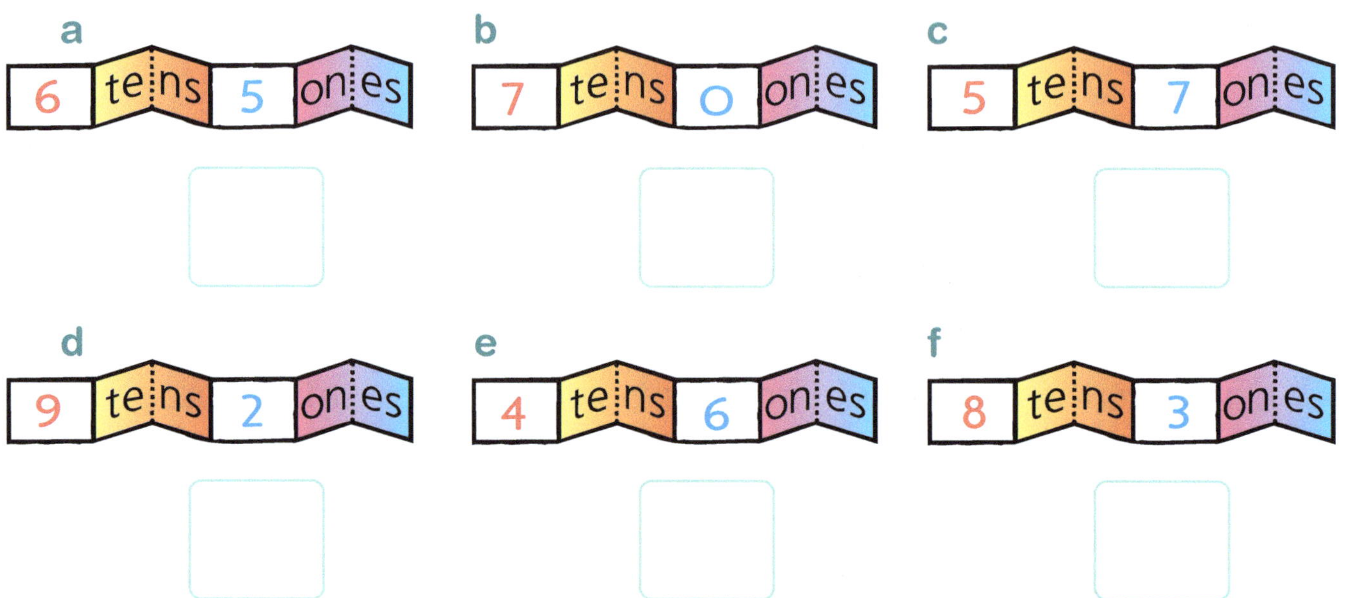


2. Complete:

a 78 = ☐ tens ☐ ones  b 80 = ☐ tens ☐ ones

c 54 = ☐ tens ☐ ones  d 61 = ☐ tens ☐ one

3. Circle the smaller number.

a 91 or 89  b 62 or 67  c 49 or 54

FUN SPOT

Three number cards are turned over. One student uses two of these to write a secret number. The other student tries to guess the secret number.

 ISBN 9780655709022

Start

1 Write the number shown by each numeral expander.

a

b

c

d

2 Expand the numbers.

a 90 = ☐ tens ☐ ones

b 73 = ☐ tens ☐ ones

c 112 = ☐ tens ☐ ones

3 Write the numerals.

a one hundred and five ☐

b eighty-three ☐

c one hundred and fifteen ☐

d one hundred ☐

ACTIVITY

Every 10th bead around this page is coloured, starting at the top.
Count the beads. Colour the beads at these numbers:

a 16 b 35 c 48 d 67 e 88 f 99 g 113

For each number say how many tens and how many ones.

120 110 100

 *AUSTRALIAN SIGNPOST MATHS NSW 1* • ISBN 9780655709022

**1** Complete each numeral expander and write the number.

a 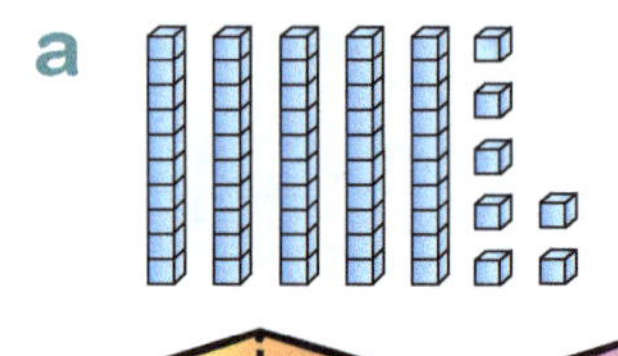

b 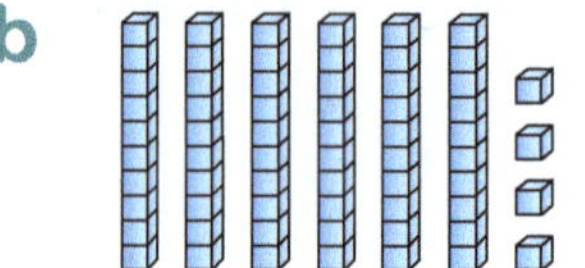

c 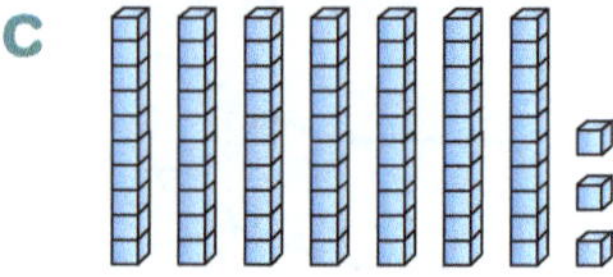

d 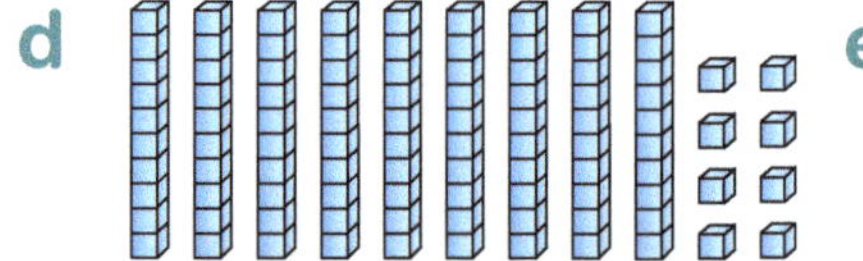

e 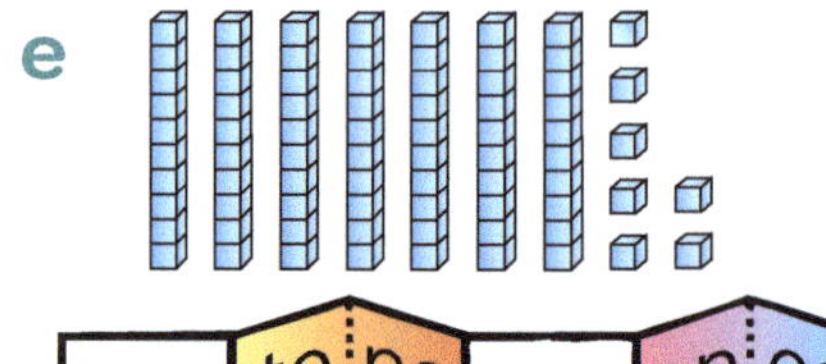

f 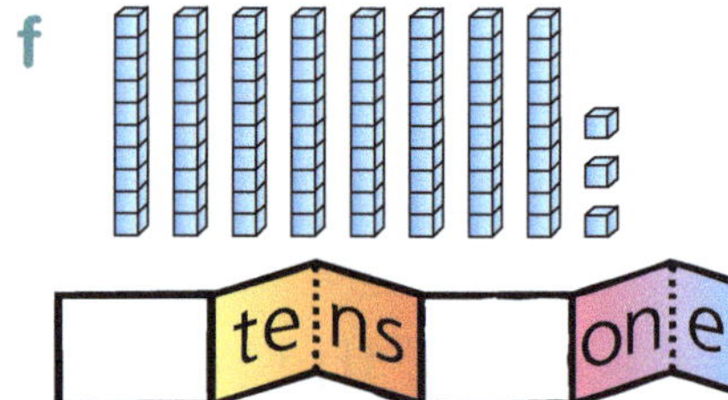

**2** Write the numeral.

a fifty-one

b thirty-eight

c eighty-two

d forty-seven

e ninety-four

f fourteen

**3** Write the numbers before (one less than) and after (one more than).

a

| before | | after |
|---|---|---|
| | 78 | |
| | 35 | |

b

| before | | after |
|---|---|---|
| | 80 | |
| | 56 | |


 • *AUSTRALIAN SIGNPOST MATHS NSW 1* • ISBN 9780655709022

# 19D Finding the nearest ten

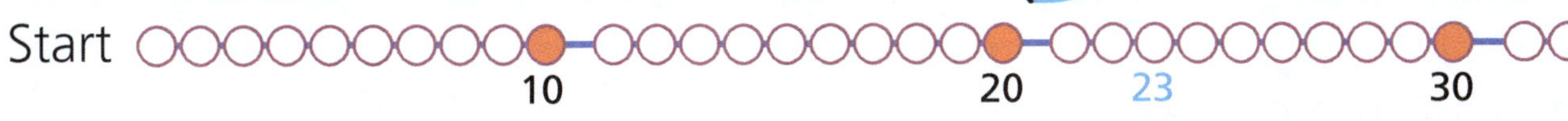


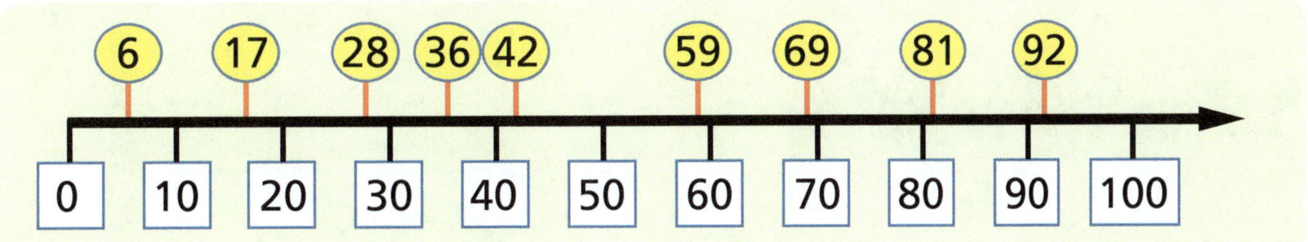


1 Use number line above to write the nearest ten to the number:

a 6 ☐ b 17 ☐ c 28 ☐

d 36 ☐ e 42 ☐ f 59 ☐

g 69 ☐ h 81 ☐ i 92 ☐

2

Use this number line to write the nearest ten to the number:

a 51 ☐ b 57 ☐ c 59 ☐

d 54 ☐ e 52 ☐ f 56 ☐

3 Use the beads around the page to write the nearest ten to the number:

a 58 ☐ b 23 ☐ c 72 ☐

d 86 ☐ e 44 ☐ f 97 ☐

# Subtraction by counting on

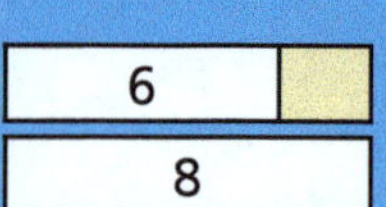

CONCEPT

How many more make 8?

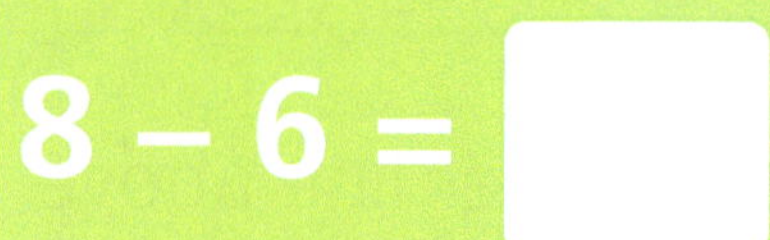


- I count on from 6 to make 8.
- I need 2 more to make 8.

**1** Draw the missing objects and complete.

**a**

How many more to make 8?

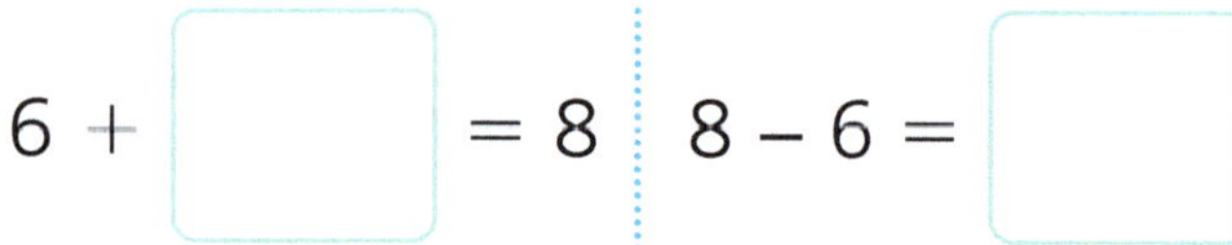

6 + ☐ = 8 | 8 – 6 = ☐

**b**

How many more to make 7?

6 + ☐ = 7 | 7 – 6 = ☐

**c**

How many more to make 9?

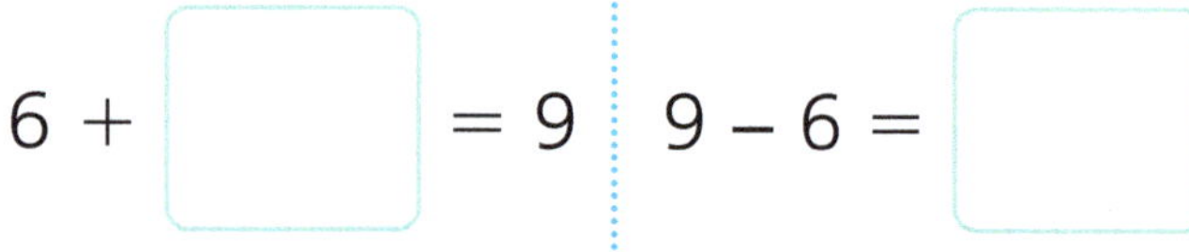

6 + ☐ = 9 | 9 – 6 = ☐

**d**

How many more to make 10?

7 + ☐ = 10 | 10 – 7 = ☐

**e**

How many more to make 8?

5 + ☐ = 8 | 8 – 5 = ☐

**f**

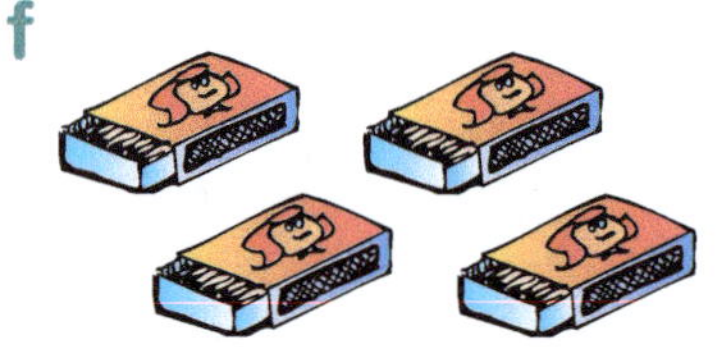

How many more to make 7?

4 + ☐ = 7 | 7 – 4 = ☐

# 20B Number relationships

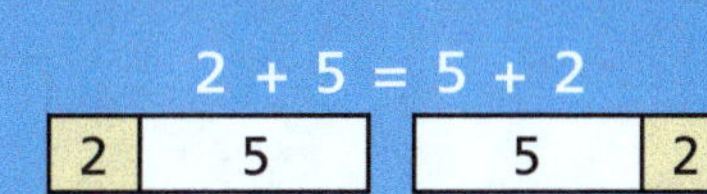

**=** can mean **is the same as**, **equals** or **is equal to**.

$2 + 2 = 1 + 3 = 4$

  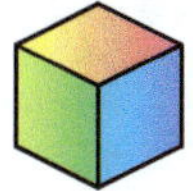 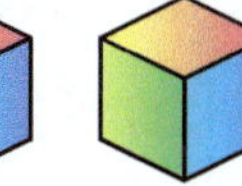 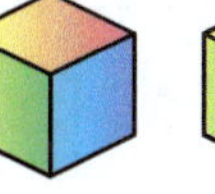 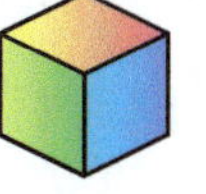       

**1**

a $1 + 4 =$ ☐ $2 + 3 =$ ☐
so $1 + 4 = 2 + 3 =$ ☐

b $5 + 2 =$ ☐ $3 + 4 =$ ☐
so $5 + 2 = 3 + 4 =$ ☐

c $3 + 1 =$ ☐ $1 + 3 =$ ☐
so $3 + 1 = 1 + 3 =$ ☐

d $6 + 2 =$ ☐ $2 + 6 =$ ☐
so $6 + 2 = 2 + 6 =$ ☐

e $4 + 5 =$ ☐ $5 + 4 =$ ☐
so $4 + 5 = 5 + 4 =$ ☐

f $7 + 3 =$ ☐ $3 + 7 =$ ☐
so $7 + 3 = 3 + 7 =$ ☐

**2** True (T) or false (F)?

a $8 + 5 = 4 + 9$ ☐

b $5 + 4 = 3 + 6$ ☐

**3** Match those that have the same answer.

| 6 + 7 | 9 + 4 | 7 + 5 | 6 + 5 | 8 + 7 | 7 + 4 |
|---|---|---|---|---|---|
| 4 + 9 | 5 + 7 | 7 + 6 | 7 + 8 | 4 + 7 | 5 + 6 |

*AUSTRALIAN SIGNPOST MATHS NSW 1* • ISBN 9780655709022

# Numbers to 100

ACTIVITY

On the number chart:

- Count by **ones** to 100.
- Count by **twos** to 50.
- Count by **fives** to 100.
- Count by **tens** to 100.

Start at any number on the chart and count backwards or forwards by ones.

| 1 | 2 | 3 | 4 | 5 | 6 | 7 | 8 | 9 | 10 |
|---|---|---|---|---|---|---|---|---|---|
| 11 | 12 | 13 | 14 | 15 | 16 | 17 | 18 | 19 | 20 |
| 21 | 22 | 23 | 24 | 25 | 26 | 27 | 28 | 29 | 30 |
| 31 | 32 | 33 | 34 | 35 | 36 | 37 | 38 | 39 | 40 |
| 41 | 42 | 43 | 44 | 45 | 46 | 47 | 48 | 49 | 50 |
| 51 | 52 | 53 | 54 | 55 | 56 | 57 | 58 | 59 | 60 |
| 61 | 62 | 63 | 64 | 65 | 66 | 67 | 68 | 69 | 70 |
| 71 | 72 | 73 | 74 | 75 | 76 | 77 | 78 | 79 | 80 |
| 81 | 82 | 83 | 84 | 85 | 86 | 87 | 88 | 89 | 90 |
| 91 | 92 | 93 | 94 | 95 | 96 | 97 | 98 | 99 | 100 |

1. Use the number chart above to locate the nearest ten to each number.

**a** 43 ☐ **b** 61 ☐ **c** 39 ☐

**d** 86 ☐ **e** 70 ☐ **f** 68 ☐

**g** 34 ☐ **h** 57 ☐ **i** 72 ☐

68 and 72 are both 2 away from 70.

2. Write the numbers before (one less than) and after (one more than).

**a**

| before | | after |
|---|---|---|
| | 69 | |
| | 100 | |

**b**

| before | | after |
|---|---|---|
| | 83 | |
| | 55 | |

3. Write the numbers given in Question 1 parts **a** to **f** in order, smallest to largest.

# 20D Chance words

FUN SPOT

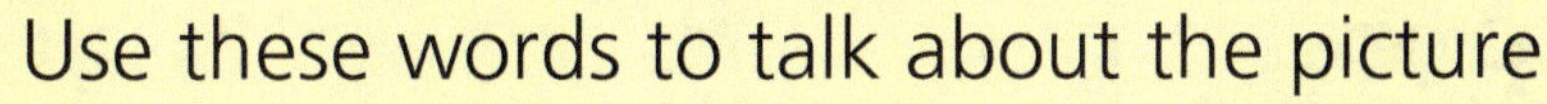

Use these words to talk about the picture.

will happen | won't happen | might happen

maybe | probably

# 21A Equal groups

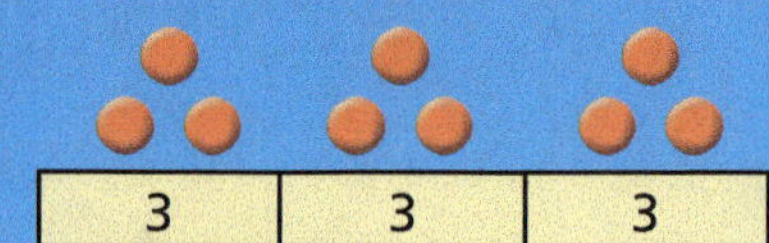

3 groups of 5 = 15

| 5 | 5 | 5 |
|---|---|---|
| 15 | | |

**1** a

☐ + ☐

☐ groups of ☐ = ☐

b

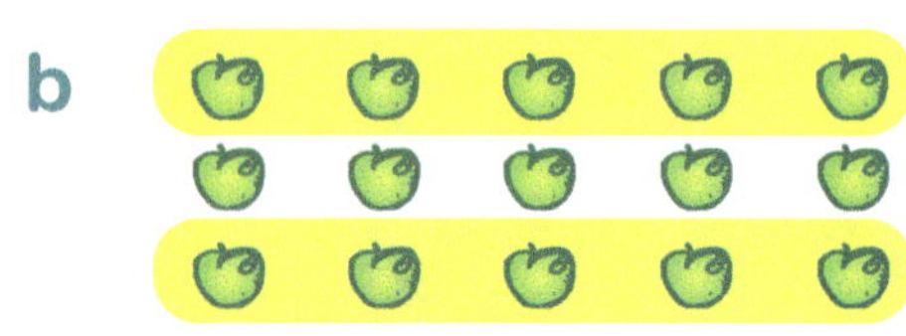

☐ + ☐ + ☐

☐ groups of ☐ = ☐

c

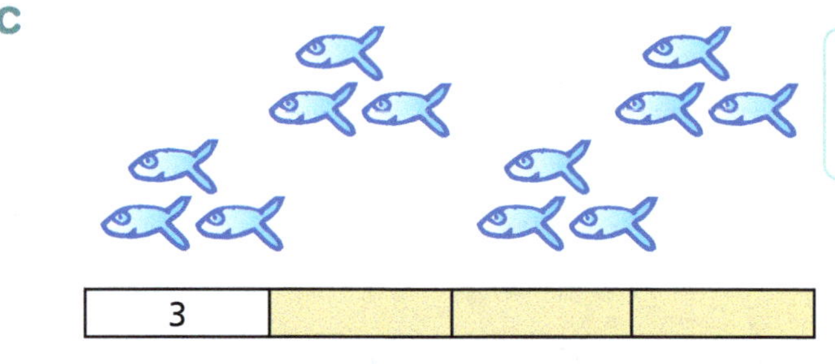

| 3 | | | |
|---|---|---|---|

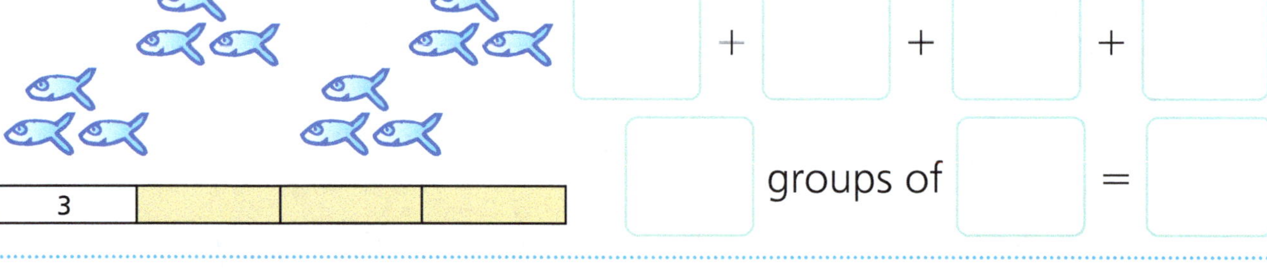

☐ + ☐ + ☐ + ☐

☐ groups of ☐ = ☐

d

| 6 | | |
|---|---|---|

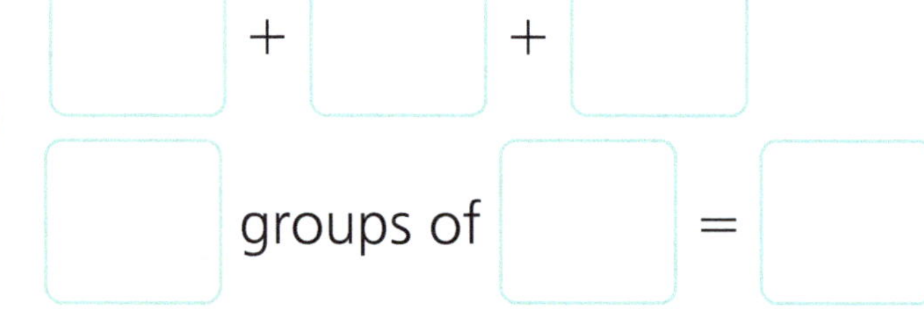

☐ + ☐ + ☐

☐ groups of ☐ = ☐

e 4 groups of 2 trees

☐ + ☐ + ☐ + ☐

☐ groups of ☐ = ☐

f 3 groups of 4 worms

☐ + ☐ + ☐

☐ groups of ☐ = ☐

 • *AUSTRALIAN SIGNPOST MATHS NSW 1* • ISBN 9780655709022

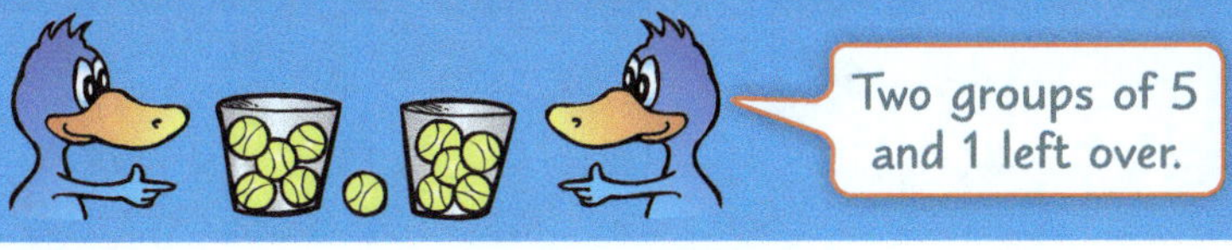

# 21B Using groups

Two groups of 5 and 1 left over.

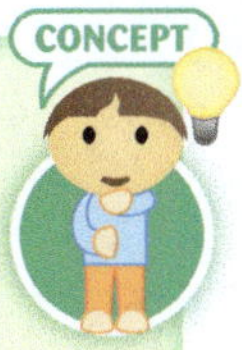

CONCEPT

Use counters to model this problem.

12 apples. Put 4 in each box.
How many boxes do we need?

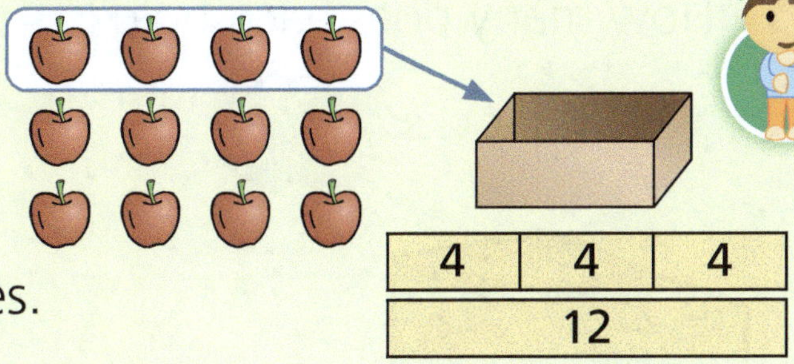

| 4 | 4 | 4 |
|---|---|---|
| 12 | | |

Answer: We would need ☐ boxes.

**1** Draw circles to show these groups or rows.

**a** groups of 3 frogs

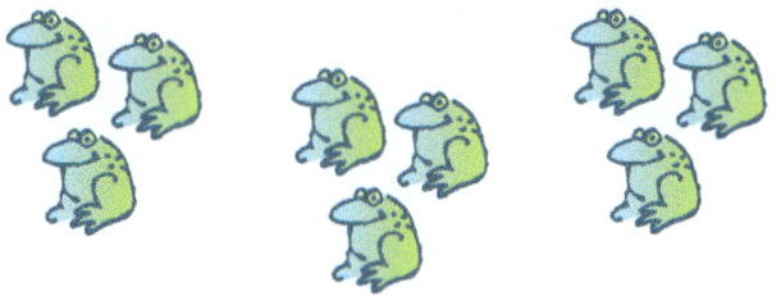

How many frogs? ☐ How many groups of 3? ☐

**b** groups of 4 jugs

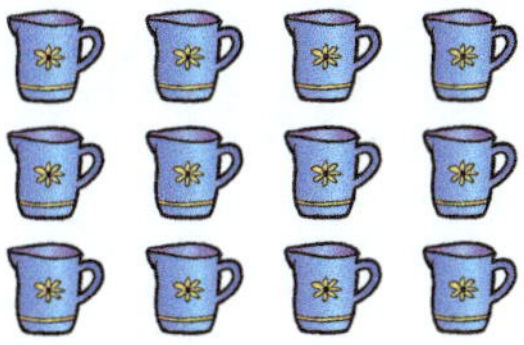

How many jugs? ☐ How many groups of 4? ☐

**c** groups of 8 fish

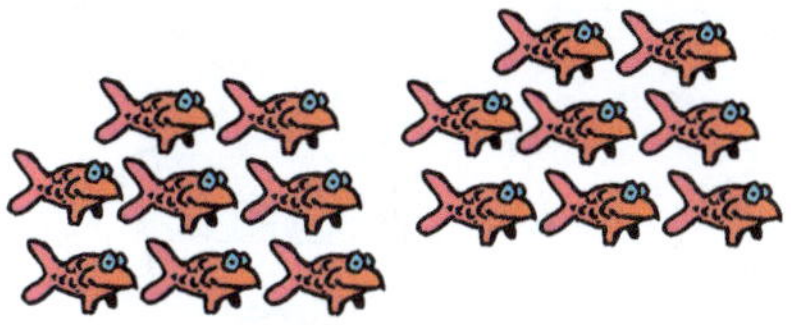

How many fish? ☐ How many groups of 8? ☐

**d**

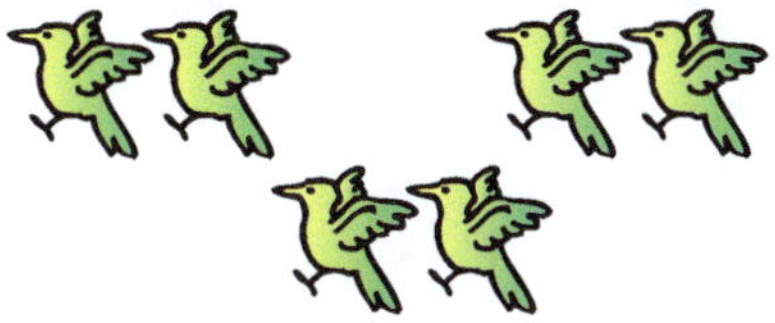

How many birds? ☐ How many groups of 2? ☐

**e**

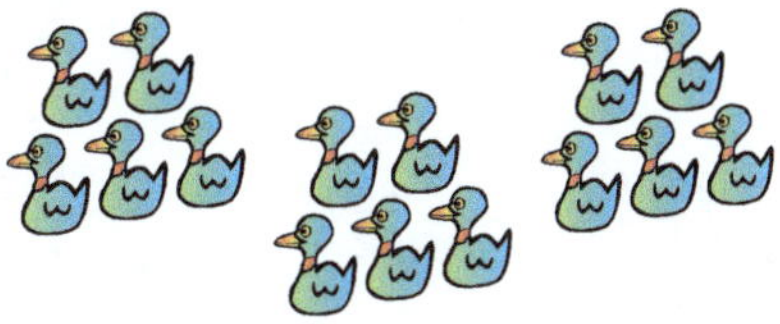

How many ducks? ☐ How many groups of 5? ☐

**f**

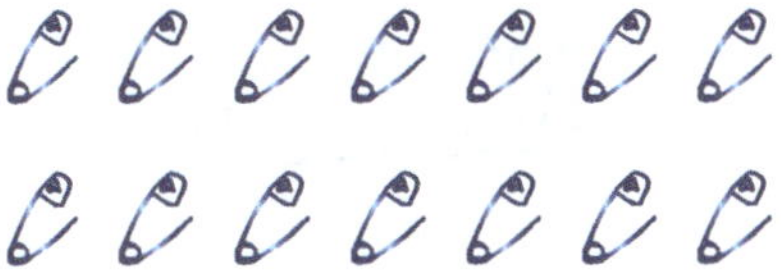

How many pins? ☐ How many groups of 7? ☐

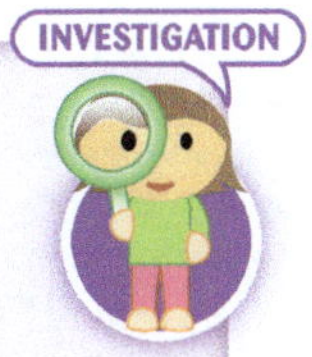

INVESTIGATION

Use 20 counters. How many students can be given:

**a** 3 counters? ☐ students with ☐ counters left over.

**b** 6 counters? ☐ students with ☐ counters left over.

# 21C Informal units of volume

INVESTIGATION

Volume is how much space an object takes up.

1. How many does each hold?

**a** Use blocks.

Fitwell Shoes — Guess ☐ Check ☐

Lunch — Guess ☐ Check ☐

**b** Use marbles.

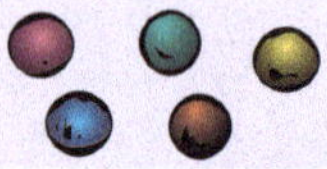

YOGHURT — Guess ☐ Check ☐

Cup — Guess ☐ Check ☐

**c** Use place-value ones blocks.

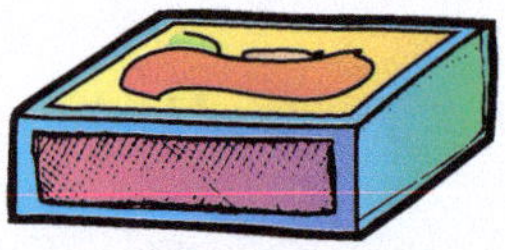

Box — Guess ☐ Check ☐

Egg cup — Guess ☐ Check ☐

**d** Use place-value tens blocks.

CHAMP dog food — Guess ☐ Check ☐

TOOTHPASTE SMILEY — Guess ☐ Check ☐

2. In each part of Question 1, circle the object that has the larger volume. Which unit is easiest to use? ☐

3. If there are gaps when packing, would this make it hard to compare jugs? ☐



 • *AUSTRALIAN SIGNPOST MATHS NSW 1* • ISBN 9780655709022

# 21D Comparing volume

No gaps is better.

1 Record the number of blocks in containers A and B.

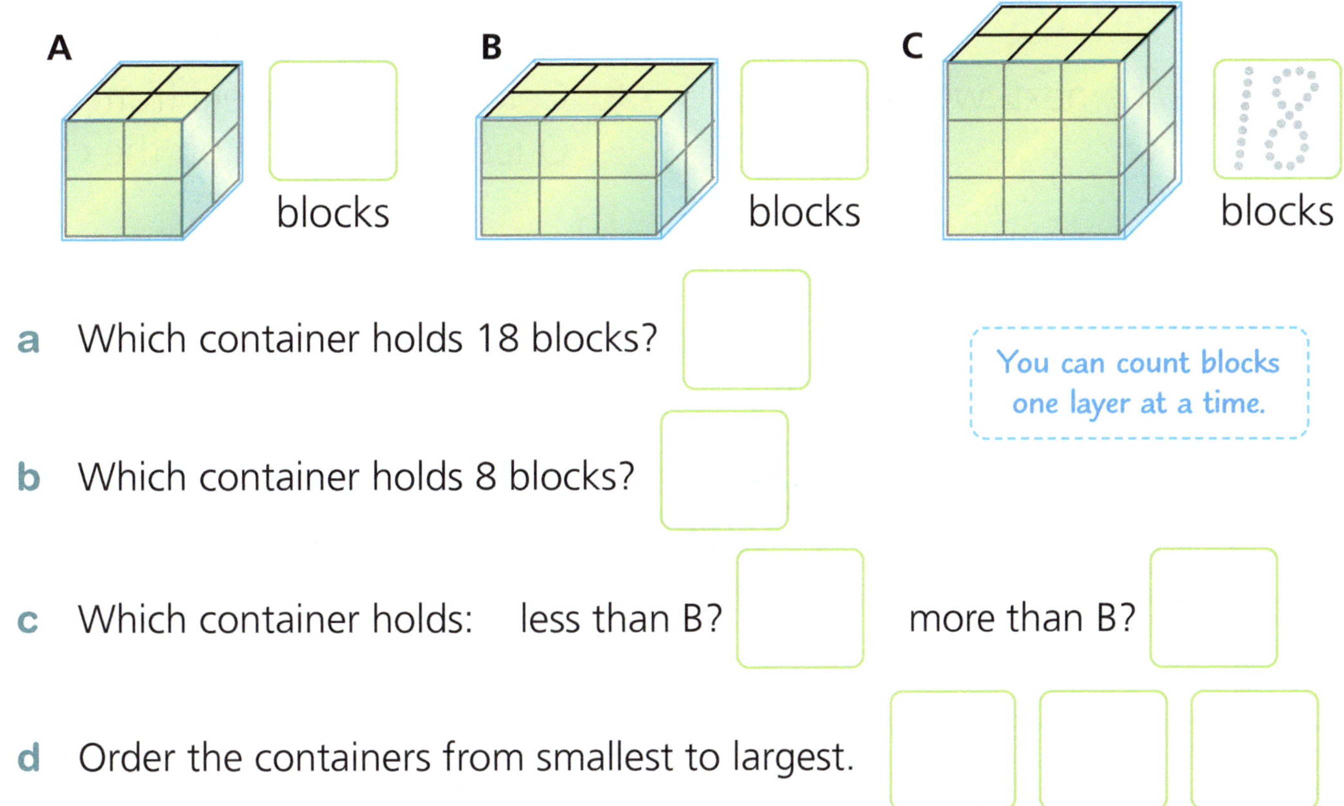


a Which container holds 18 blocks? ☐

b Which container holds 8 blocks? ☐

You can count blocks one layer at a time.

c Which container holds: less than B? ☐ more than B? ☐

d Order the containers from smallest to largest. ☐ ☐ ☐

ACTIVITY

Pack blocks into two containers. Record the number of blocks needed to fill each container.

| Container | Guess | Volume | Hold less or more? |
|---|---|---|---|
| 1 | ☐ blocks | ☐ blocks | |
| 2 | ☐ blocks | ☐ blocks | |

The number between 27 and 29 is 28.

## 1 Write the missing numbers.

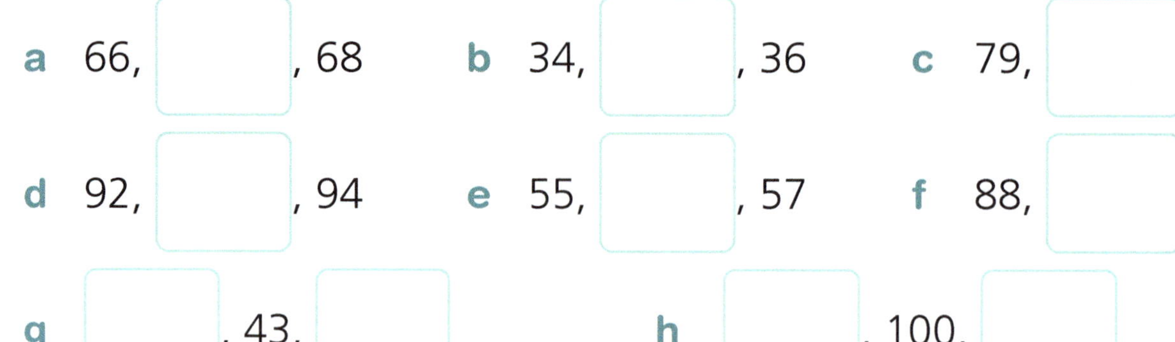

a 66, ☐, 68   b 34, ☐, 36   c 79, ☐, 81

d 92, ☐, 94   e 55, ☐, 57   f 88, ☐, 90

g ☐, 43, ☐   h ☐, 100, ☐

## 2 Write the next two numbers.

a 37, ☐, ☐

b 86, ☐, ☐

c 40, ☐, ☐

d 105, ☐, ☐

e 118, ☐, ☐

Practise counting to 120.

## 3 Colour your answers from Questions 1 and 2 on the chart.

| 1 | 2 | 3 | 4 | 5 | 6 | 7 | 8 | 9 | 10 |
|---|---|---|---|---|---|---|---|---|---|
| 11 | 12 | 13 | 14 | 15 | 16 | 17 | 18 | 19 | 20 |
| 21 | 22 | 23 | 24 | 25 | 26 | 27 | 28 | 29 | 30 |
| 31 | 32 | 33 | 34 | 35 | 36 | 37 | 38 | 39 | 40 |
| 41 | 42 | 43 | 44 | 45 | 46 | 47 | 48 | 49 | 50 |
| 51 | 52 | 53 | 54 | 55 | 56 | 57 | 58 | 59 | 60 |
| 61 | 62 | 63 | 64 | 65 | 66 | 67 | 68 | 69 | 70 |
| 71 | 72 | 73 | 74 | 75 | 76 | 77 | 78 | 79 | 80 |
| 81 | 82 | 83 | 84 | 85 | 86 | 87 | 88 | 89 | 90 |
| 91 | 92 | 93 | 94 | 95 | 96 | 97 | 98 | 99 | 100 |
| 101 | 102 | 103 | 104 | 105 | 106 | 107 | 108 | 109 | 110 |
| 111 | 112 | 113 | 114 | 115 | 116 | 117 | 118 | 119 | 120 |

## 4 Count by tens to join the dots.

a

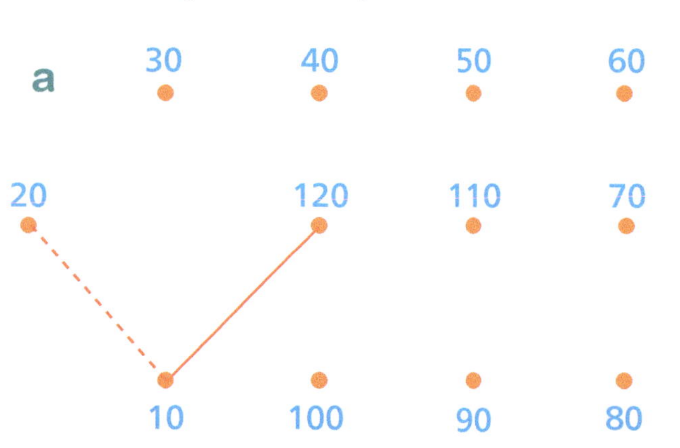


b

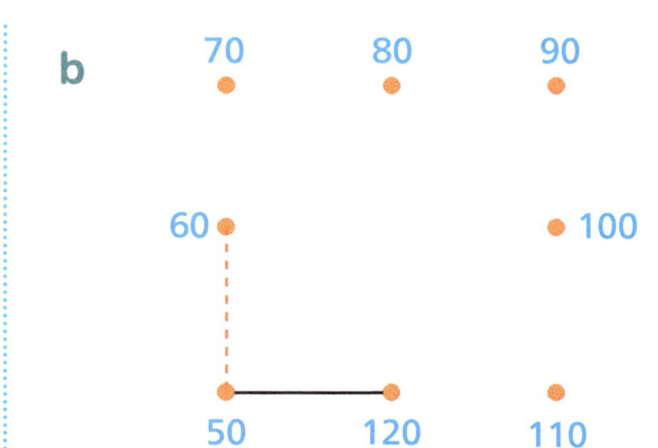




 ISBN 9780655709022

# 22B Skip counting patterns

Skip counting by 2 2, 4, 6, 8, 10, …
Skip counting by 5 5, 10, 15, 20, 25, …
Skip counting by 10 10, 20, 30, 40, 50, …

20, 18, 16, 14 … counting by 2 backwards

25, 20, 15, 10 … counting by 5 backwards

1 Do these patterns count by 2, 5 or 10?

a 8, 10, 12, 14, … ☐

b 20, 30, 40, 50, … ☐

c 5, 10, 15, 20, … ☐

d 12, 14, 16, 18, … ☐

2 Write the missing numbers in each skip counting pattern.

a 2, 4, 6, 8, 10, 12, ☐, ☐, ☐, 20

b 10, 20, 30, 40, 50, ☐, ☐, ☐, 90, 100

c 5, 10, 15, 20, 25, ☐, ☐, ☐, 45, 50

d 90, 80, 70, 60, 50, ☐, ☐, ☐, 10

e 50, 45, 40, 35, 30, ☐, ☐, ☐, 10

How did you continue the pattern in part **a**? ☐

How did you continue the pattern in part **b**? ☐

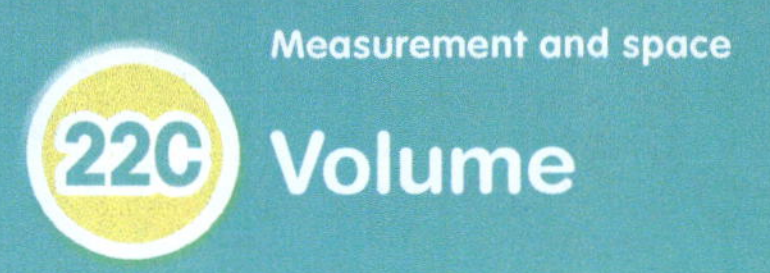

# 22C Volume

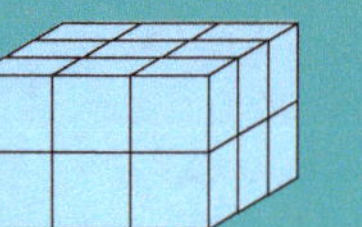

Each layer has 9 blocks.

Find the volume of each model.

1 a 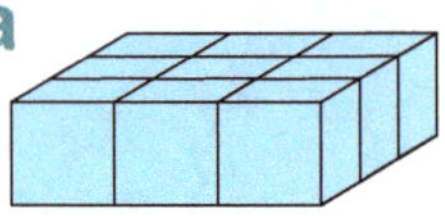 ☐ blocks

b 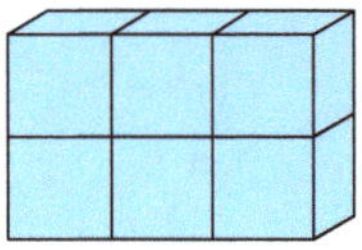 ☐ blocks

c 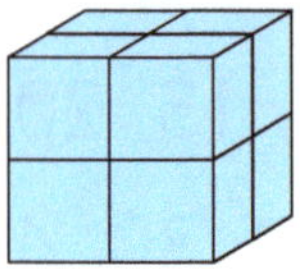 ☐ blocks

d 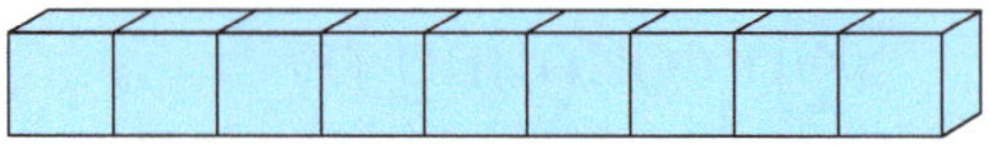 ☐ blocks

Part c is 2 groups of 4.

2 a 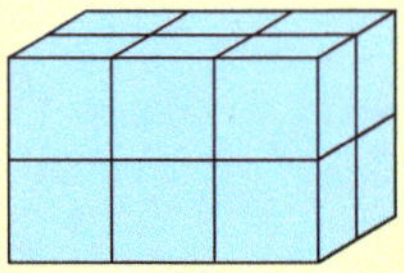 ☐ blocks

b 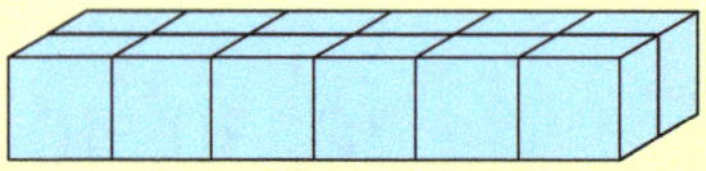 ☐ blocks

c 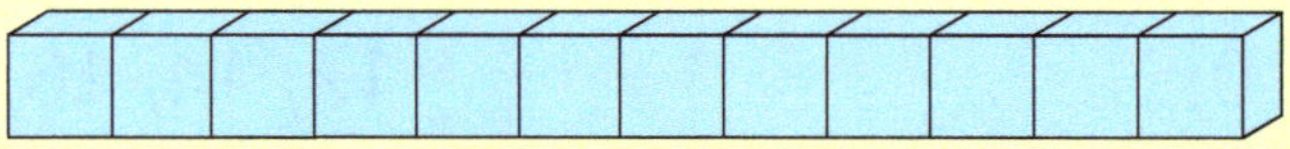 ☐ blocks

Can different models have the same volume? ☐

3 a 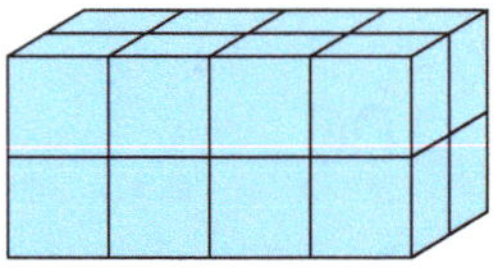 ☐ blocks

b 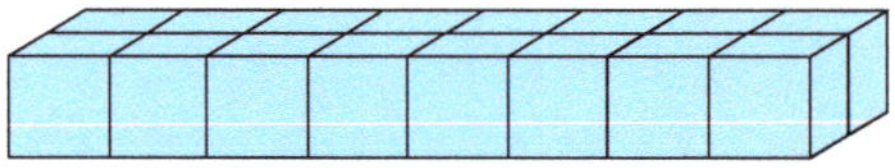 ☐ blocks

c 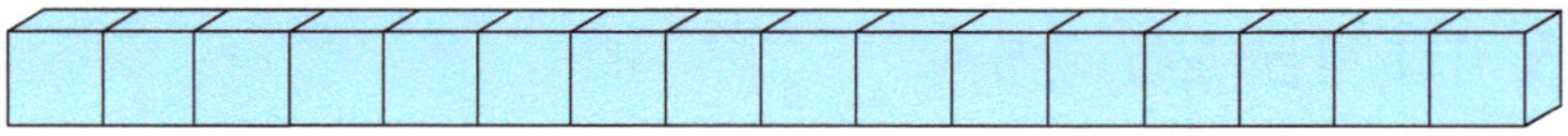 ☐ blocks

ACTIVITY

- Make different models using 8 blocks. How many did you make? ☐
- Make different models using 10 blocks. How many did you make? ☐

 ISBN 9780655709022

# 22D Halves and quarters

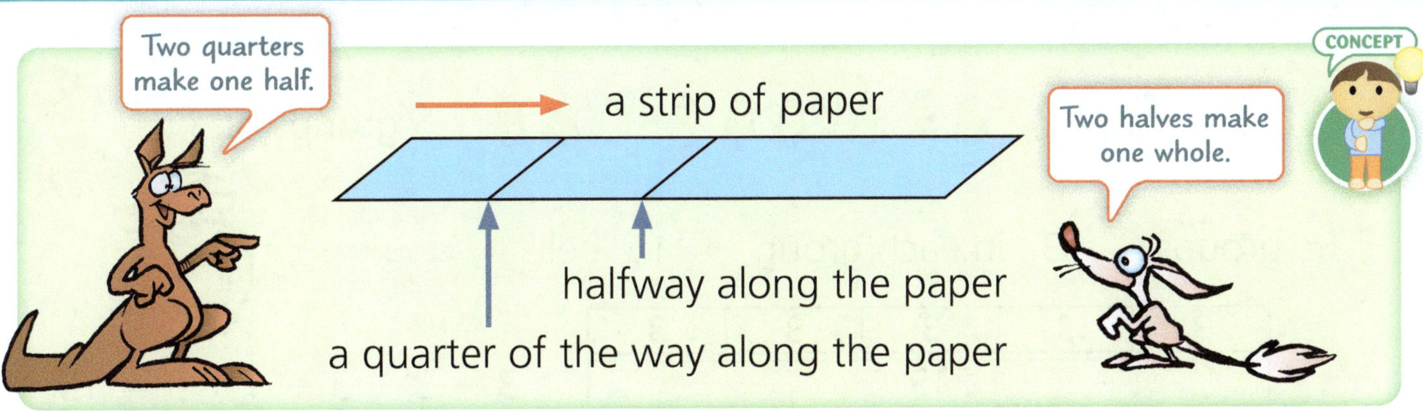


1 Circle the shapes that show halves. Tick the shapes that show quarters.

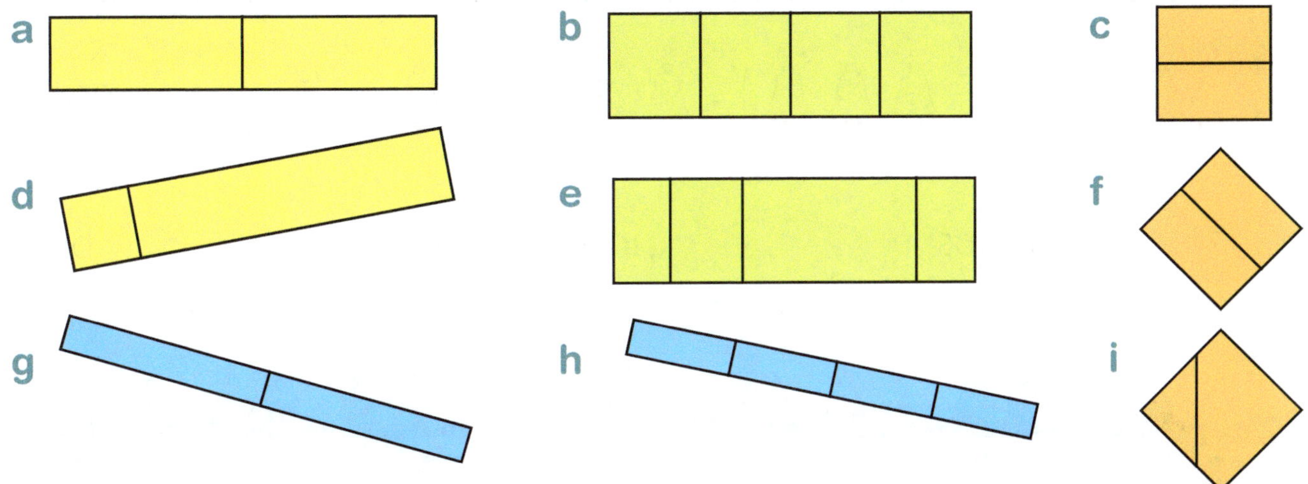


2 Write the letter that best shows the position of the dot along the line.

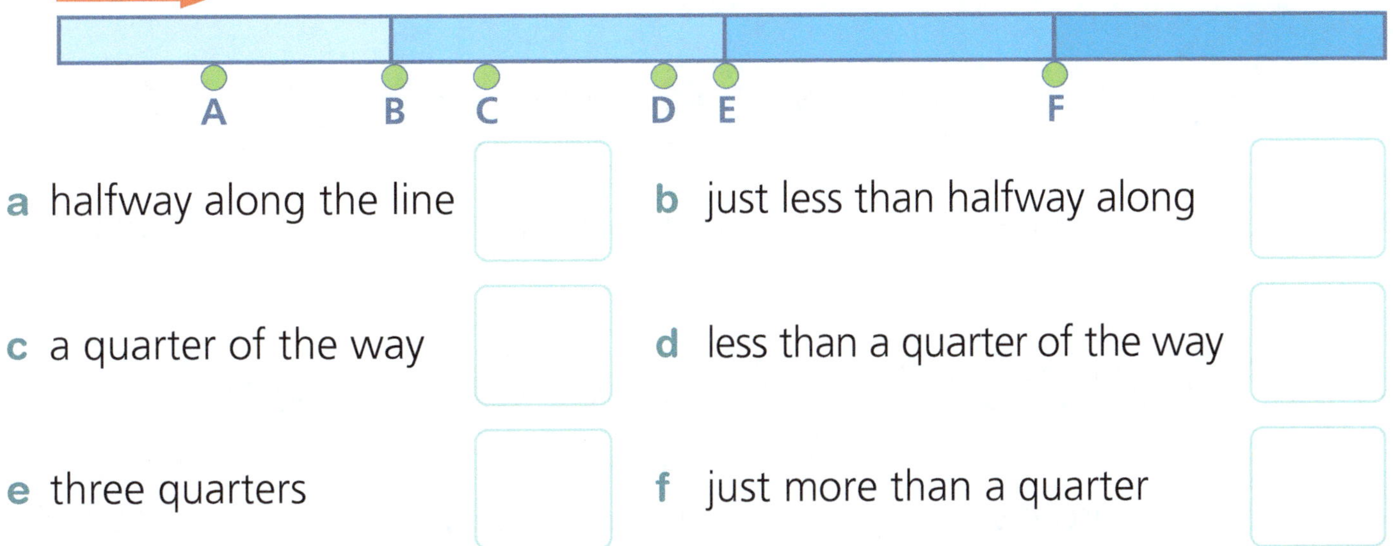


a halfway along the line

b just less than halfway along

c a quarter of the way

d less than a quarter of the way

e three quarters

f just more than a quarter

Fold a square into halves in as many different ways as you can.
Fold a square into quarters in as many different ways as you can.

 • *AUSTRALIAN SIGNPOST MATHS NSW 1* • ISBN 9780655709022

# 23A Equal groups

4 groups of 2 eyes

| 2 | 2 | 2 | 2 |
|---|---|---|---|

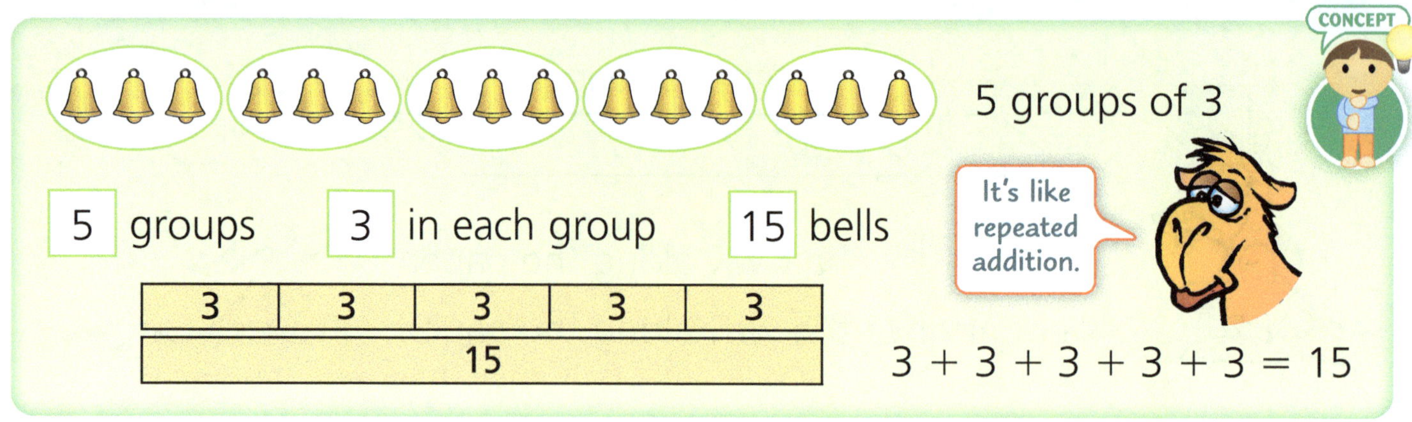


1 How many groups? How many in each group? How many altogether?

a     4 groups of 3

☐ groups ☐ in each group ☐ bells

b 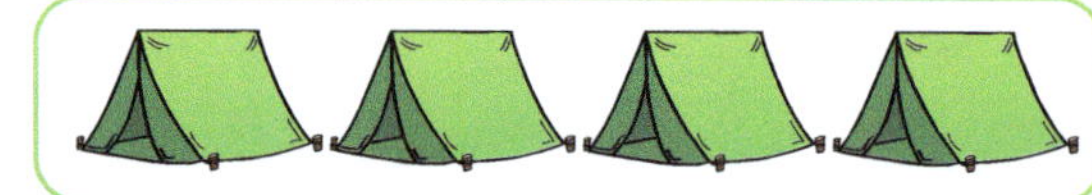 

☐ groups ☐ in each group ☐ tents

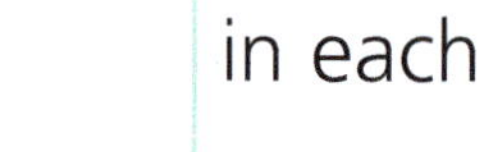

c 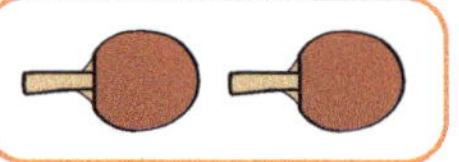 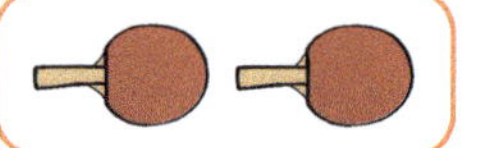 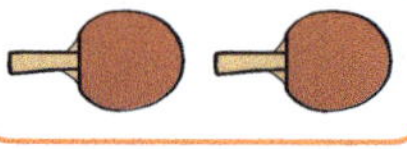 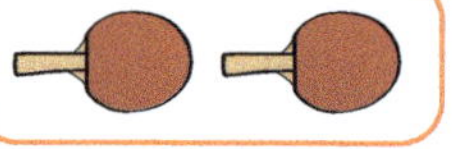 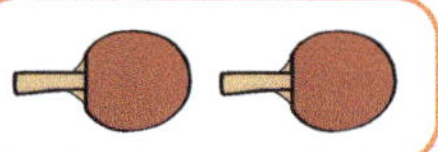

☐ groups ☐ in each group ☐ bats

d  

☐ groups ☐ in each group ☐ balls

2 a 5 groups of 2 = ☐ b 2 groups of 5 = ☐



 • *AUSTRALIAN SIGNPOST MATHS NSW 1* • ISBN 9780655709022

# 23B Using groups

CONCEPT

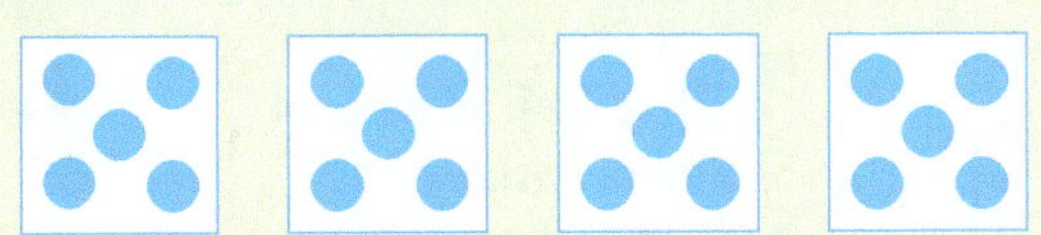

4 groups of 5 is the same as 20.

Skip counting: 5, 10, 15, 20 … or 5 + 5 + 5 + 5 = 20

1 Use skip counting to find the total number of objects in:

a 3 groups of 5

b 5 groups of 5

c 6 groups of 5

d 7 groups of 5

2 Use counters to make these groups. Skip count to find the total.

a 3 groups of 2

b 6 groups of 2

c 2 groups of 10

d 5 groups of 10

e 2 groups of 4

f 4 groups of 2

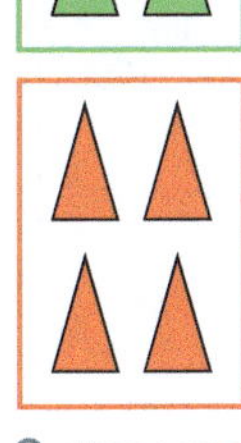

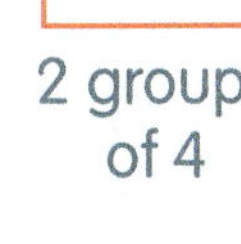

2 groups
of 4

3 a

How many groups?

How many in each group?

How many altogether?

b

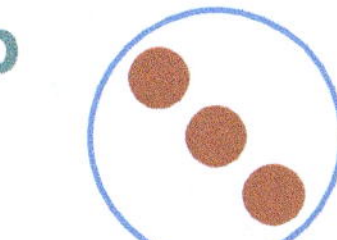 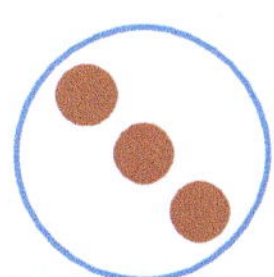 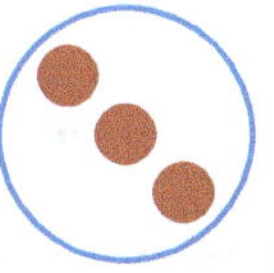

How many groups?

How many in each group?

How many altogether?

# Halves and quarters

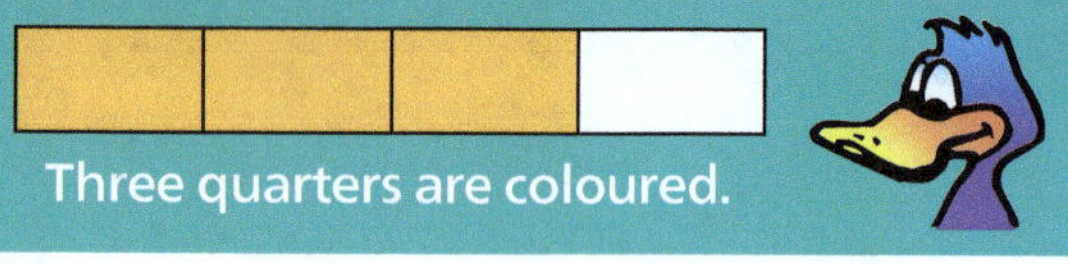

Three quarters are coloured.

One half is coloured.

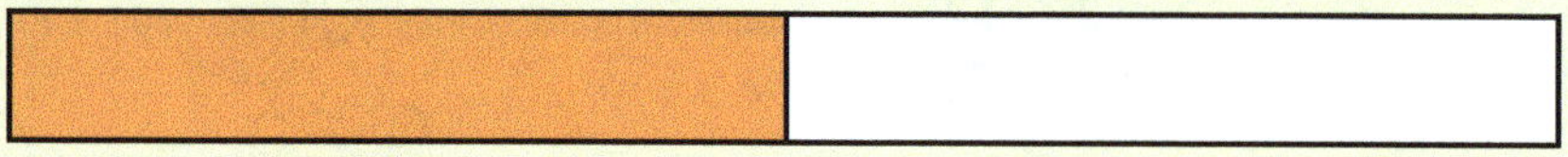

One quarter is coloured.

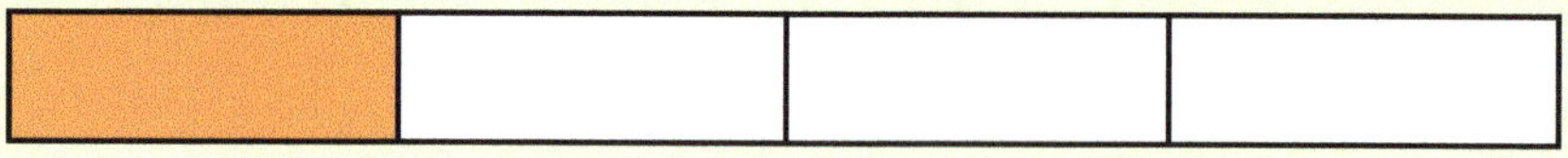

(Two quarters is the same as one half.)

One half is one of two equal parts.

One quarter is one of four equal parts.

## Making halves

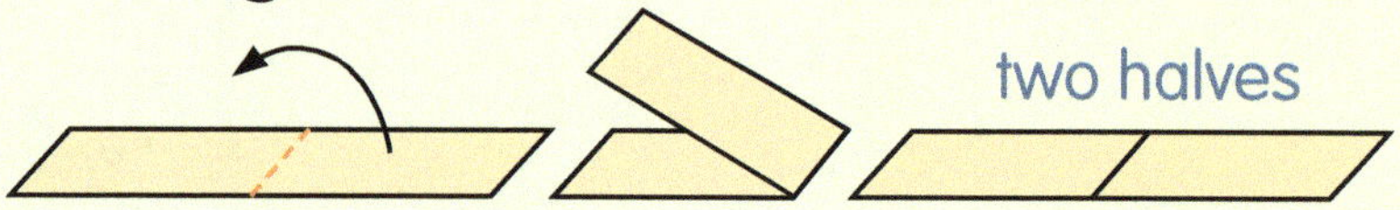

two halves

We folded the strip of paper into two halves.

## Making quarters

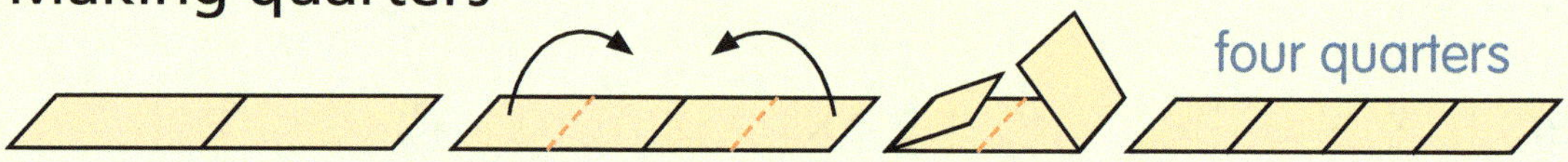

four quarters

We have folded each half in half.

1 Draw a line to cut each shape in half. Colour half of each shape.

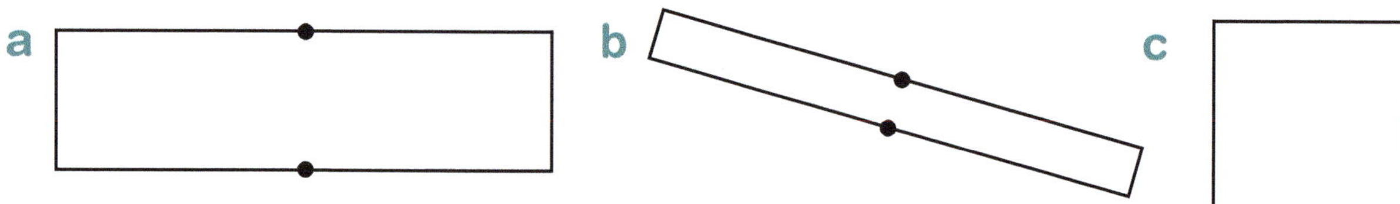

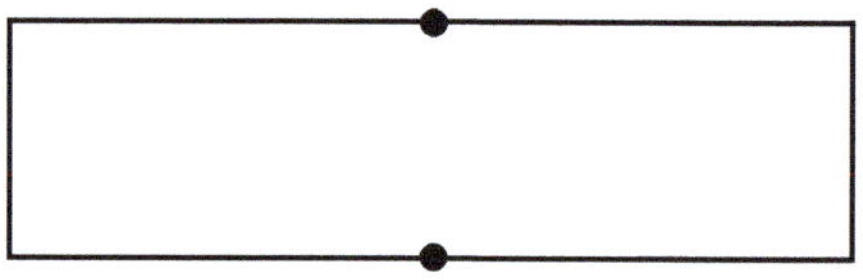

2 Draw lines to cut each shape into quarters. Colour one quarter of each.

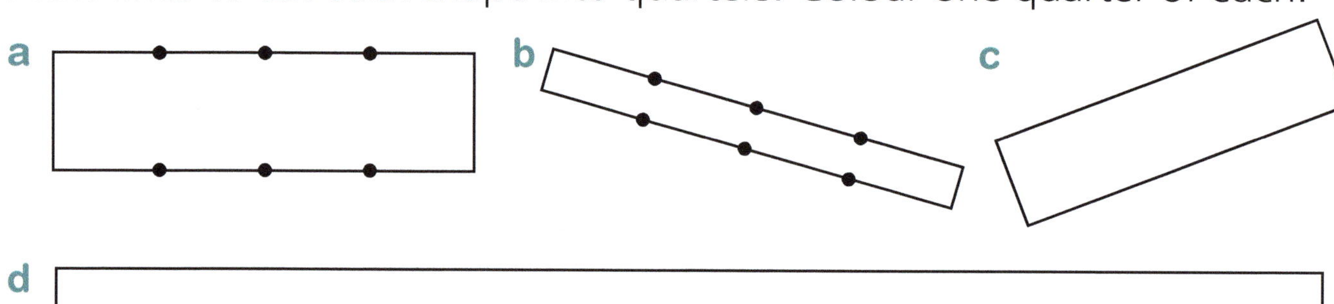


d

Fold lengths of paper into halves and quarters.

Draw lines on the folds. Label each part.

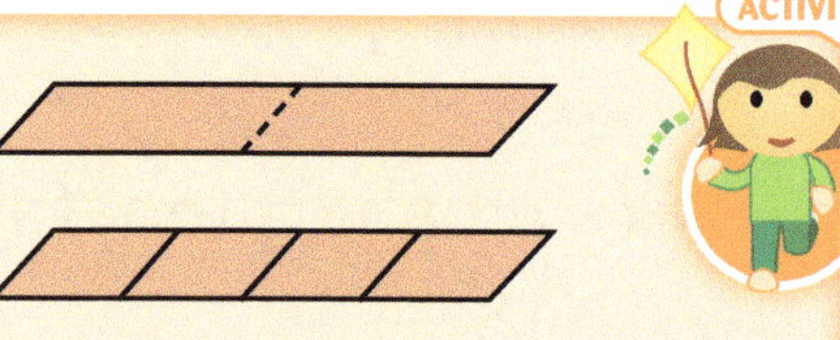



 • *AUSTRALIAN SIGNPOST MATHS NSW 1* • ISBN 9780655709022

# 23D Symmetry

CONCEPT

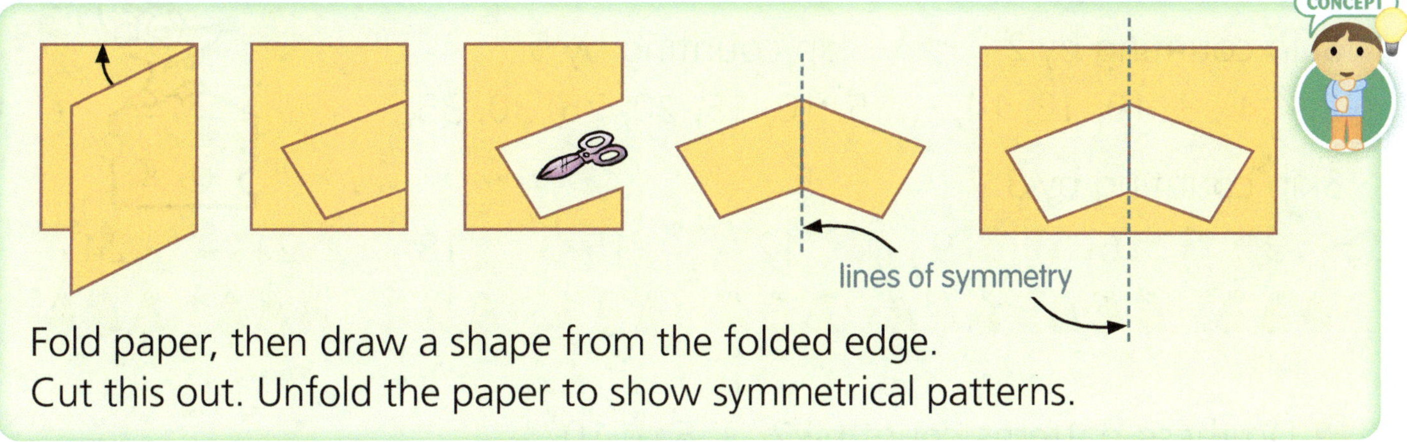


Fold paper, then draw a shape from the folded edge.
Cut this out. Unfold the paper to show symmetrical patterns.

**1** Draw a line of symmetry for each.

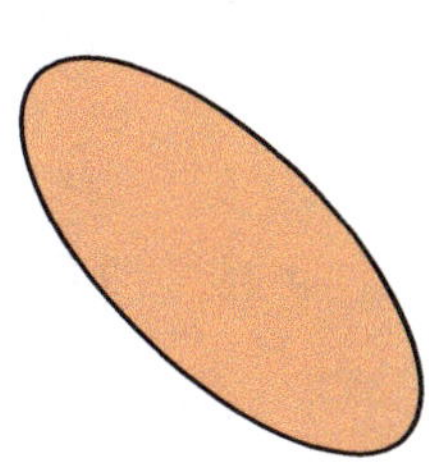

When you fold a shape along a line of symmetry, the parts on each side match.

two lines of symmetry

**2** Circle the shapes where a line of symmetry is shown correctly.

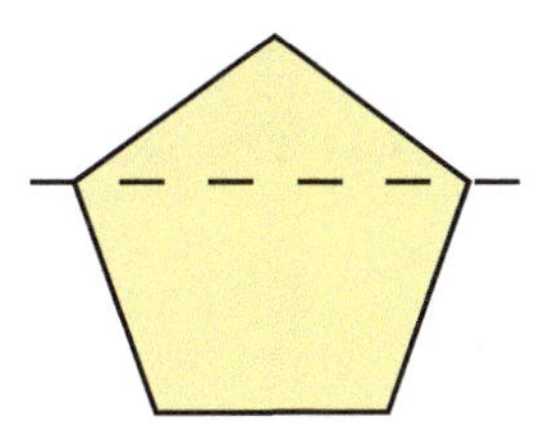
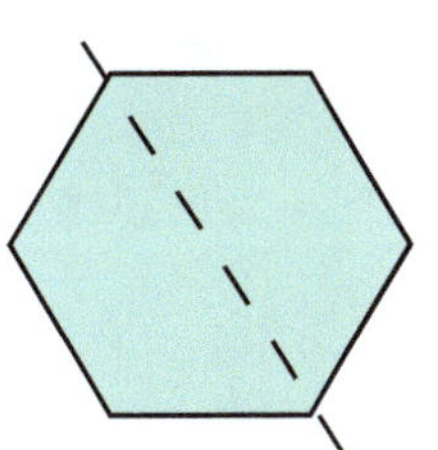
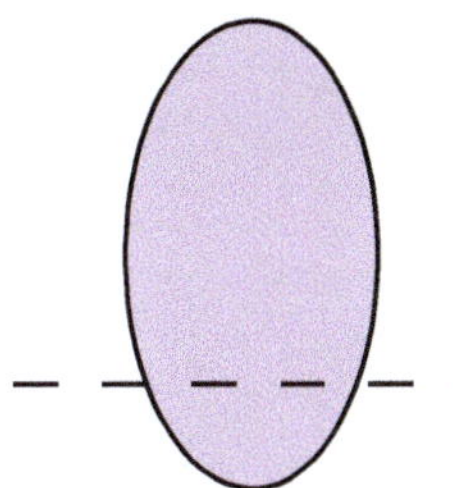
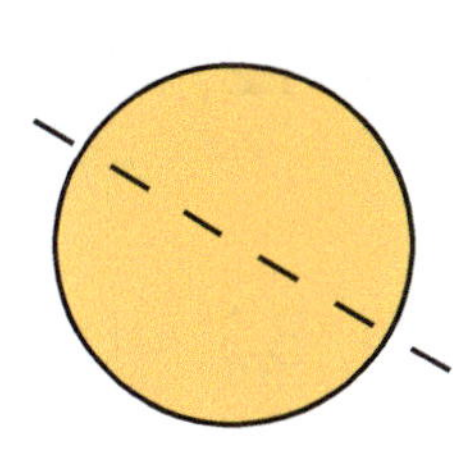

**3** Use pattern blocks to make these designs.
Draw each line of symmetry.

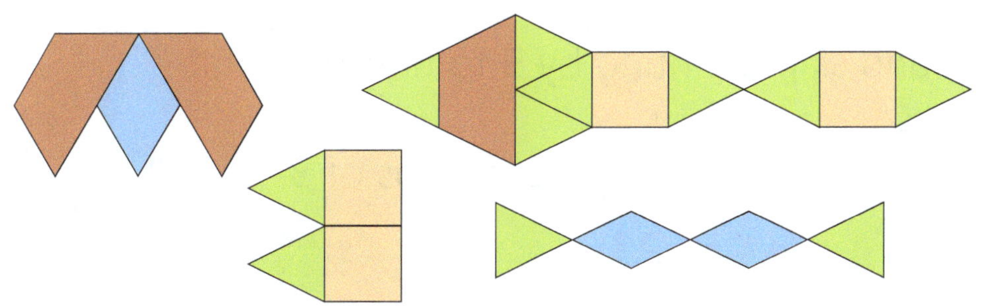

Slide back the edge of this page to see the edge of page 95 beside it. What do you notice?

ACTIVITY

Make symmetrical designs using paper folding, pattern blocks, drawing, computer software or by folding paper that has wet paint (or ink blots) on it.

 • *AUSTRALIAN SIGNPOST MATHS NSW 1* • ISBN 9780655709022

# 24A Skip counting

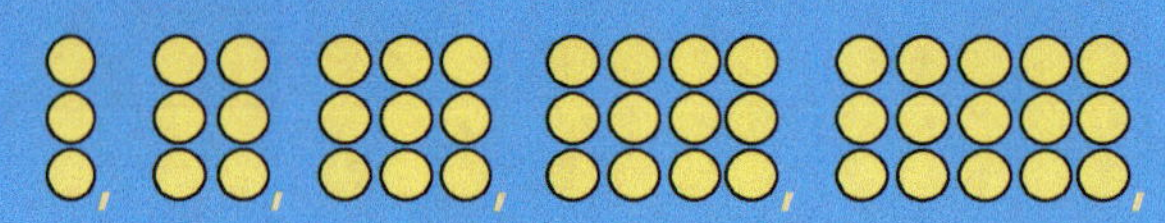

Skip counting by 2:
2, 4, 6, 8, 10, 12, 14,…

Skip counting by 5:
5, 10, 15, 20, 25, 30, 35,…

Skip counting by 3:

3 6 9 12 15 18 21 24

CONCEPT

Try rhythmic counting.

1 Do these patterns count by 2, 3, 5 or 10?

a 12, 14, 16, 18, … ☐

b 10, 15, 20, 25, … ☐

c 3, 6, 9, 12, 15 … ☐

d 10, 20, 30, 40, … ☐

2 Write the next four numbers in each skip counting pattern.

a 3, 6, 9, 12, 15, 18, ☐, ☐, ☐, ☐

b 10, 20, 30, 40, 50, ☐, ☐, ☐, ☐

c 2, 4, 6, 8, 10, 12, ☐, ☐, ☐, ☐

3 Use the bells above and skip counting by 3 to find the total.

a 2 groups of 3 ☐

b 5 groups of 3 ☐

c 4 groups of 3 ☐

d 3 groups of 3 ☐

e 7 groups of 3 ☐

f 9 groups of 3 ☐


 • *AUSTRALIAN SIGNPOST MATHS NSW 1* • ISBN 9780655709022

# 24B Number patterns

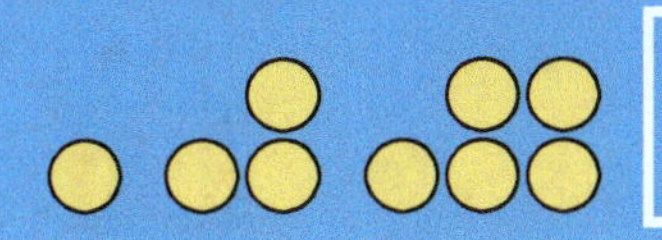

4, 10, 16, ☐, 28, 34

4 add 6 makes 10.
10 add 6 makes 16.
16 add 6 makes 22,
**so 22 is the missing number.**
**Check:** 22 + 6 = 28 and 28 + 6 = 34

**add 6**

15, 12, 9, ☐, 3, 0

15 take away 3 leaves 12.
12 take away 3 leaves 9.
9 take away 3 leaves 6,
**so 6 is the missing number.**
**Check:** 6 – 3 = 3 and 3 – 3 = 0

**subtract 3**

0 1 2 3 4 5 6 7 8 9 10 11 12 13 14 15 16 17 18 19 20

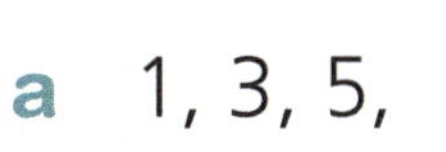

1. Complete each number pattern.

   **a** 1, 3, 5, ☐ **b** 8, 11, 14, ☐

   **c** 9, 7, 5, ☐ **d** 15, 10, 5, ☐

Discuss how you found the answer to part **d**.

2. Complete each number pattern and write the rule.

   **a** 2, 4, ☐, 8, 10 The rule is: add ☐.

   **b** 9, 7, ☐, 3, 1 The rule is: subtract ☐.

   **c** 3, 6, ☐, 12, 15 The rule is: add ☐.

   **d** 0, 4, ☐, 12, 16 The rule is: add ☐.

   **e** 20, ☐, 10, 5, 0 The rule is: subtract ☐.

# 24C Months of the year

January, February, March, April, May, June, July, August, September, October, November, December

1 Discuss the calendar below.

| January | February | March | April |
|---|---|---|---|
| | School starts | Tom's birthday | Easter holidays |
| **May** | **June** | **July** | **August** |
| | Ella's birthday | | |
| **September** | **October** | **November** | **December** |
| | | Speech night | Christmas holidays |

a Which month is Tom's birthday?

b How many months from Tom's birthday until Christmas?

c How many months from January to Easter holidays?

d If it is August now, how many months ago was Ella's birthday?

AUGUST

Use a real calendar to find the number of months until or after Christmas.



 • *AUSTRALIAN SIGNPOST MATHS NSW 1* • ISBN 9780655709022

## Find our favourite colour.

- Put many counters of 4 colours into a container.
- Each student chooses one counter and puts it into another container.
- Place the counters chosen into 4 lines to make a data display.

## Steps to gather and organise data.

- Make up a question and list the possible answers.

Question: What is our favourite colour?

4 possible answers:

- Show the data in a data display.

  Write the colours in the left column below.
  Record the numbers chosen next to each colour.

- Make a picture graph using the data we have gathered.

  Write the colours in spaces at the bottom of the graph.
  Colour a face for each person who chose that colour.

**Our favourite colour**



 • *AUSTRALIAN SIGNPOST MATHS NSW 1* • ISBN 9780655709022

# 25A Number patterns

Even numbers end in 0, 2, 4, 6 or 8.

Odd numbers end in 1, 3, 5, 7 or 9.

We can use the columns to add 10,
**3, 13, 23, 33, ...**
or to take away 10,
**49, 39, 29, 19.**

| 1 | 2 | 3 | 4 | 5 | 6 | 7 | 8 | 9 | 10 |
|---|---|---|---|---|---|---|---|---|---|
| 11 | 12 | 13 | 14 | 15 | 16 | 17 | 18 | 19 | 20 |
| 21 | 22 | 23 | 24 | 25 | 26 | 27 | 28 | 29 | 30 |
| 31 | 32 | 33 | 34 | 35 | 36 | 37 | 38 | 39 | 40 |
| 41 | 42 | 43 | 44 | 45 | 46 | 47 | 48 | 49 | 50 |

1. Write the next two numbers in each pattern.

   a 4, 14, 24, ☐, ☐

   b 7, 17, 27, ☐, ☐

   c 45, 35, 25, ☐, ☐

   d 14, 16, 18, ☐, ☐

   e 50, 49, 48, ☐, ☐

   f 3, 6, 9, ☐, ☐

2. Complete each pattern for 8 more hops.

   a

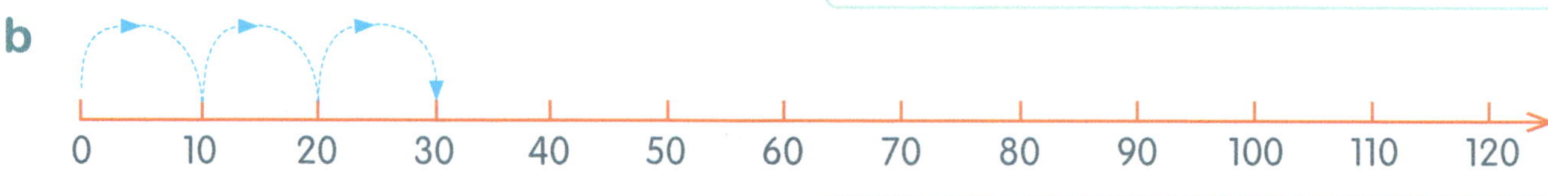


   This is counting by twos.
   What is the rule being used? ☐

   b

   0 10 20 30 40 50 60 70 80 90 100 110 120

   This is counting by tens.
   What is the rule being used? ☐

3. Use the number chart at the top of the page.

   a Colour the even numbers red. Circle the smallest even number.

   b Colour the odd numbers green. Tick the largest odd number.



 ISBN 9780655709022

# 25B Counting by 2s, 5s and 10s

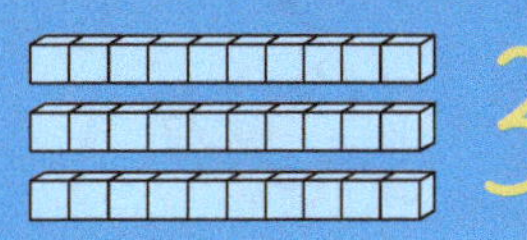

30

Start 10 20 30 40 50 60 70 80 90 100 110 120

| 1 | 2 | 3 | 4 | 5 | 6 | 7 | 8 | 9 | 10 |
|---|---|---|---|---|---|---|---|---|---|
| 11 | 12 | 13 | 14 | 15 | 16 | 17 | 18 | 19 | 20 |
| 21 | 22 | 23 | 24 | 25 | 26 | 27 | 28 | 29 | 30 |
| 31 | 32 | 33 | 34 | 35 | 36 | 37 | 38 | 39 | 40 |
| 41 | 42 | 43 | 44 | 45 | 46 | 47 | 48 | 49 | 50 |

1. Count by twos to finish this pattern of even numbers.

2, 4, 6, ☐, ☐, ☐, ☐, ☐, ☐, ☐

| 1 | 2 | 3 | 4 | 5 | 6 | 7 | 8 | 9 | 10 |
|---|---|---|---|---|---|---|---|---|---|
| 11 | 12 | 13 | 14 | 15 | 16 | 17 | 18 | 19 | 20 |
| 21 | 22 | 23 | 24 | 25 | 26 | 27 | 28 | 29 | 30 |
| 31 | 32 | 33 | 34 | 35 | 36 | 37 | 38 | 39 | 40 |
| 41 | 42 | 43 | 44 | 45 | 46 | 47 | 48 | 49 | 50 |

2. Count by fives to finish the pattern.

5, 10, 15, ☐, ☐, ☐, ☐, ☐, ☐

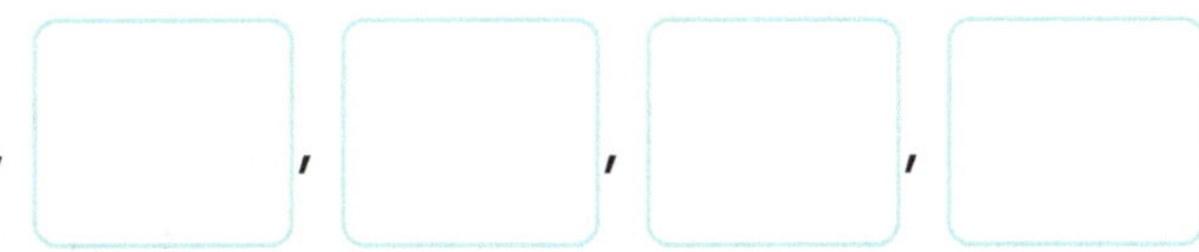

3. Count by tens to finish the pattern.

10, 20, 30, ☐, ☐, ☐, ☐, ☐, ☐

4. Look at the beads around the page. Colour every 5th bead black.

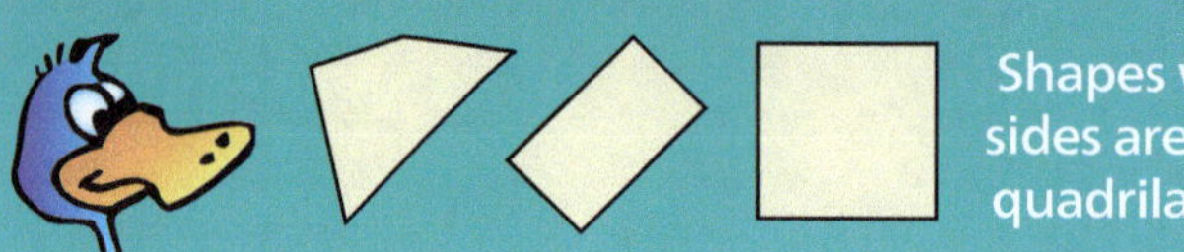

Shapes with 4 sides are called quadrilaterals.

## Shape words

circle triangle square rectangle quadrilateral hexagon pentagon octagon

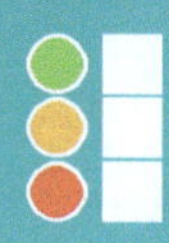

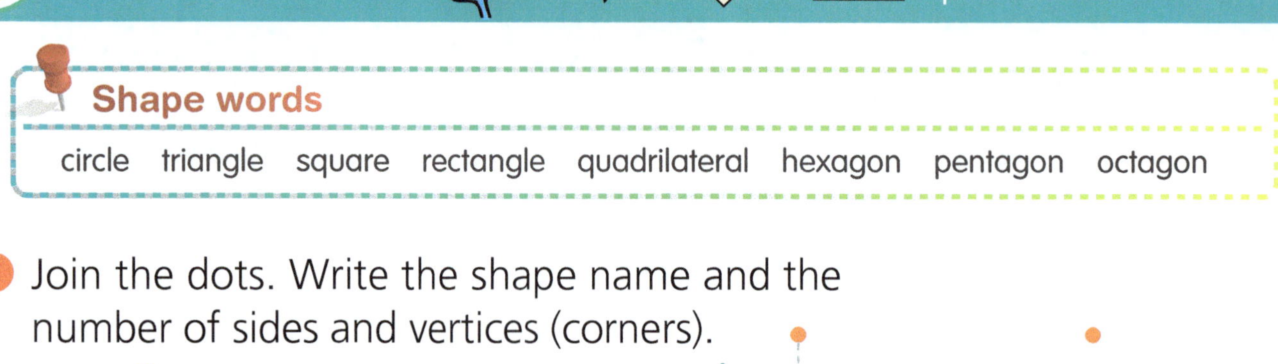

**1** Join the dots. Write the shape name and the number of sides and vertices (corners).

**a**

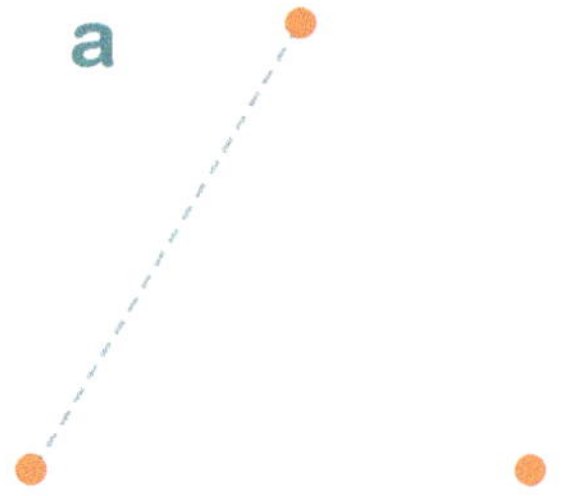

Sides | Vertices

Shape name:

**b**

Sides | Vertices

Shape name:

**c**

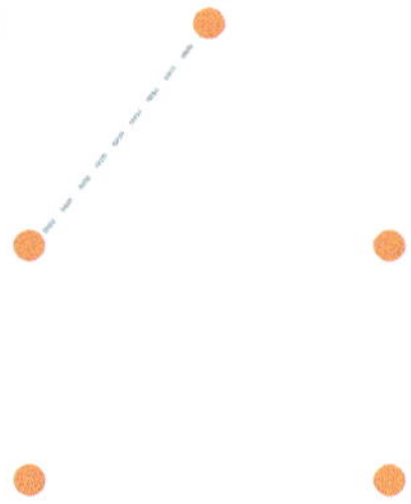

Sides | Vertices

Shape name:

**d**

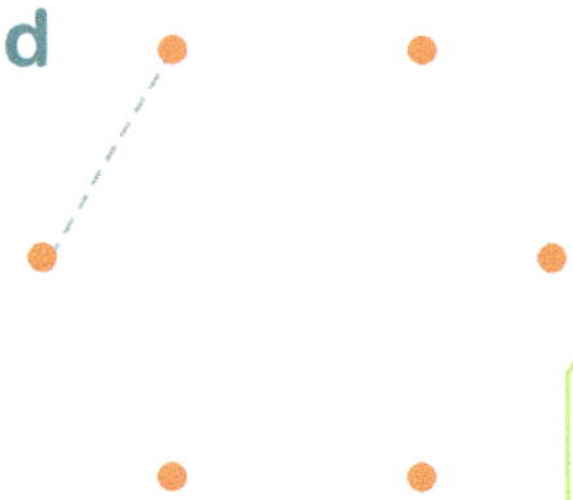

Sides | Vertices

Shape name:

INVESTIGATION

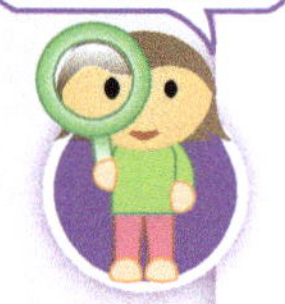

Draw a square and a rectangle. These shapes are quadrilaterals.

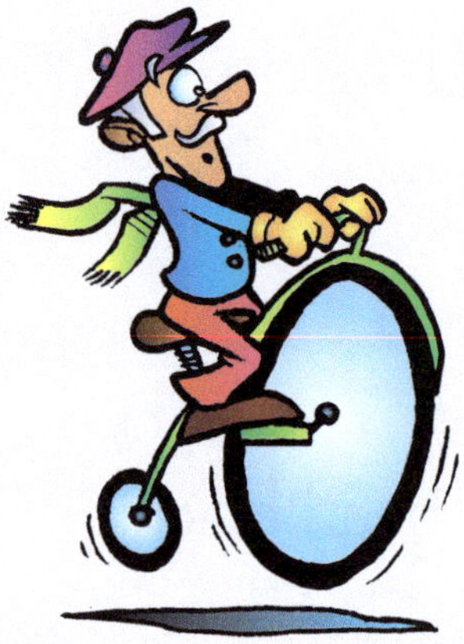

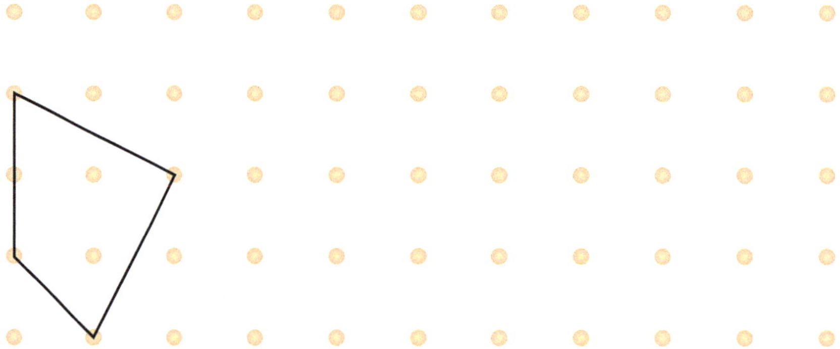

# 25D Properties of shapes

1 a Complete this table. (A vertex is a corner. Vertices are corners.)

| Shape | Name | Number of vertices | Number of sides |
|---|---|---|---|
| triangle shape | | | |
| square shape | | 4 | |
| rectangle shape | | | |
| pentagon shape | | | |
| hexagon shape | | | |
| circle shape | circle | | |
| octagon shape | | | 8 |

Hexagons have 6 sides and 6 vertices.

Describe a shape. Ask a classmate to name the shape.

b Colour in the shapes that have all sides equal.

c Circle the shapes that have four sides. These are quadrilaterals.

d Write the name of the shape that has:

3 vertices ______ 6 sides ______

e Name another shape, like the hexagon, that can make a pattern with no gaps or overlaps. ______.

INVESTIGATION

Find out what you can about these shapes.

oval kite parallelogram

# 26A Half of a group

Two halves make one whole.

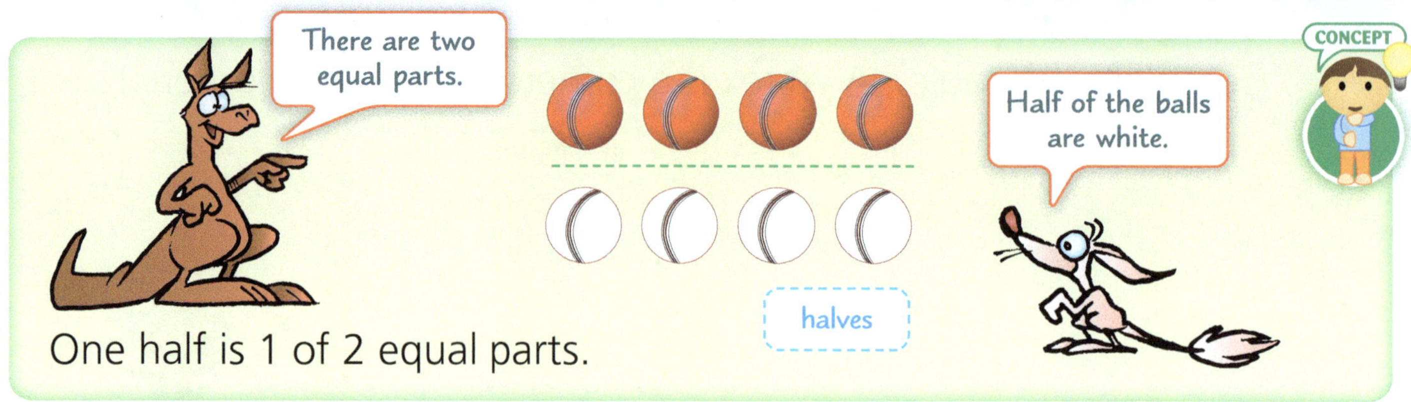


1 Circle the groups that are divided into halves.

Colour one half of each of the circled groups.

2 Circle half of each group.

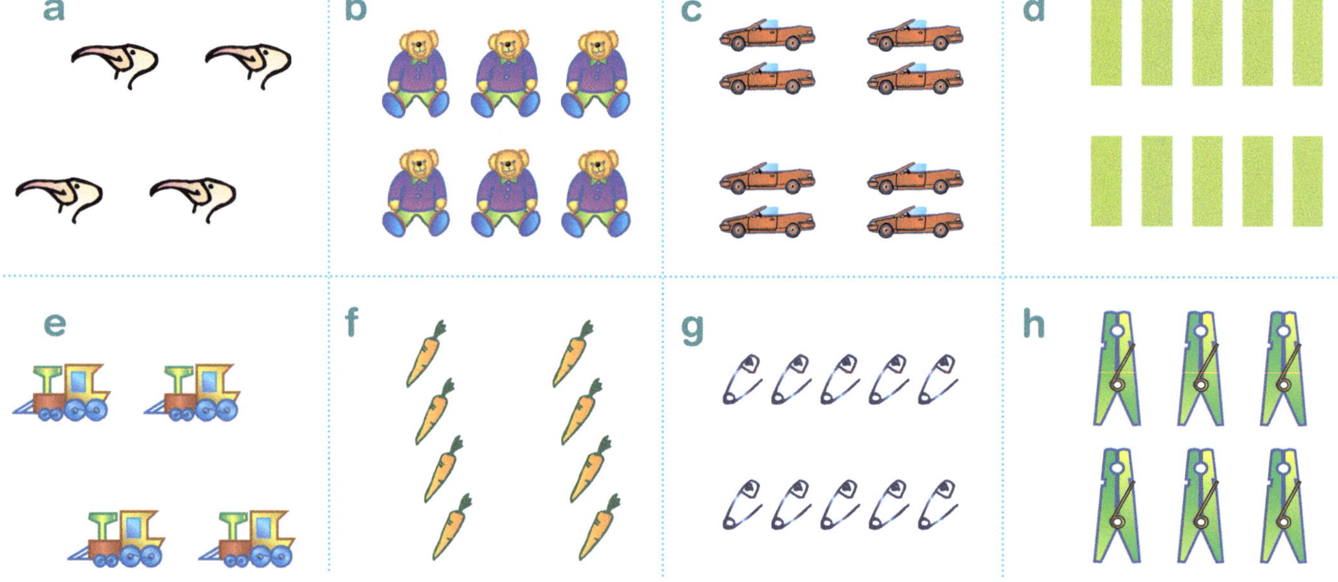




 • *AUSTRALIAN SIGNPOST MATHS NSW 1* • ISBN 9780655709022

# 26B Halves

half half

Two halves make one whole.

One half is one of two equal parts.

1. Draw a line to halve each group.

2. Circle half of each collection.

3. True or false?

When two halves of a collection are put together you have the whole collection.

Share a collection of 20 counters into two halves.
Count each half.

What is half of 20 counters?

Find half of other collections.

 • *AUSTRALIAN SIGNPOST MATHS NSW 1* • ISBN 9780655709022

# 26C Calendar

Which month has the least number of days?

Thirty days has September,
April, June and November,
All the rest have thirty-one
Except February alone
Which has twenty-eight days clear,
And twenty-nine days each leap year.

1 How many days are there in these months?

a September ______ b May ______ c February ______

d January ______ e April ______ f July ______

| March | | | | | | |
|---|---|---|---|---|---|---|
| Sun | Mon | Tue | Wed | Thu | Fri | Sat |
| | | 1 | 2 | 3 | 4 | 5 |
| 6 | 7 | 8 | 9 | 10 | 11 | 12 |
| 13 | 14 | 15 | 16 | 17 | 18 | 19 |
| 20 | 21 | 22 | 23 | 24 | 25 | 26 |
| 27 | 28 | 29 | 30 | 31 | | |

Use a real calendar to mark important dates.

2 a How many days are in March? ______

b On what day does March begin? ______

c On what day does March end? ______

d How many Wednesdays are in March? ______

# 26D The calendar

Practise using a calendar at home.

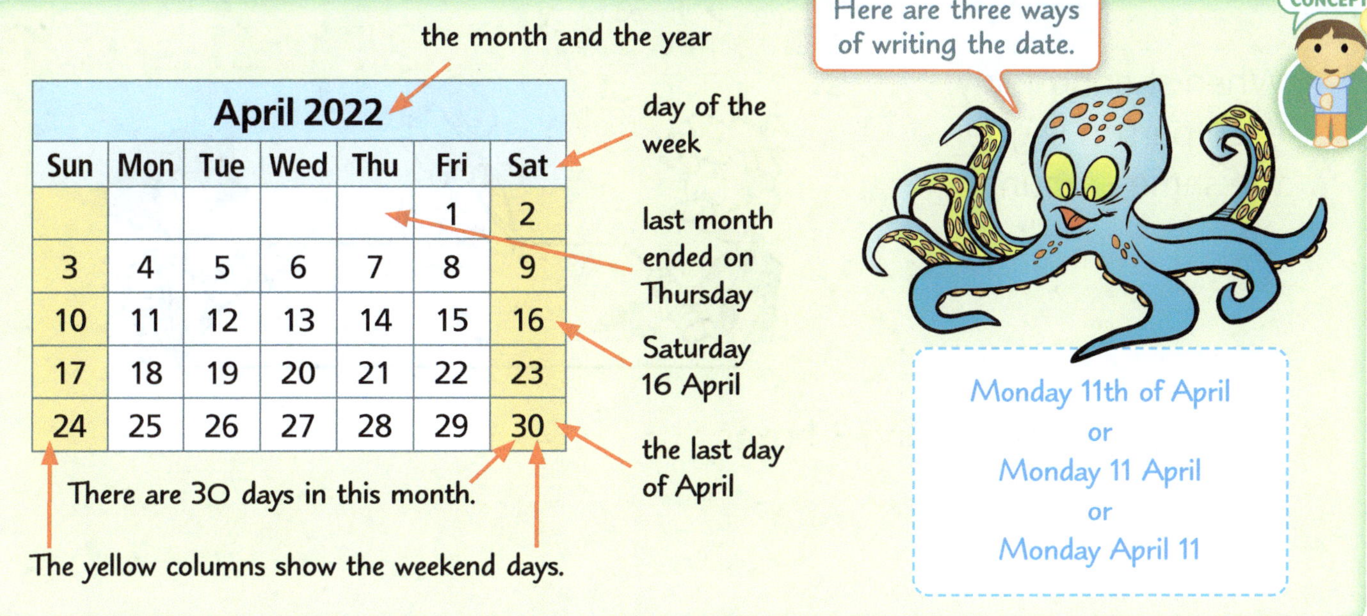


| April 2022 | | | | | | |
|---|---|---|---|---|---|---|
| Sun | Mon | Tue | Wed | Thu | Fri | Sat |
| | | | | | 1 | 2 |
| 3 | 4 | 5 | 6 | 7 | 8 | 9 |
| 10 | 11 | 12 | 13 | 14 | 15 | 16 |
| 17 | 18 | 19 | 20 | 21 | 22 | 23 |
| 24 | 25 | 26 | 27 | 28 | 29 | 30 |

1. On the calendar, colour these dates blue.
   - a Monday 4th of April
   - b Friday 8th of April
   - c Tuesday April 12
   - d Thursday April 14
   - e Wednesday 20 April
   - f Thursday 21 April

Sunday, Monday, Tuesday, Wednesday, Thursday, Friday, Saturday

2. On the calendar, circle these dates.
   - a Sunday 3rd of April
   - b Saturday 9th April
   - c the first day of the month
   - d the last day of the month
   - e the first Wednesday
   - f the last Tuesday

3. What day of the week is:
   - a April 13? ______
   - b April 1? ______
   - c April 24? ______
   - d April 10? ______
   - e 19 April? ______
   - f 11 April? ______

 • *AUSTRALIAN SIGNPOST MATHS NSW 1* • ISBN 9780655709022

# Sharing

CONCEPT

When sharing fairly, each person is given the same amount.

1. Share 6 counters among 3 boxes.

One share = ☐

2. Share 8 blocks between 2 groups.

One share = ☐

3. Share 10 blocks between 2 groups.

One share = ☐

INVESTIGATION

Share 12 counters:

a between 2.
One share = ☐

b between 3.
One share = ☐

c between 4.
One share = ☐

d between 6.
One share = ☐

# 27B Sharing

CONCEPT

When we share, each person gets the same number of items.

(One could be left over.)

Five each.

Half of 10 is 5.

1 Share 9 counters among these boxes.

How many are in each box?

2 Share 8 counters among these boxes.

How many are in each box?

3

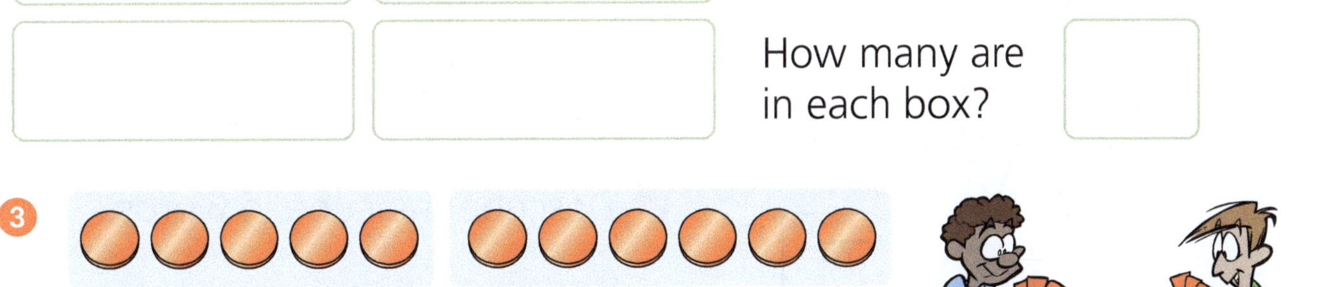

Is this a fair share?

Circle the group with the unequal share.

INVESTIGATION

Share 14 counters into 3 equal groups.

How many did you put in each group?

What was left over?

# 27C The cube

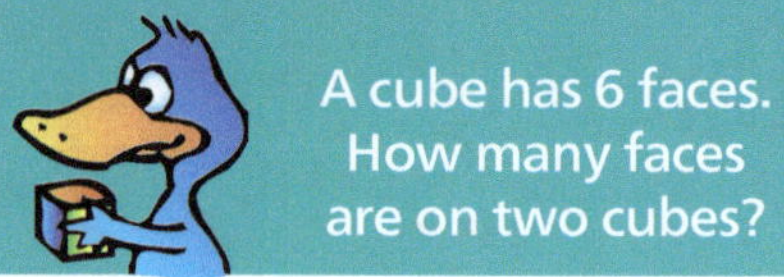

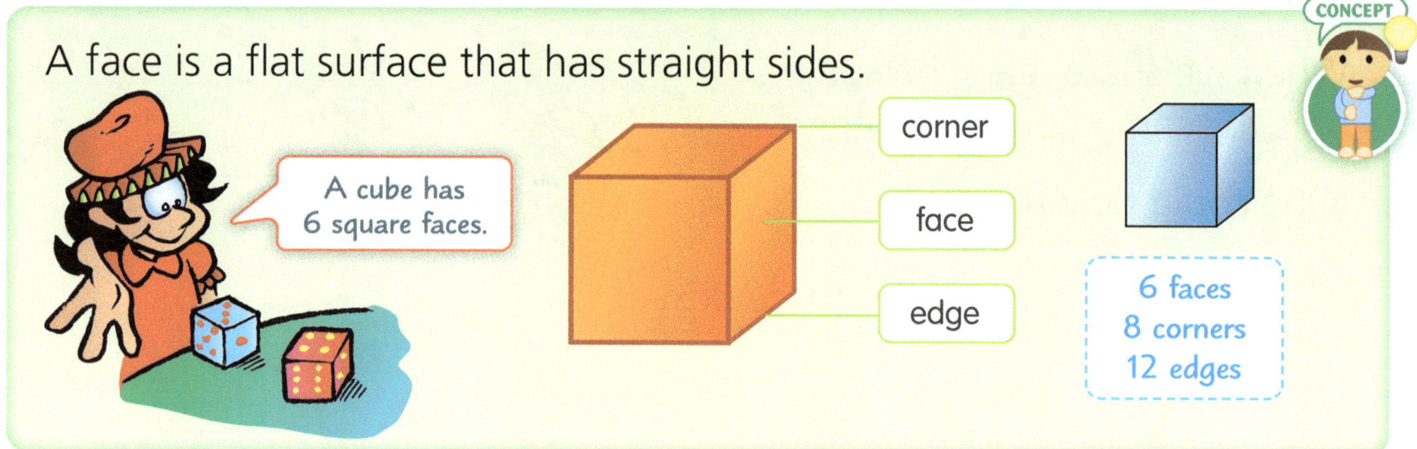


1. Colour the cubes red, the sphere blue, the cone and the cylinder yellow.

2. Circle the objects that can be stacked.

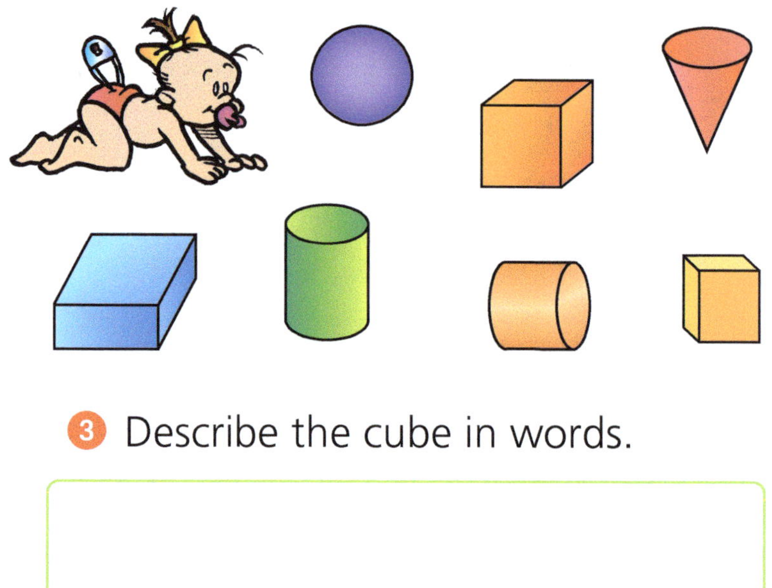

3. Describe the cube in words.

# Giving directions

FUN SPOT

1 Use a counter to follow the instructions.

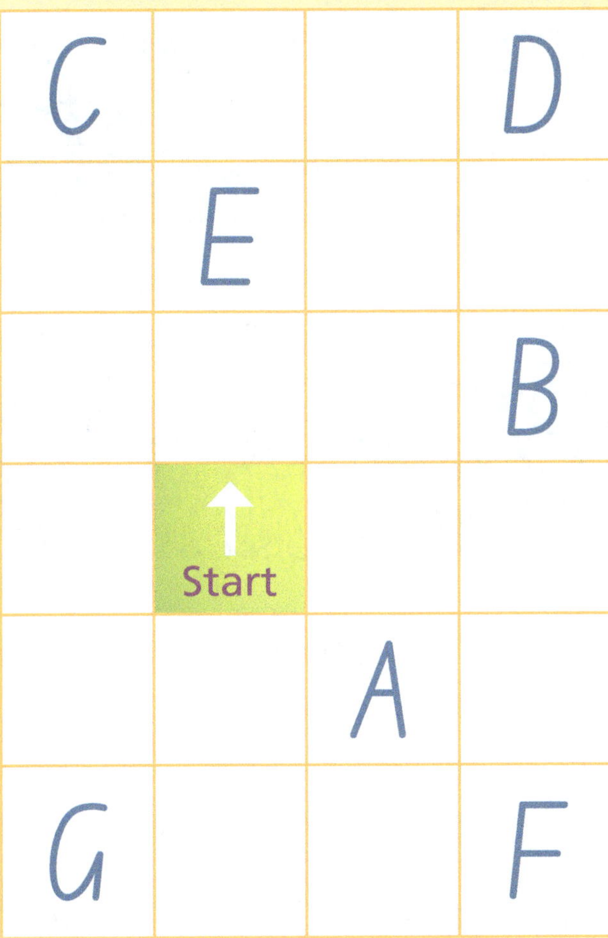


1 Place your counter on the space marked Start.

2 Move the counter 3 spaces up. Colour that square red.

3 From the red square, move the counter 2 spaces right. Colour that square blue.

4 From the blue square, move the counter 5 spaces down. Colour that square green.

5 From the green square, move the counter 3 spaces left.

The counter is now at ☐.

2 Follow these directions from Start on the diagram above. Where do you finish?

a 2 up, 2 right, 3 down, 1 left ☐

b 1 up, 1 left, 3 down, 3 right ☐

3 Work with a partner.

Take turns to give each other directions.

## Challenge

4 You are at the Start. Write the letter where you finish if you:

a move 2 forward, turn to your right, move 2 forward, turn right, move 4 forward, turn right, move 3 forward. ☐

b move 1 backward, turn to your left, move 1 forward, turn right, move 4 forward, turn right, move 3 forward. ☐

 • *AUSTRALIAN SIGNPOST MATHS NSW 1* • ISBN 9780655709022

# 28A Grouping to share

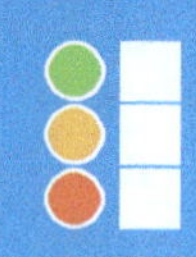

CONCEPT

**14 eggs**

How many groups of 3 eggs can be given away?

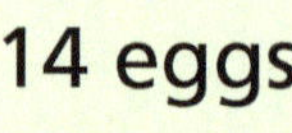

4 groups of 3 2 left over

1 How many groups of 4 students can play tennis at the same time?

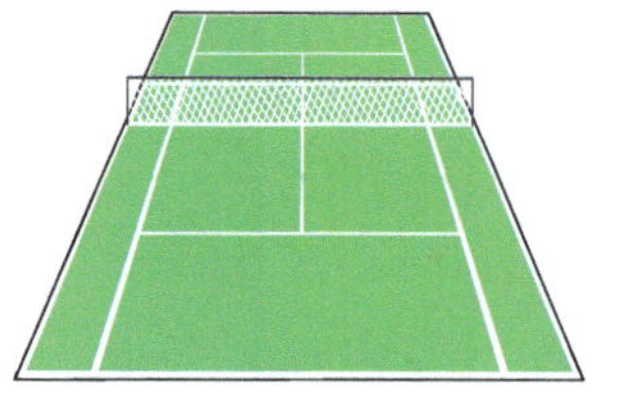

☐ groups of 4 with ☐ left over.

2 

a How many teachers can be given 4 tennis balls? ☐ teachers

b How many girls can be given 3 tennis balls? ☐ girls

c How many boys can be given 2 tennis balls? ☐ boys

INVESTIGATION

Use 20 counters.

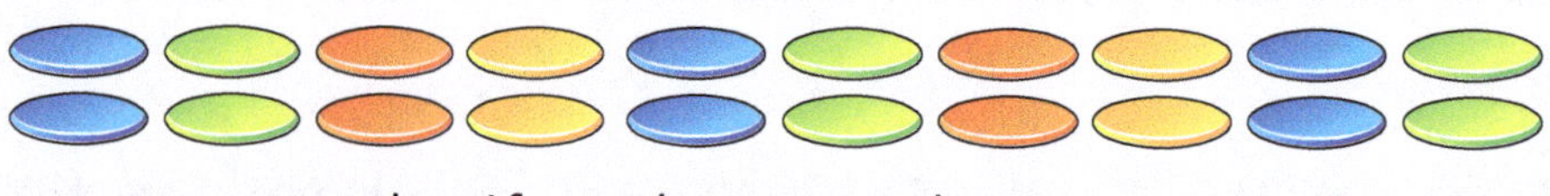

How many groups can you make if each group has:

| 2 counters? | 4 counters? | 10 counters? | 5 counters? |
|---|---|---|---|
| ☐ groups | ☐ groups | ☐ groups | ☐ groups |

 • *AUSTRALIAN SIGNPOST MATHS NSW 1* • ISBN 9780655709022

# 28B How many groups?

CONCEPT

We have 12 tennis balls. How many girls can be given 2 tennis balls?

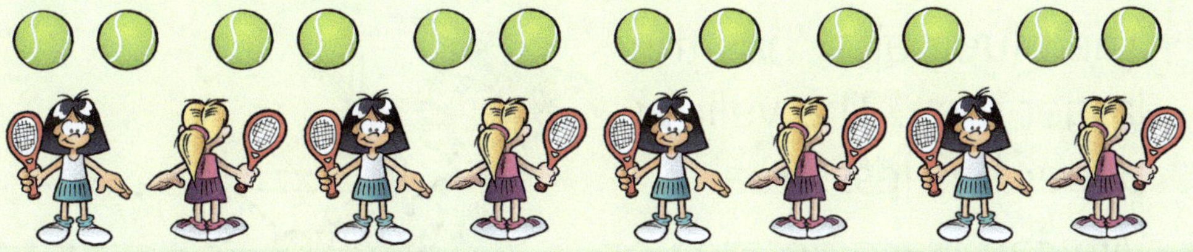

6 girls

1 a 8 counters. How many girls can be given 2 counters? ___ girls

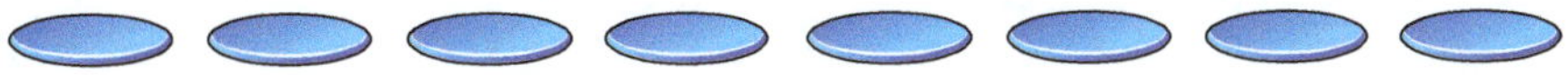

b 9 counters. How many boys can be given 3 counters? ___ boys

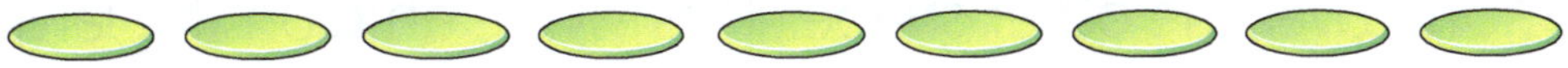

c 20 marbles. How many students can be given 5 marbles? 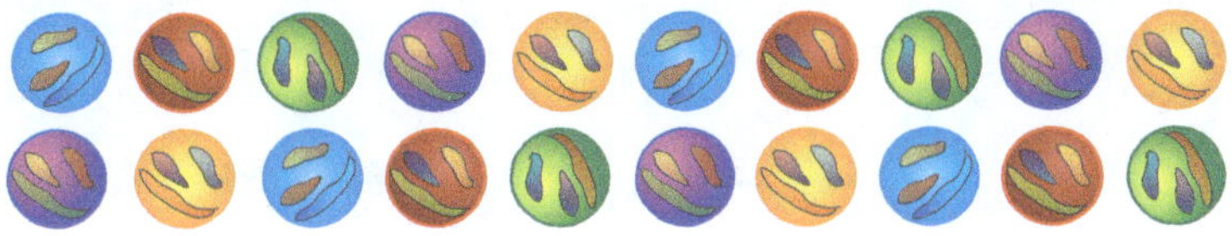 ___ students

2 How many altogether? ___

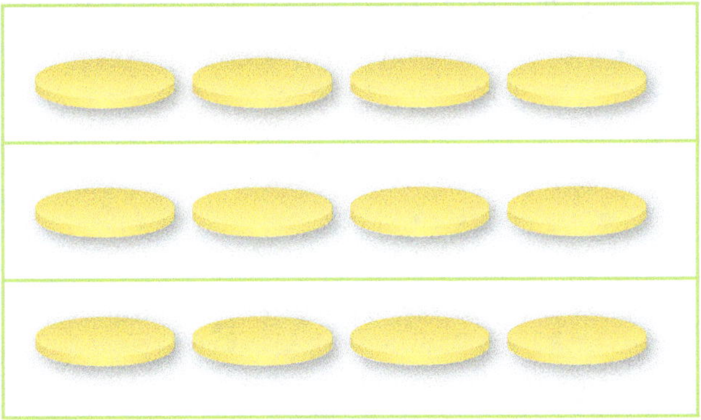

How many groups? ___

How many in each group? ___

3 Circle the groups. How many groups are there?

a 10 hats, 2 in each group. ___ groups

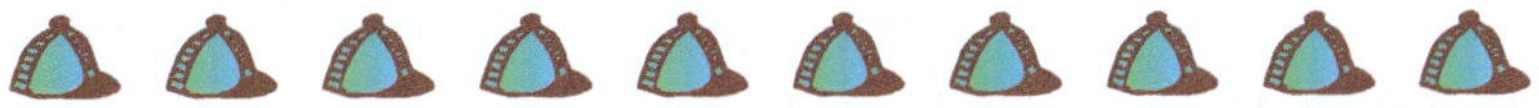

b 12 carrots, 3 in each group. ___ groups

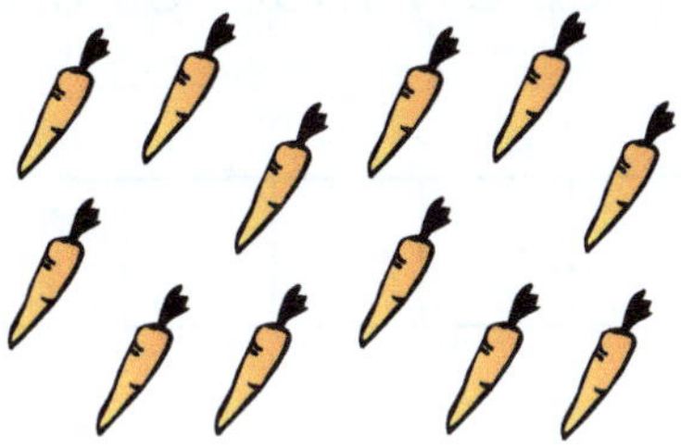

# 28C Comparing areas

Area is the amount of surface on a shape.

CONCEPT

**Compare areas** by putting one on top of the other.

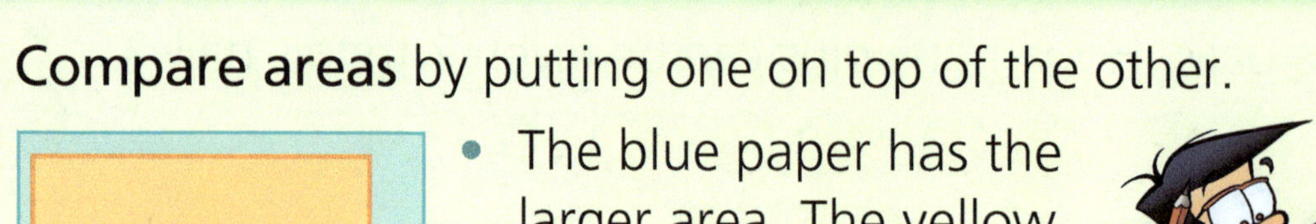

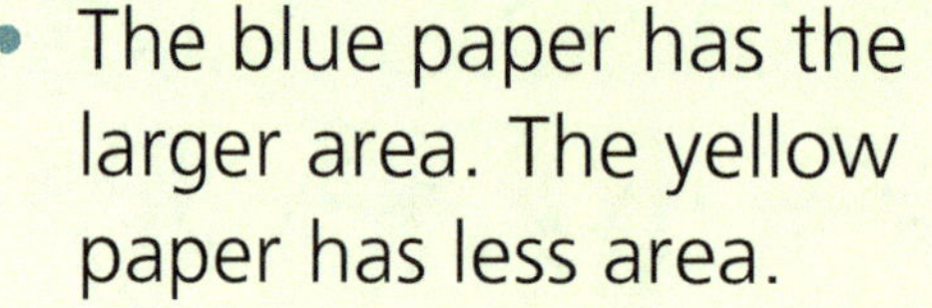

- The blue paper has the larger area. The yellow paper has less area.
- We can trace an area on paper and put it on top of another area.

1. Predict which shape has the larger area. Check by tracing one area and placing the tracing over the other shape. Then write an **L** on the larger area.

a

b

2. - Shravan used 12 tiles to make pattern **A**.
   - He then used the tiles to make pattern **B**.

**A**

**B**

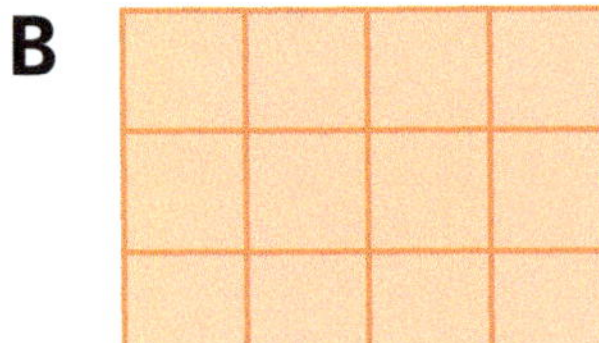

Do the patterns have the same area?

Colour a different pattern below that has the same area as the patterns Shravan made.

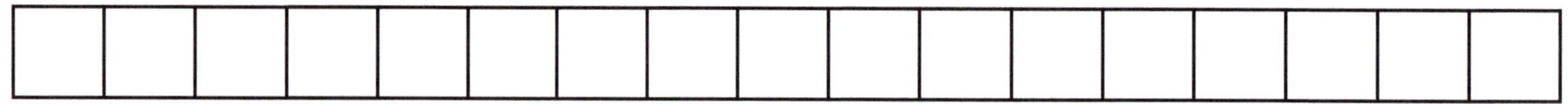



 • *AUSTRALIAN SIGNPOST MATHS NSW 1* • ISBN 9780655709022

# 28D Area using units

Area is the amount of surface on a shape.

1 Use the given unit to find each area. Complete the table.

| Area | Unit | Number of units | |
|---|---|---|---|
| | | Estimate | Measure |
| top of desk | book | books | books |
| carpet or board | newspaper | sheets | sheets |

2 Use small sticky notes and then 50c coins to cover the green square.

a Number of sticky notes needed.

b Number of 50c coins needed.

c Which used more units?
Discuss why this happened.

Why is it best to use shapes that do not leave spaces or overlap?

# Looking for tens

7 + 4 + 8 + 6 + 3

= 2 tens + 8 = 28

Combine numbers that make 10, then answer the question.

1 a 3 + 4 + 7 b 8 + 5 + 2 c 5 + 3 + 5
d 7 + 6 + 4 e 1 + 9 + 8 f 6 + 3 + 7
g 2 + 4 + 6 h 9 + 9 + 1 i 8 + 7 + 3

2 a 8 cows, 5 sheep, 2 goats. How many animals?

b 8 cars, 3 trucks, 7 bikes. What is the total?

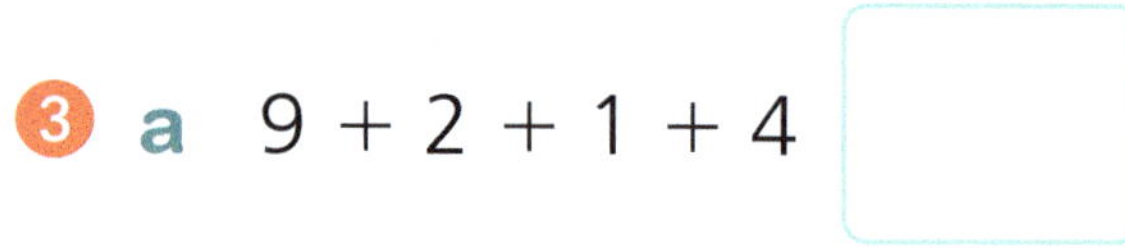

3 a 9 + 2 + 1 + 4 b 7 + 1 + 8 + 3

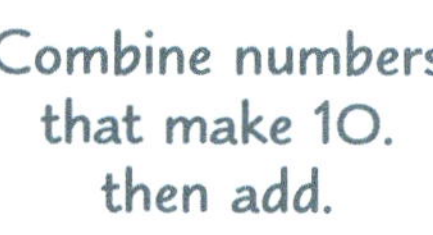

c 3 + 6 + 3 + 4 d 6 + 5 + 4 + 5
e 3 + 4 + 5 + 7 f 4 + 3 + 7 + 5

4 a \$3 + \$2 + \$6 + \$4 \$ b \$2 + \$7 + \$8 + \$3 \$

c \$5 + \$4 + \$1 + \$6 \$ d \$8 + \$3 + \$1 + \$7 \$

5 a 8 + 9 + 2 + 1 + 6 b 6 + 5 + 5 + 4 + 2
c 6 + 3 + 4 + 2 + 7 d 1 + 5 + 8 + 9 + 5

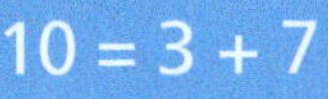

1 Use the number bonds to find the answers.

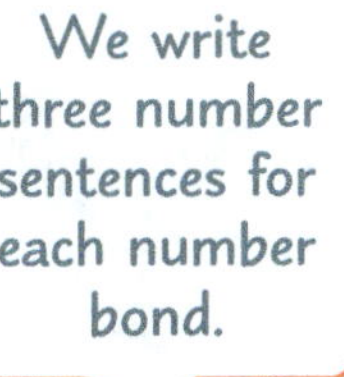

**a**
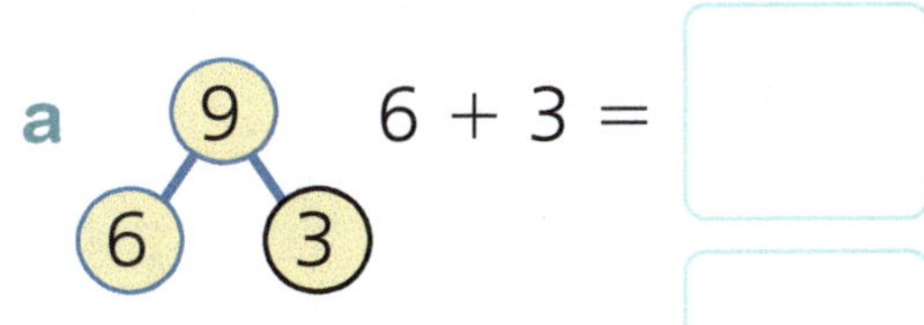


$6 + 3 =$ ☐

$9 - 6 =$ ☐

$9 - 3 =$ ☐

**b** 7, 4, 3

$7 - 4 =$ ☐

$7 - 3 =$ ☐

$4 + 3 =$ ☐

**c** 12, 5, 7

$5 + 7 =$ ☐

$12 - 7 =$ ☐

$12 - 5 =$ ☐

**d** 15, 8, 7

$15 - 8 =$ ☐

$15 - 7 =$ ☐

$8 + 7 =$ ☐

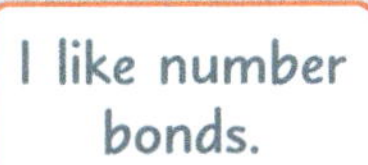

**e**
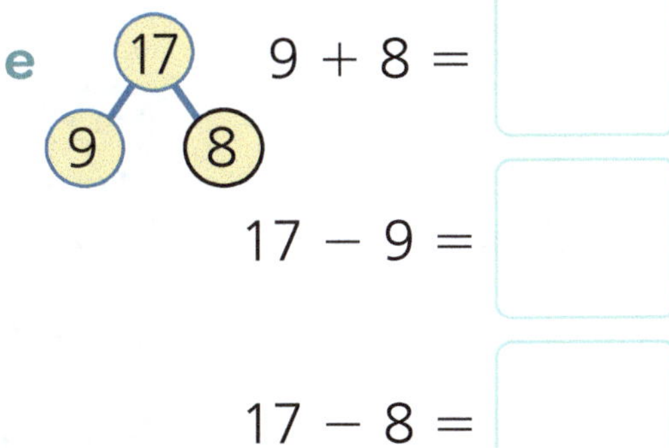


$9 + 8 =$ ☐

$17 - 9 =$ ☐

$17 - 8 =$ ☐

**f**
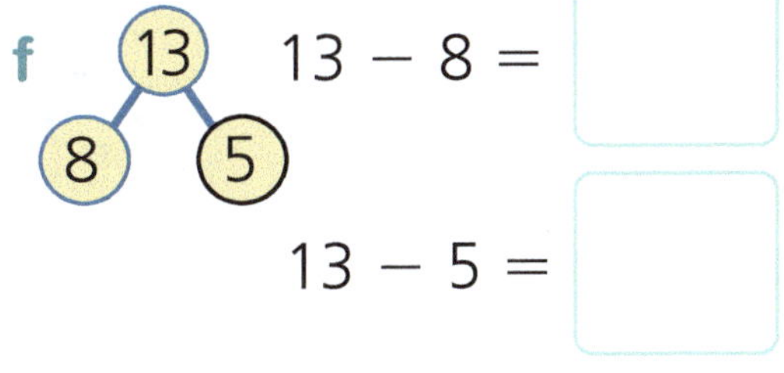


$13 - 8 =$ ☐

$13 - 5 =$ ☐

$8 + 5 =$ ☐

**g**
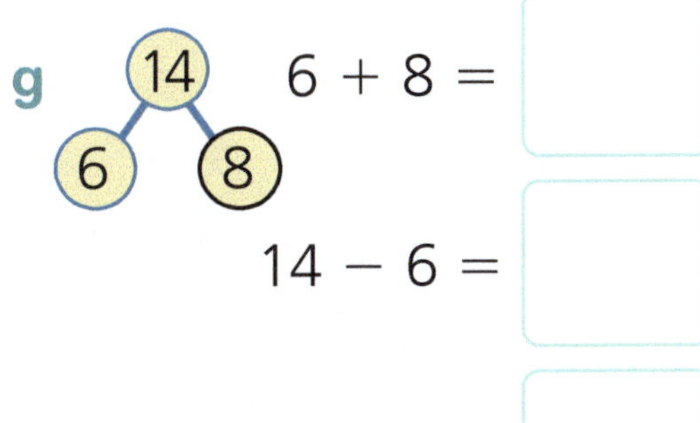


$6 + 8 =$ ☐

$14 - 6 =$ ☐

$14 - 8 =$ ☐

**h**
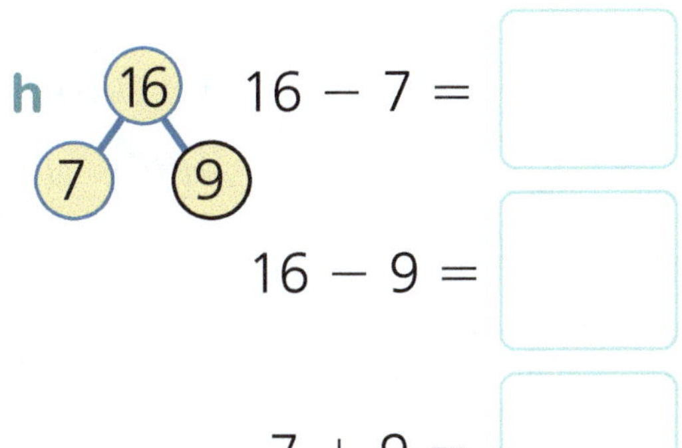


$16 - 7 =$ ☐

$16 - 9 =$ ☐

$7 + 9 =$ ☐

 • *AUSTRALIAN SIGNPOST MATHS NSW 1* • ISBN 9780655709022

# 29C Relating addition and subtraction

10 = ☐ + 7

1 Complete the number bonds and answer the number sentences.

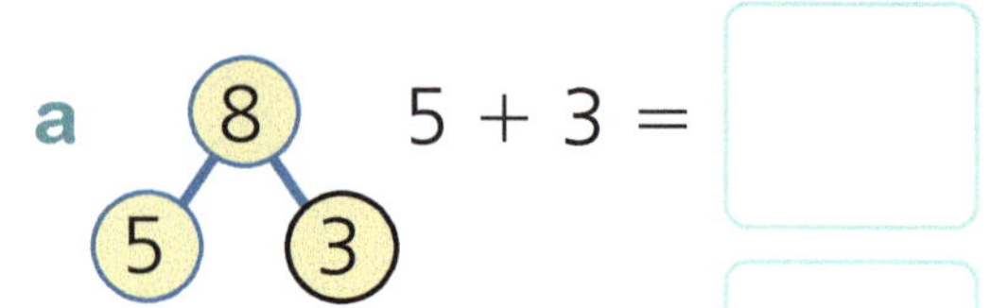

**a** (8: 5, 3)

5 + 3 = ☐

8 − 3 = ☐

8 − 5 = ☐

**b** (9: 2, 7)

2 + 7 = ☐

9 − 2 = ☐

9 − 7 = ☐

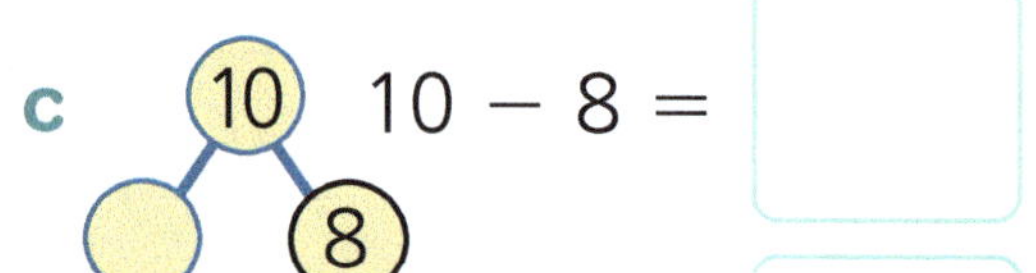

**c** (10: ☐, 8)

10 − 8 = ☐

8 + 2 = ☐

10 − 2 = ☐

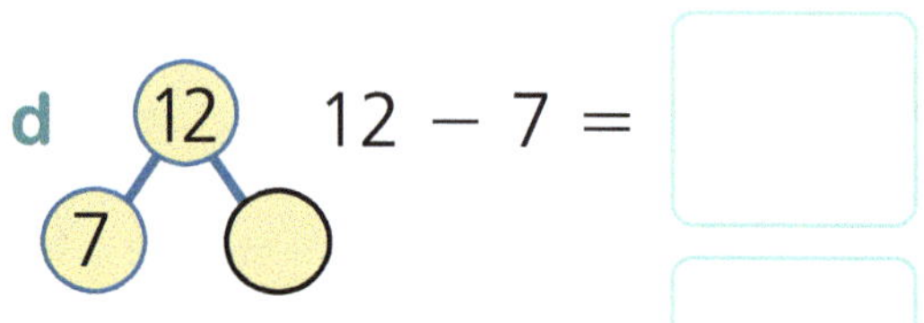

**d** (12: 7, ☐)

12 − 7 = ☐

5 + 7 = ☐

12 − 5 = ☐

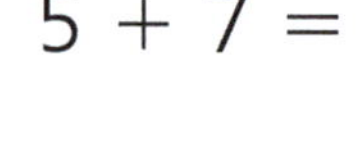

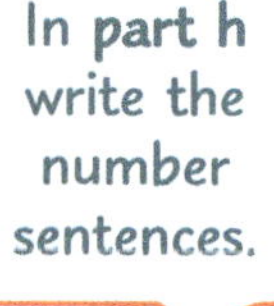


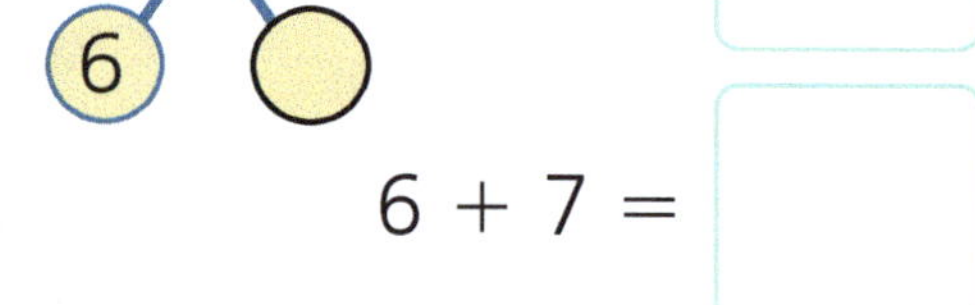

**e** (13: 6, ☐)

13 − 6 = ☐

6 + 7 = ☐

13 − 7 = ☐

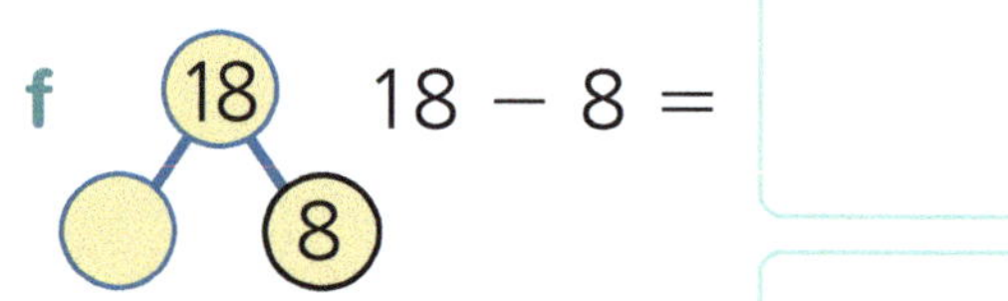

**f** (18: ☐, 8)

18 − 8 = ☐

8 + 10 = ☐

18 − 10 = ☐

**g** (17: 10, ☐)

17 − 10 = ☐

10 + 7 = ☐

17 − 7 = ☐

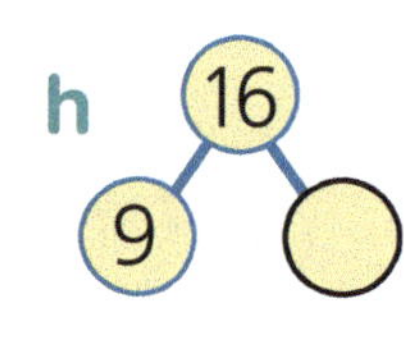

**h** (16: 9, ☐)

☐ =

☐ =

☐ =

# 29D Comparing mass

ACTIVITY

1 Compare the masses of these objects by hefting.

book

shoe

cup

You could compare other items too.

The [ ] is heaviest. The [ ] is lightest.

**Use balance scales to check.**

2 Find two collections of objects that balance. Draw them below.

You could use counters or blocks.

3 Use balance scales to answer these questions.

a 1 tens block has a mass equal to [ ] ones blocks.

b 2 tens blocks have a mass equal to [ ] ones blocks.

c 3 tens blocks have a mass equal to [ ] ones blocks.

4 How many marbles balance 10 tens blocks? [ ]

# 30A Bridging to 10

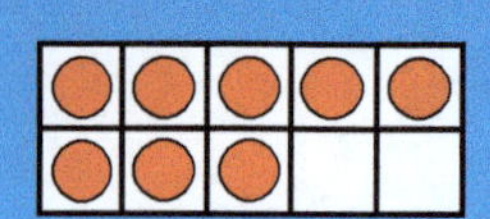

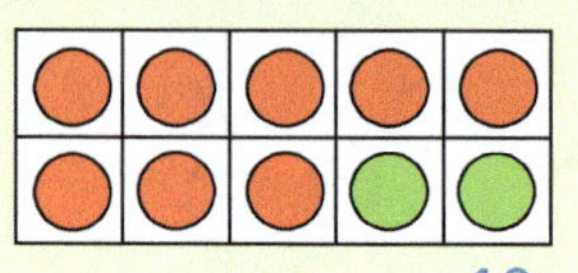

10 11 12 13 14

$8 + 6$
$= 8 + 2 + 4$
$= 10 + 4$
$= 14$

Make a group of 10, then count on.

This is called bridging to 10.

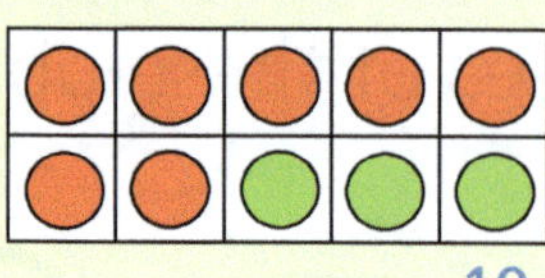

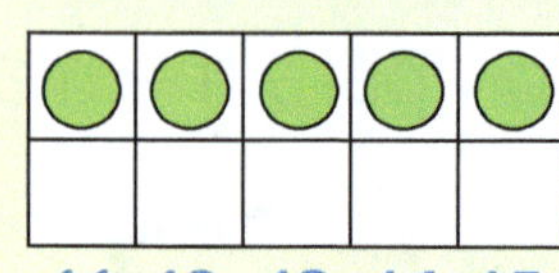

10 11 12 13 14 15

$7 + 8$
$= 7 + 3 + 5$
$= 10 + 5$
$= 15$

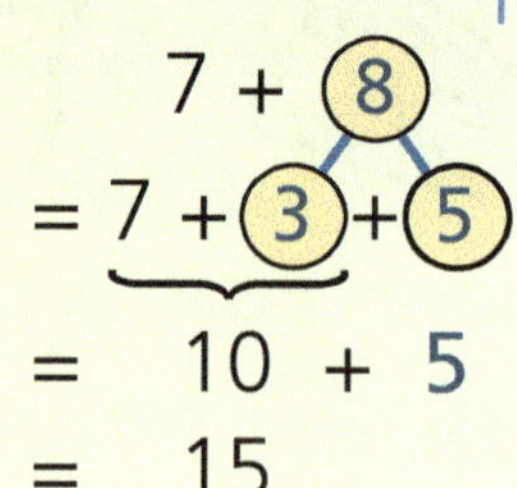

1. Finish each question.

a $9 + 5 = 9 + 1 + 4$
$= 10 + \square = \square$

b $8 + 8 = 8 + 2 + 6$
$= 10 + \square = \square$

2. Fill the first tens frame, then draw the rest in the second tens frame.

a $7 + 5$

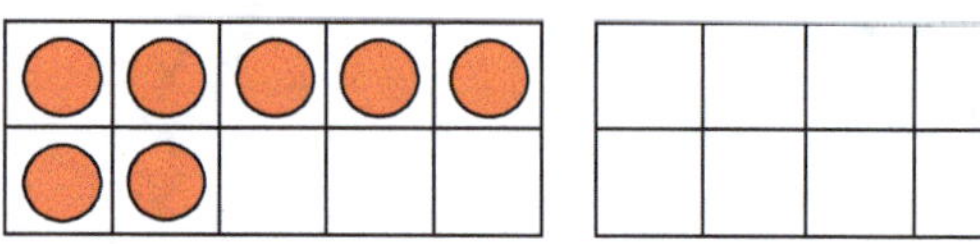

b $9 + 8$

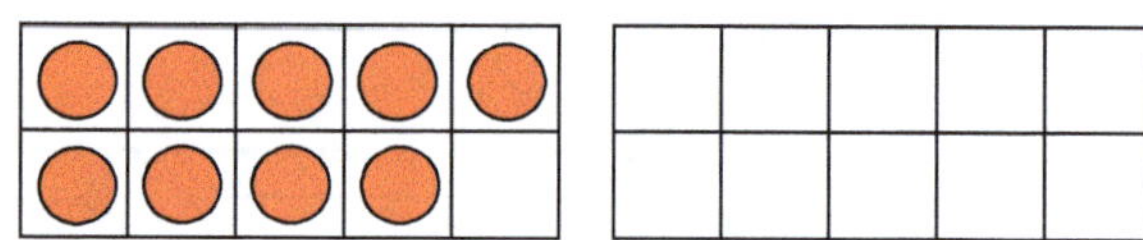

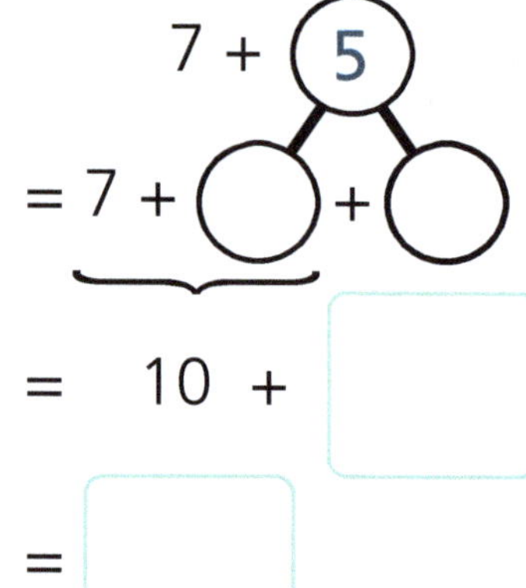

$7 + 5$
$= 7 + \bigcirc + \bigcirc$
$= 10 + \square$
$= \square$

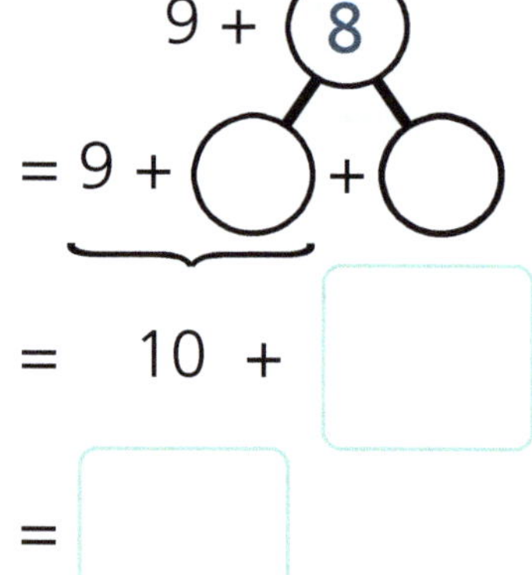

$9 + 8$
$= 9 + \bigcirc + \bigcirc$
$= 10 + \square$
$= \square$

3. Use bridging to ten to answer these questions.

a $7 + 6$ $\square$

b $8 + 5$ $\square$

c $9 + 4$ $\square$

d $8 + 7$ $\square$

 ISBN 9780655709022

# Bridging to 10s

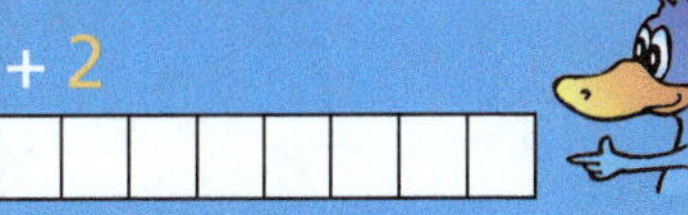

1 Use the number bonds to make the first 10.

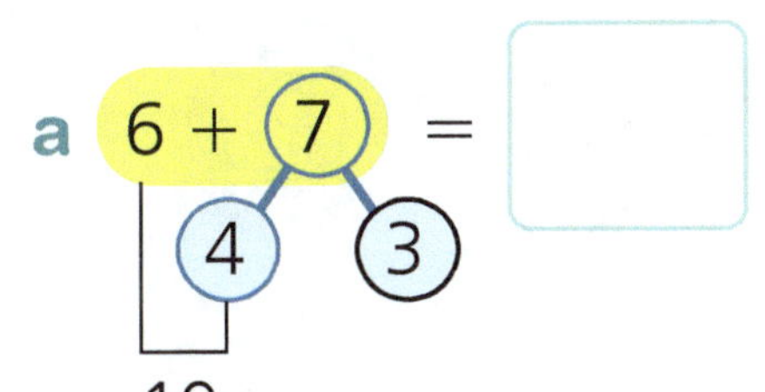


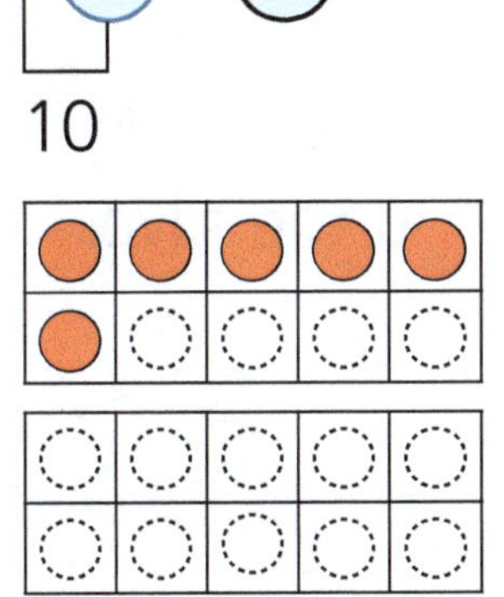

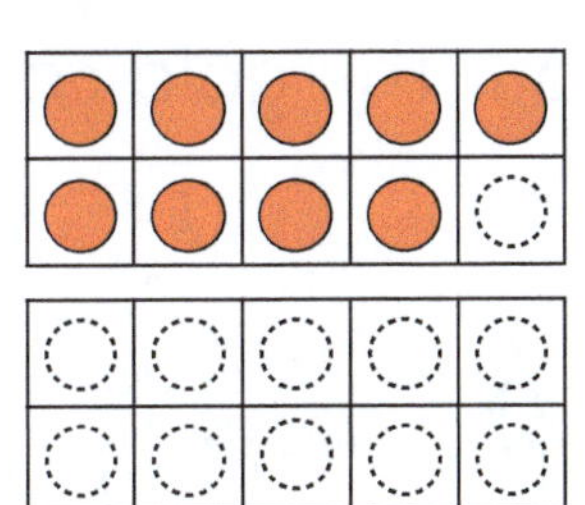

2 Use the number bonds to bridge to the next 10.

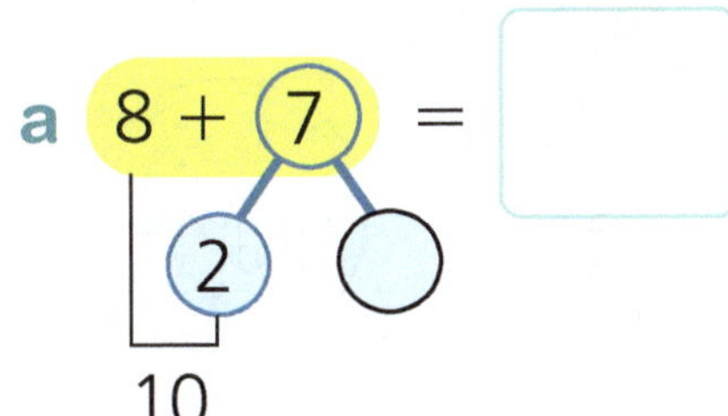


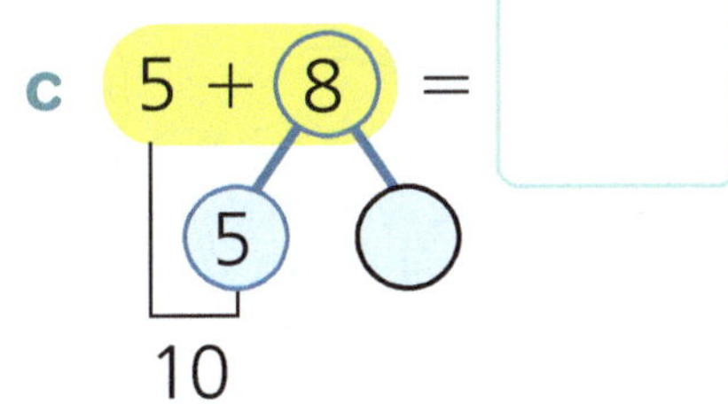


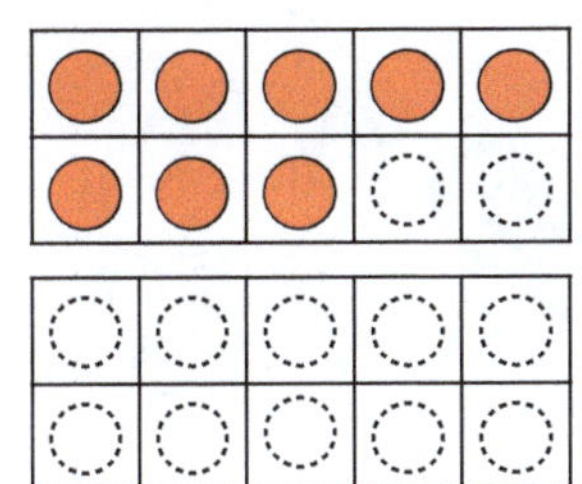

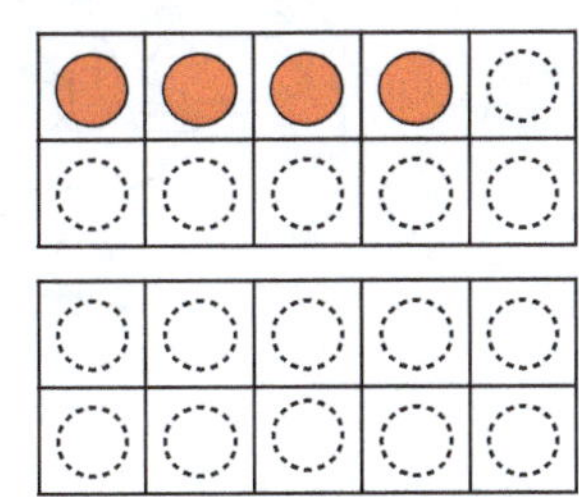

3 Use the number bonds to bridge to the next 10.

a 18 + 7
18 + 2 + 5
20 + 5 =

b 24 + 9
24 + 6 +
30 + ..... =

c 15 + 8
15 + 5 +
20 + ..... =

d 27 + 7 =
30

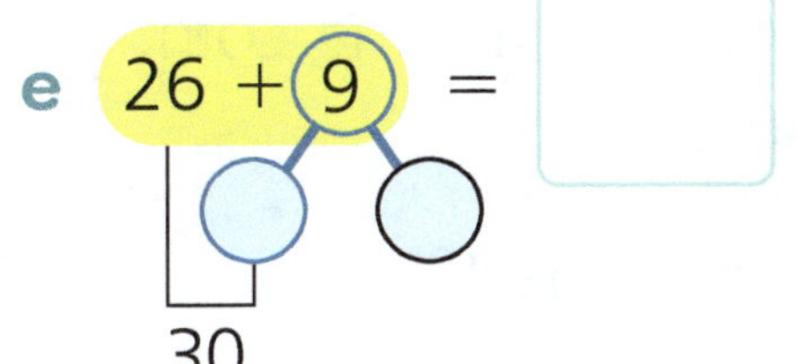


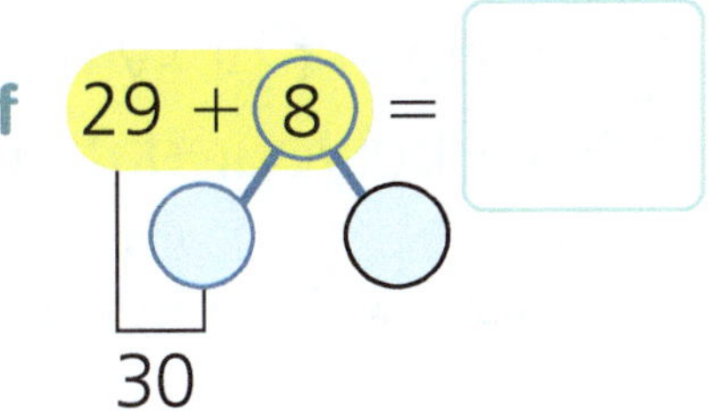

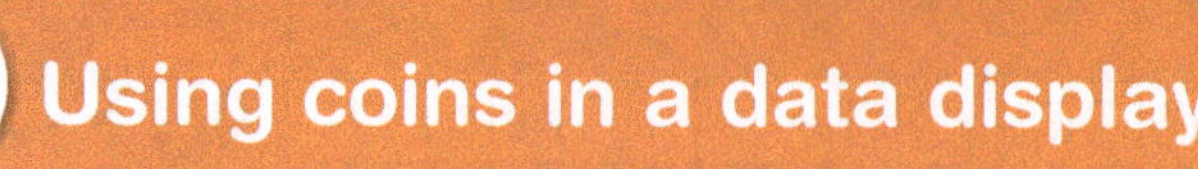

Statistics and probability

# 30C Using coins in a data display

1 dollar is equal to 100 cents.

CONCEPT

1 Discuss these coins. Colour the gold coins yellow and the silver coins green.

How many of each coin are there?

| | | | | | |
|---|---|---|---|---|---|
| 5c | | 10c | | 20c | |
| 50c | | $1 | | $2 | |

ACTIVITY

Make a data display using Question 1.

One object or symbol represents one coin.

Describe your data display.

Which coin occurred most often?

| ○ | ○ | ○ | ○ | ○ | ○ |
|---|---|---|---|---|---|
| ○ | ○ | ○ | ○ | ○ | ○ |
| ○ | ○ | ○ | ○ | ○ | ○ |
| ○ | ○ | ○ | ○ | ○ | ○ |
| 5c | 10c | 20c | 50c | $1 | $2 |



 • *AUSTRALIAN SIGNPOST MATHS NSW 1* • ISBN 9780655709022

# 30D Reflecting a shape

1. Circle the pictures that show reflection of one shape to make another.

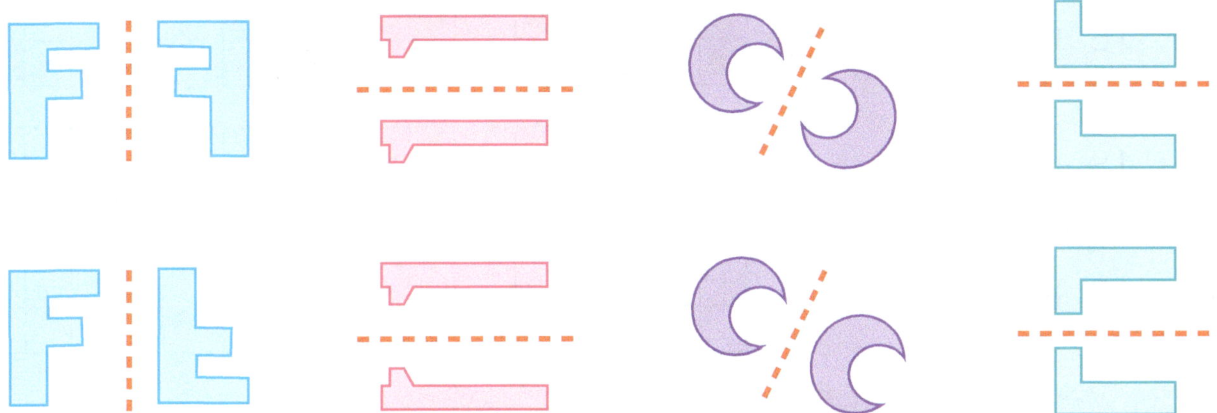

2. Flip each shape across the dotted line and draw the reflection.

Slide back the edge of this page to see the edge of the page 123 beside it.

# 31A Bridging to 10s

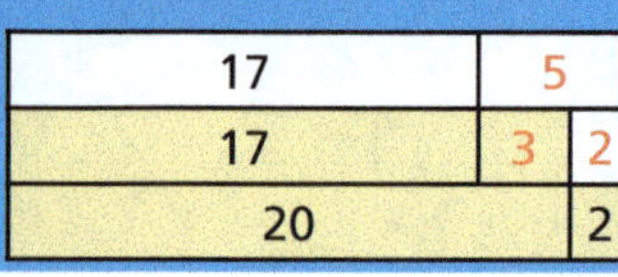

## Bridging to ten

CONCEPT

We can break up (partition) the smaller number to bridge to the next ten.

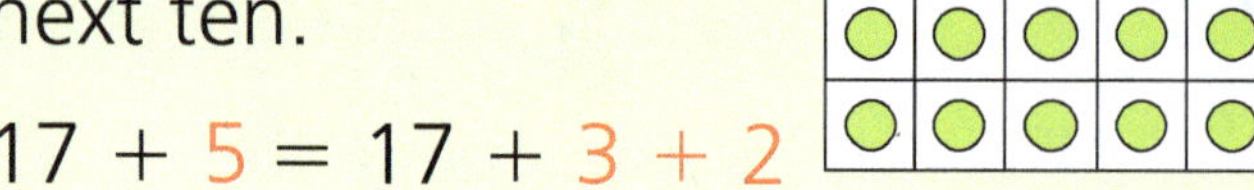

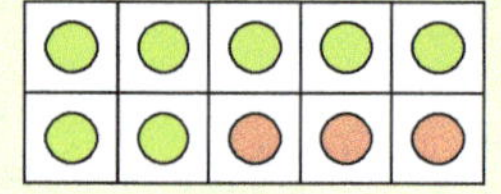

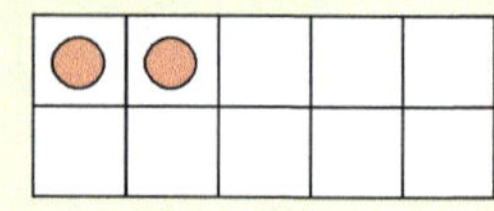

17 + 5 = 17 + 3 + 2
= 22

17 and 3 is 20, and 2 more makes 22.

1 Use the ten frames to answer these questions.

a 18 + 7 = ☐

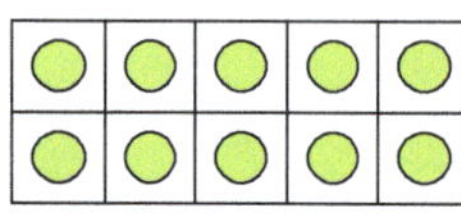

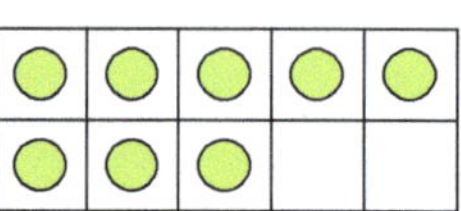

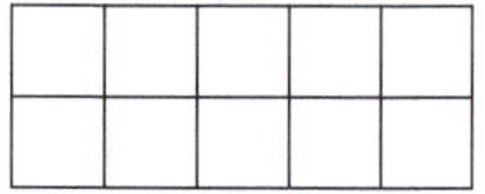

b 15 + 6 = ☐

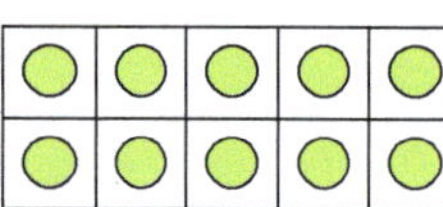

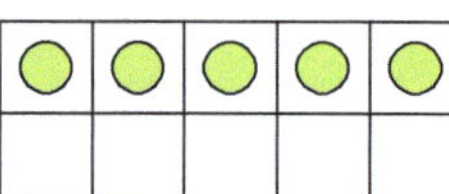

c 19 + 5 = ☐

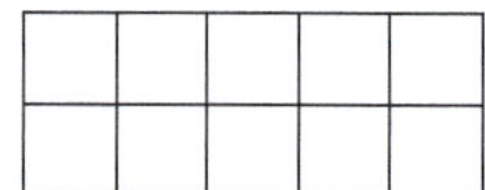

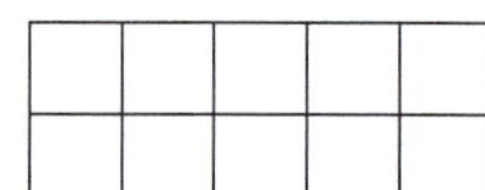

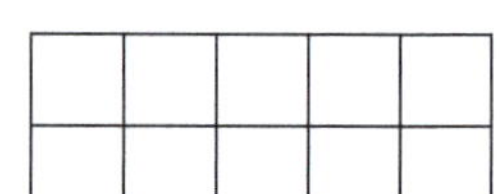

## Using the number line

CONCEPT

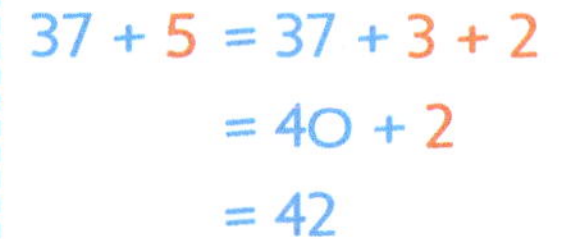


Break up the number to bridge to the next ten.

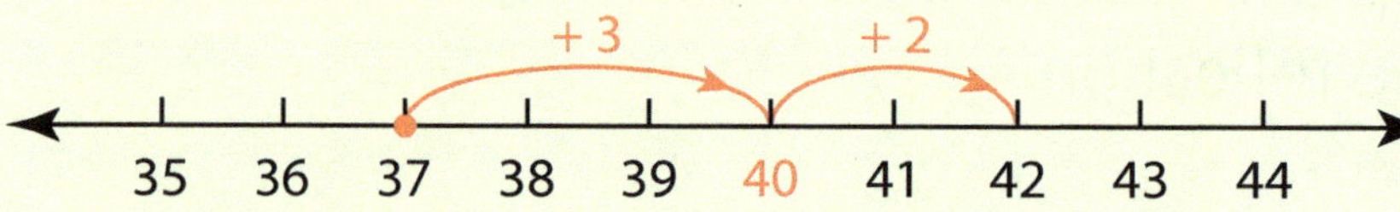


2 Use the number line to bridge to the next ten and answer these questions.

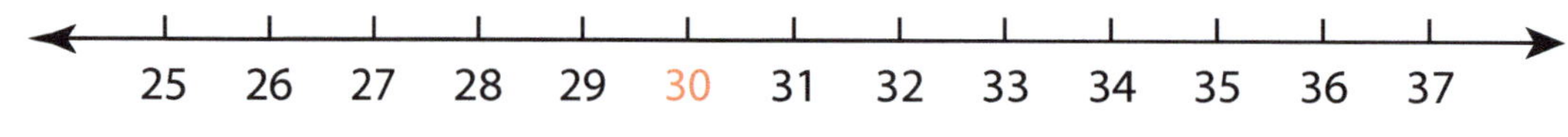


a 28 + 4 = 28 + ☐ + ☐
= ☐ + ☐
= ☐

b 27 + 6 = 27 + ☐ + ☐
= ☐ + ☐
= ☐

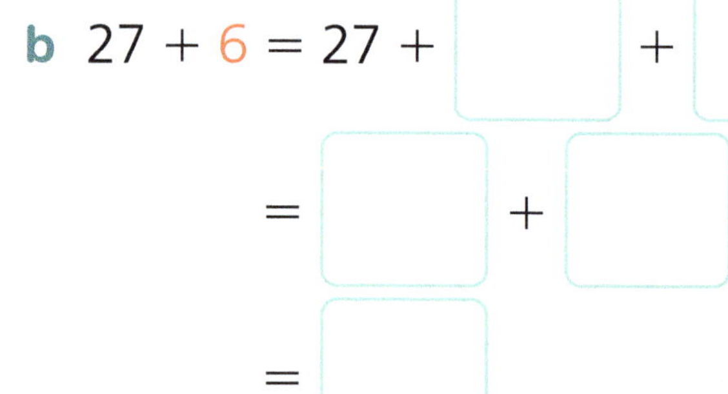



 • *AUSTRALIAN SIGNPOST MATHS NSW 1* • ISBN 9780655709022

# Sliding a shape

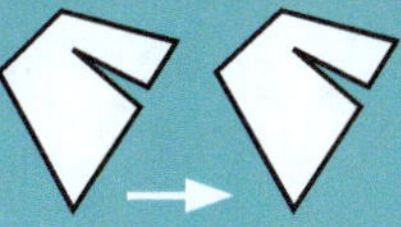

1. Circle the pictures that show a slide.

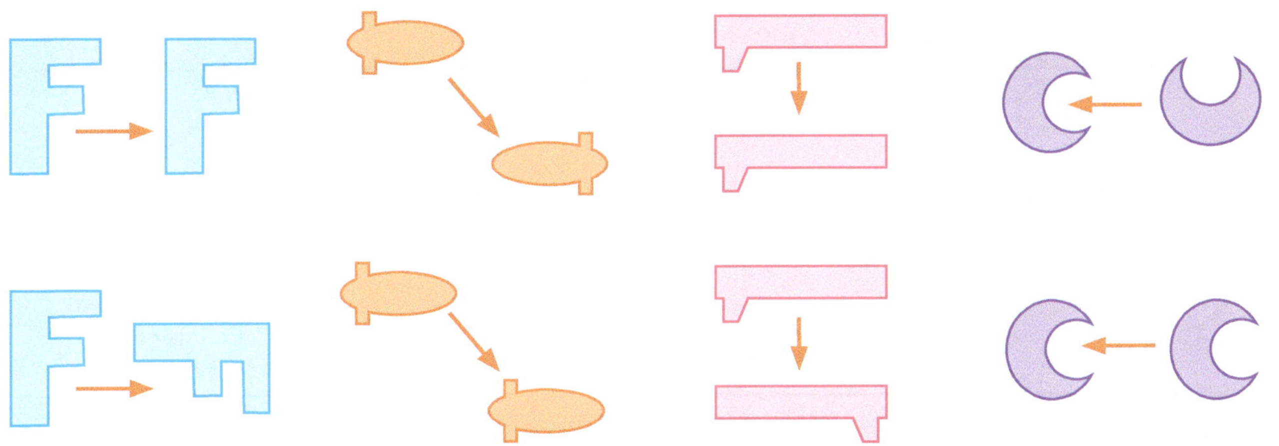

2. Trace each shape. Slide the shape across the page to finish the pattern.

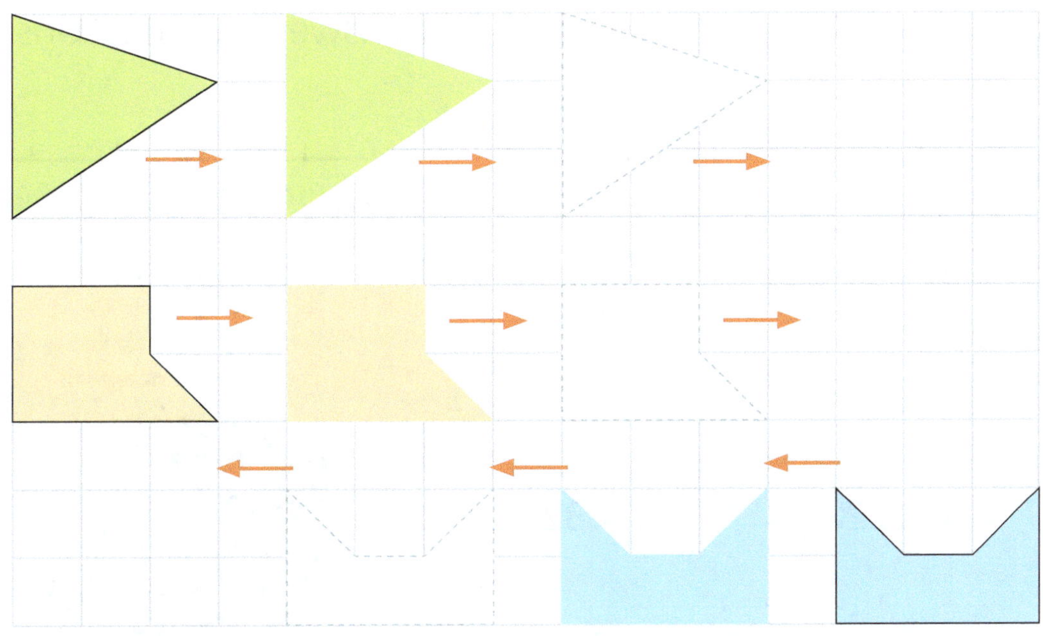

# 31C Counting back

$13 - 5 = 13 - 3 - 2$

CONCEPT

Use the number line.

$24 - 7 = 24 - 4 - 3$
$= 20 - 3$
$= 17$

7, 4, ?

Break up the 7 to go back to the last ten.

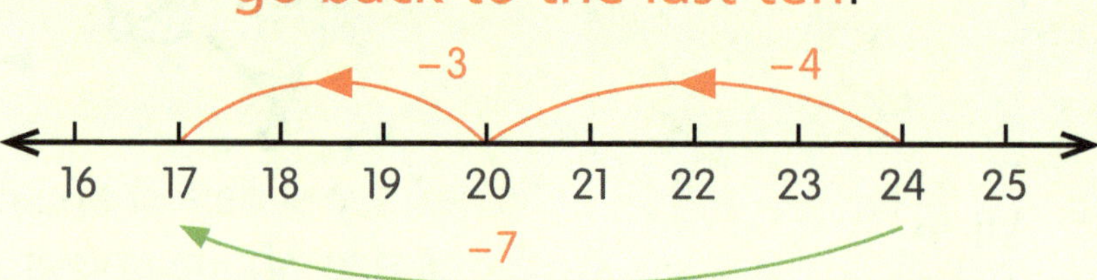


1 Use the number line to subtract across 10.

**a**

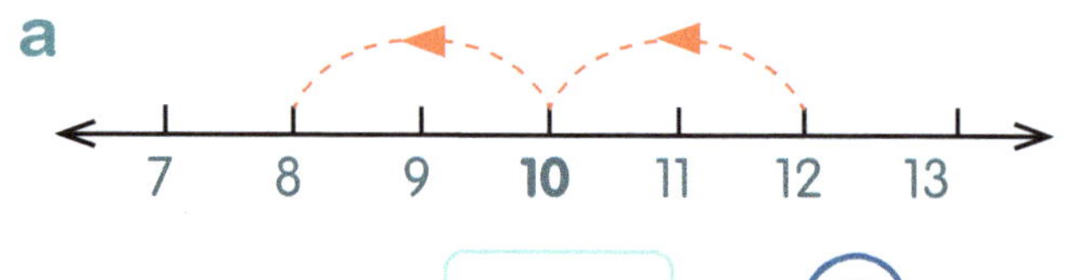


$12 - 4 =$ ☐

**b**

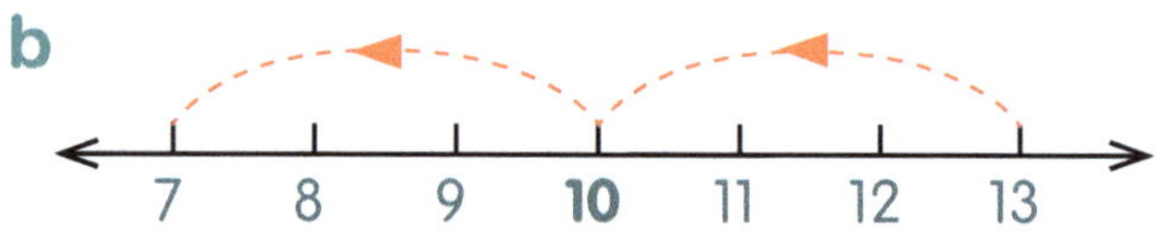


$13 - 6 =$ ☐

6, 3

**c**

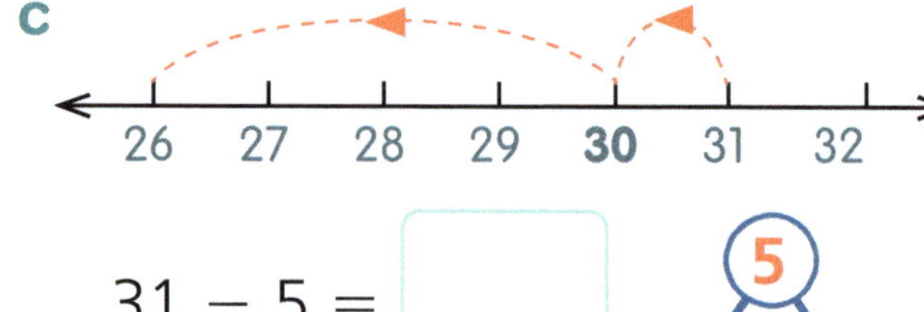


$31 - 5 =$ ☐

5, 1

**d**

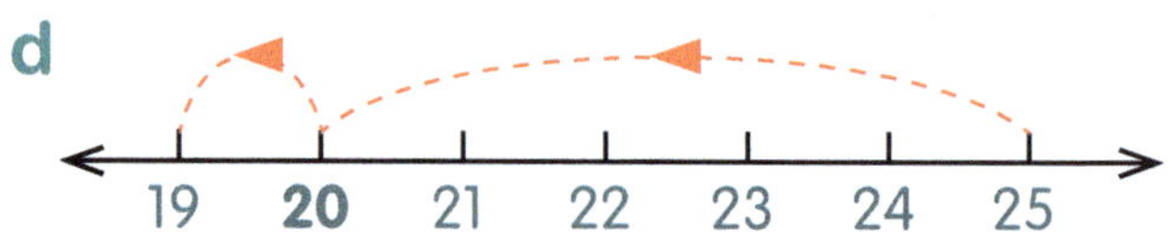


$25 - 6 =$ ☐

6, 5

2 Use the number line to bridge to the last 10 to answer the questions.

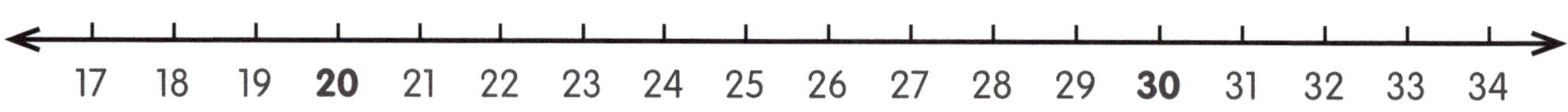


**a** $23 - 4$

**b** $31 - 3$

**c** $25 - 6$

**d** $34 - 5$

**e** $22 - 4$

**f** $32 - 8$

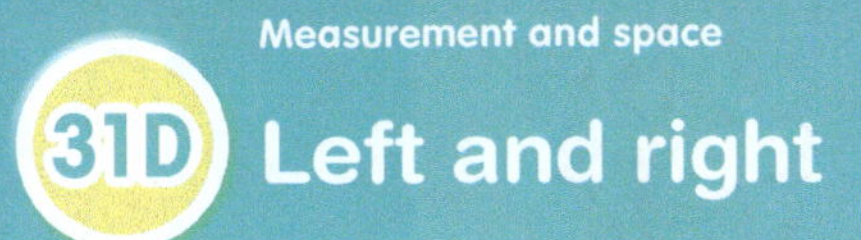


# Left and right

CONCEPT

If a friend is facing me, their **right hand side** is on my **left**.

All the children have the bat in their right hand.

1 Draw an arrow to show how each car will turn.

a Turn right.
b Turn left.
c Turn right.
d Turn left.

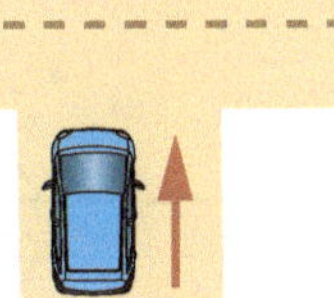
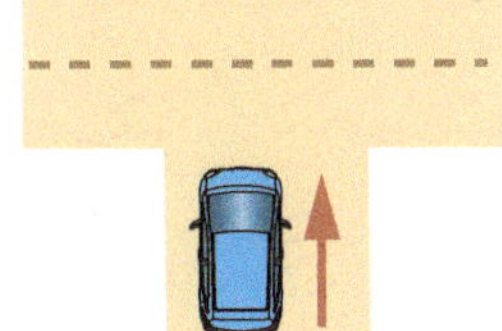

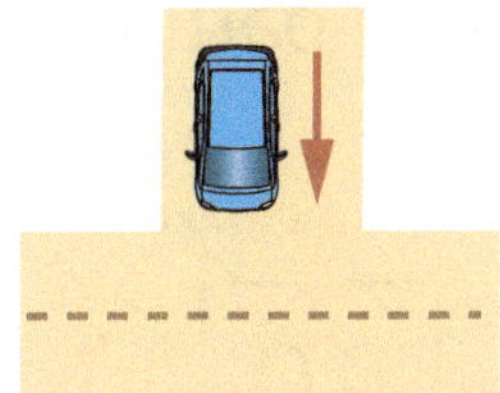

2 Write the letters the truck will go through if **L** means the truck goes left, and **R** means it goes right.

a **L**, **L**

b **L**, **L**, **L**

c **L**, **L**, **L**, **L**

d **L**, **R**, **R**, **R**

e **L**, **R**, **R**, **R**, **L**

# 32A Using partitioning

CONCEPT

Using partitioning can help when adding.

$38 + 4 = 30 + 12$
$= 30 + 10 + 2$
$= 40 + 2$
$= 42$

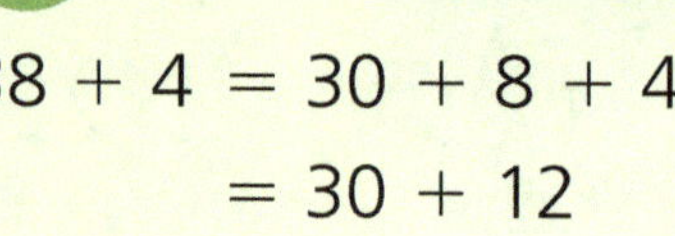

$38 + 4 = 30 + 8 + 4$
$= 30 + 12$
$= 42$

$38 + 4 = 30 + 12$
$= 42$

1. a $20 + 10 =$ ☐   b $30 + 10 =$ ☐   c $10 + 10 =$ ☐

2. Use partitioning to split the numbers.

a 24

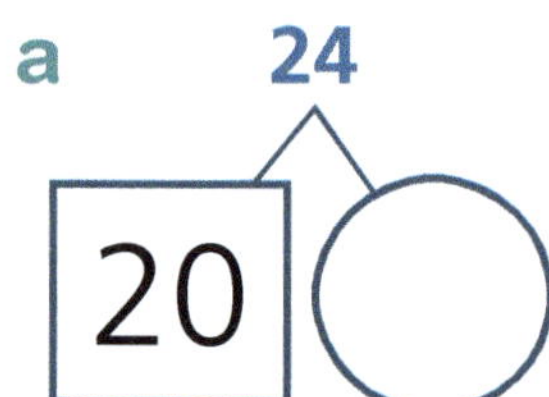


b 39

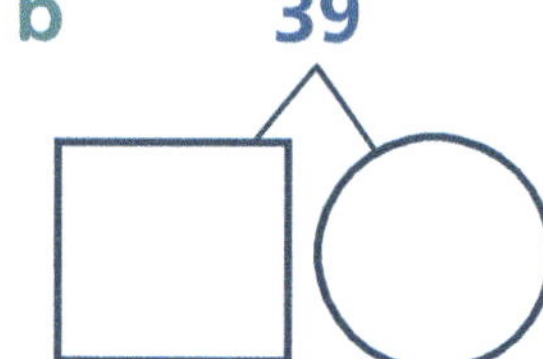

c 18

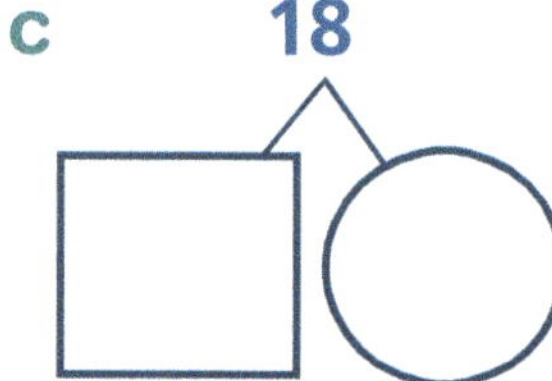

d 27

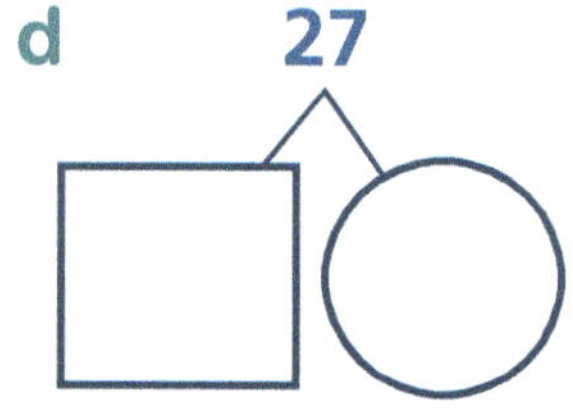

3. Use partitioning to find the answers.

a $24 + 7$
$= 20 + 4 + 7$
$= 20 +$ ☐
$=$ ☐

b $39 + 4$
$= 30 + 9 + 4$
$= 30 +$ ☐
$=$ ☐

c $18 + 5$
$= 10 + 8 + 5$
$= 10 +$ ☐
$=$ ☐

d $35 + 3$
$= 30 +$ ☐
$=$ ☐

e $26 + 4$
$= 20 +$ ☐
$=$ ☐

f $17 + 7$
$= 10 +$ ☐
$=$ ☐

g $32 + 3$
$=$ ☐

h $37 + 8$
$=$ ☐

i $25 + 6$
$=$ ☐


 ISBN 9780655709022

# 32B Using partitioning to add

1 a 27 + 6 = 20 + 7 + 6
= 20 + 13
= 20 + 10 + 3
= 30 + 3
= ☐

b 38 + 4 = 30 + 8 + 4
= 30 + 12
= 30 + 10 + 2
= 40 + 2
= ☐

2 Use partitioning to split the first number, then add.

a 39 + 5 = 30 + 14
(39 → 30 and 9; 9 + 5 = 14)
= 30 + 10 + 4
= ☐

b 26 + 4 = 20 + 10
(26 → 20 and 6; 6 + 4 = 10)
= ☐

39 + 4
= 30 + 13

c 18 + 7 = 10 + 15
(18 → 10 and 8; 8 + 7 = 15)
= 10 + 10 + 5
= ☐

d 39 + 4 = 30 + 13
(39 → 30 and 9; 9 + 4 = 13)
= 30 + 10 + 3
= ☐

e 46 + 8 = 40 + 14
(46 → 40 and 6; 6 + 8 = 14)
= 40 + 10 + 4
= ☐

f 27 + 7 = 20 + 14
(27 → 20 and 7; 7 + 7 = 14)
= 20 + 10 + 4
= ☐

g 27 + 7 = 20 + ☐
(27 → 20 and 7)
= 20 + ☐ + ☐
☐ = ☐

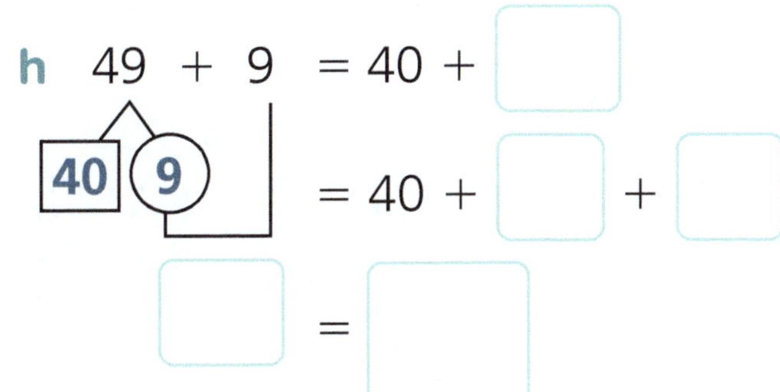

h 49 + 9 = 40 + ☐
(49 → 40 and 9)
= 40 + ☐ + ☐
☐ = ☐

 • *AUSTRALIAN SIGNPOST MATHS NSW 1* • ISBN 9780655709022

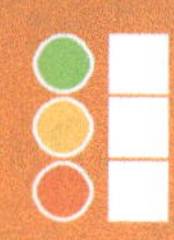

ACTIVITY

Talk about the picture. What might happen next week?

If something **could happen** we say it is possible.

Which of these activities are possible?

If something could not happen we say it is not possible (or impossible).

Which of these activities are not possible?

1 John's story begins with: 'I was standing on my desk at home when my dog jumped up onto the desk.' What might happen next?

# 32D Following directions

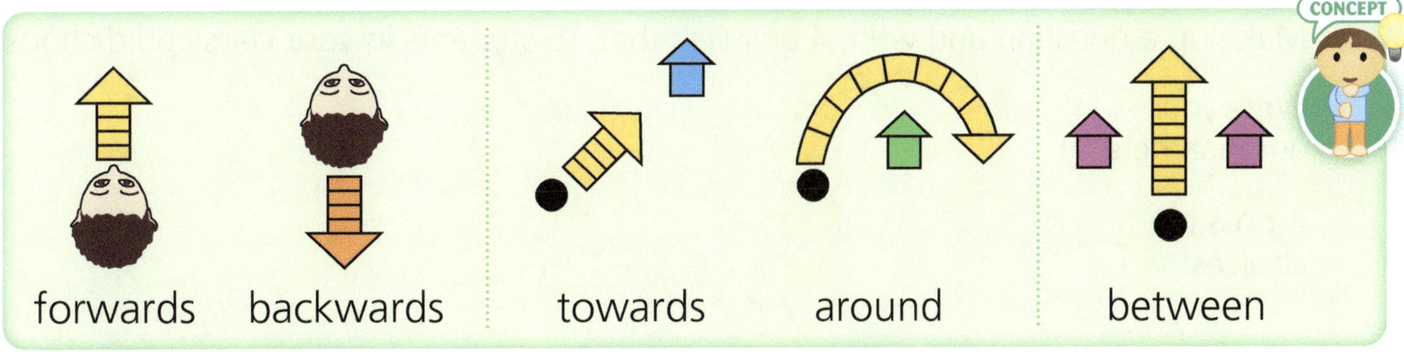


1. Talk about the paths taken by student A and B.
Give directions to student C to take him to the finish.

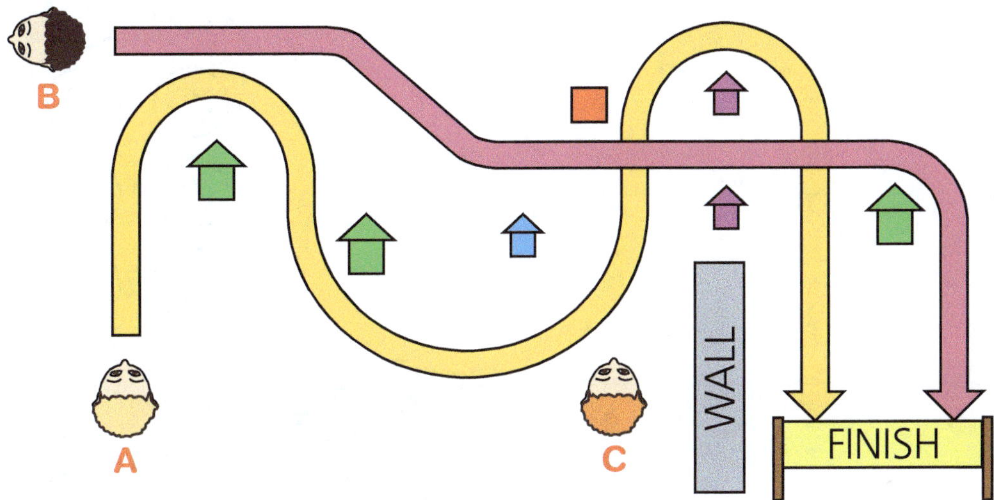


2. Talk about the paths taken by girl D (forwards) and girl E (backwards).

Give directions to a partner for moving around the room. Take turns.

# 33A Gather and organise data

A picture graph is a data display with pictures.

1 Make up a question and write 4 answers that 15 students in your class could choose.

Write your question here.

4 possible choices:

2 Collect information from 15 students. Show answers in this table.
Put your 4 possible choices in the left column.
Trace one line in black for each student.

3 Make a picture graph on the right. Put your 4 possible choices in the spaces at the bottom of the graph. Use the information above to colour a face for each student who chose that answer.

CONCEPT

## Tally marks

Each mark stands for 1 choice.

Tallies are usually placed in groups of 5.

||||| ||||| = 10

The fifth mark is often drawn across the other four marks.

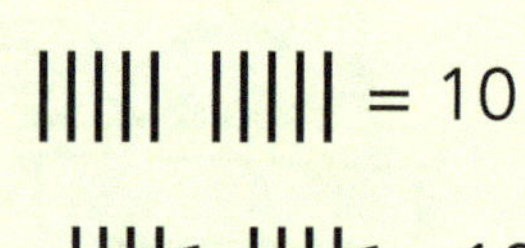

= 10

## Identifying and addressing areas of need

An essential part of a teacher's role is identifying and addressing areas of student need.

This includes recognising areas where memory is fading and discovering any concepts that have been missed or misunderstood.

**Testing is a great way to identify areas of need, but is only really useful when the results are used to help the student.**

It is important to build a strong foundation when teaching new concepts and skills.

It is also important to revise/re-teach areas of weakness you discover so that these areas will not be barriers to the future learning of related concepts.

## Progress tests and retests (see adjacent page)

Progress tests 1 to 5 are found on pages 133–158 of the online Teacher Resource.

After each test, notes and answers are supplied.

Progress test questions are cross-referenced to appropriate Student Book pages.

Progress retests 1 to 5 are found on pages 159–184 of the online Teacher Resource.

**The remediation records pages** are used to provide a record of each student's progress.

These are found on pages 133–134 and 159–160 of the online Teacher Resource.

For each error recorded, the question should be discussed, and using the Student Book cross-reference provided, practice should occur. Retesting should follow using the progress retests.

**Summary**

1 Test recent work.

2 Enter any mistakes in the remediation records.

3 Use this record to direct your revision/re-teaching.

4 Retest using the matching retest questions to ensure understanding.

## Teaching and learning

Successfully teaching content and skills is a complex process.

A **good textbook** is an important tool alongside **effective teaching and planning**.

Knowledge, understanding and skills must be embedded in the student's mind so that recall continues with time. This will be done using:

(1) instruction (2) practice (3) drill (4) review.

**Instruction** involves explicit explanation, investigation and the use of good educational resources.

**Practice** forms neural pathways within the brain.

**Drill** strengthens neural pathways. The stronger the pathways become, the longer the understanding or knowledge is retained. 'Overlearning' prolongs recall.

**Review** revitalises weakened neural pathways.

## Progress test

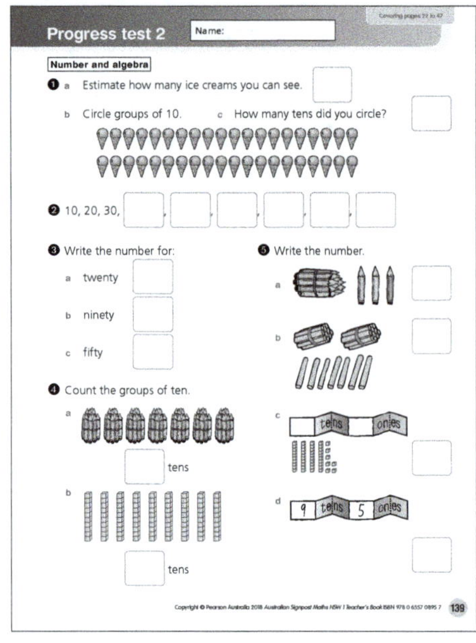

Progress test 2 Name:

Number and algebra

1 a Estimate how many ice creams you can see.

b Circle groups of 10. c How many tens did you circle?

2 10, 20, 30,

3 Write the number for:

a twenty

b ninety

c fifty

4 Count the groups of ten.

a tens

b tens

5 Write the number.

a

b

c tens ones

d 9 tens 5 ones

Copyright © Pearson Australia 2018 Australian Signpost Maths NSW 1 Teacher's Book ISBN 978 0 6557 0895 7 139

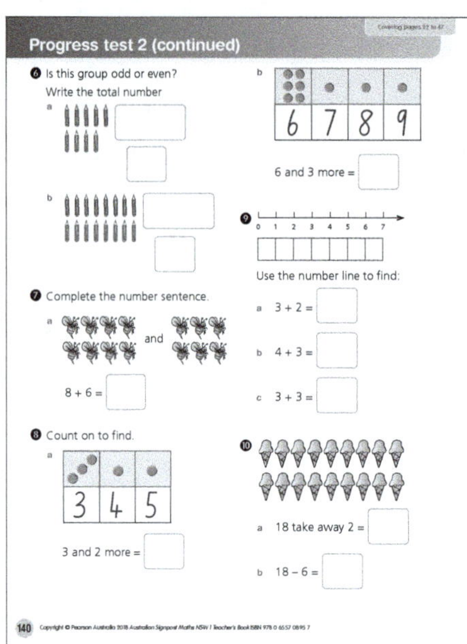

Progress test 2 (continued)

6 Is this group odd or even?

Write the total number

a

b

7 Complete the number sentence.

a and

8 + 6 =

8 Count on to find.

a 3 4 5

3 and 2 more =

b 6 7 8 9

6 and 3 more =

9 0 1 2 3 4 5 6 7

Use the number line to find:

a 3 + 2 =

b 4 + 3 =

c 3 + 3 =

10

a 18 take away 2 =

b 18 − 6 =

140 Copyright © Pearson Australia 2018 Australian Signpost Maths NSW 1 Teacher's Book ISBN 978 0 6557 0895 7

## Progress retest

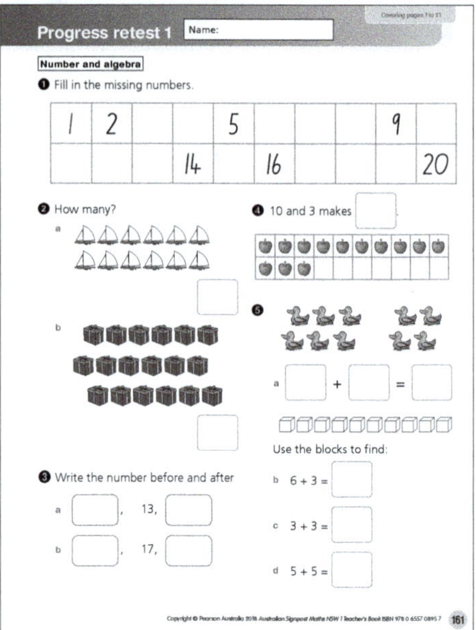

Progress retest 1 Name:

Number and algebra

1 Fill in the missing numbers.

| 1 | 2 | | | 5 | | | | 9 | |
|---|---|---|---|---|---|---|---|---|---|
| | | | 14 | | 16 | | | | 20 |

2 How many?

a

b

3 Write the number before and after

a , 13,

b , 17,

4 10 and 3 makes

5

a + =

Use the blocks to find:

b 6 + 3 =

c 3 + 3 =

d 5 + 5 =

Copyright © Pearson Australia 2018 Australian Signpost Maths NSW 1 Teacher's Book ISBN 978 0 6557 0895 7 161

## Notes and Answers for Progress test 2

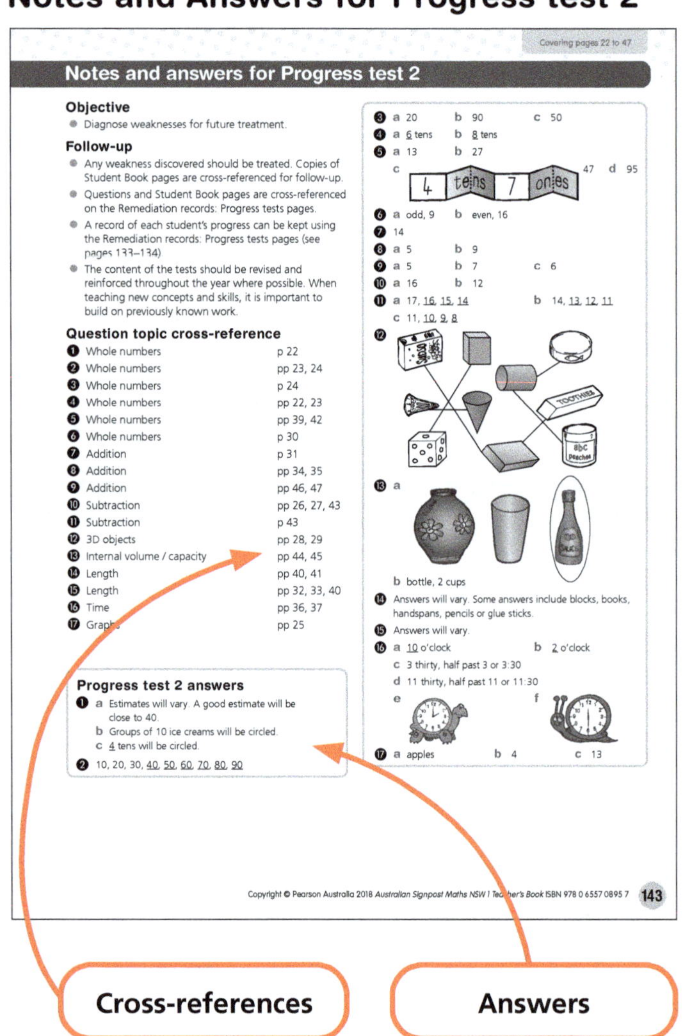

Covering pages 22 to 47

Notes and answers for Progress test 2

**Objective**

- Diagnose weaknesses for future treatment.

**Follow-up**

- Any weakness discovered should be treated. Copies of Student Book pages are cross-referenced for follow-up.
- Questions and Student Book pages are cross-referenced on the Remediation records: Progress tests pages.
- A record of each student's progress can be kept using the Remediation records: Progress tests pages (see pages 133–134).
- The content of the tests should be revised and reinforced throughout the year where possible. When teaching new concepts and skills, it is important to build on previously known work.

**Question topic cross-reference**

| | | |
|---|---|---|
| 1 | Whole numbers | p 22 |
| 2 | Whole numbers | pp 23, 24 |
| 3 | Whole numbers | p 24 |
| 4 | Whole numbers | pp 22, 23 |
| 5 | Whole numbers | pp 39, 42 |
| 6 | Whole numbers | p 30 |
| 7 | Addition | p 31 |
| 8 | Addition | pp 34, 35 |
| 9 | Addition | pp 46, 47 |
| 10 | Subtraction | pp 26, 27, 43 |
| 11 | Subtraction | p 43 |
| 12 | 3D objects | pp 28, 29 |
| 13 | Internal volume / capacity | pp 44, 45 |
| 14 | Length | pp 40, 41 |
| 15 | Length | pp 32, 33, 40 |
| 16 | Time | pp 36, 37 |
| 17 | Graphs | pp 25 |

**Progress test 2 answers**

1 a Estimates will vary. A good estimate will be close to 40.
b Groups of 10 ice creams will be circled.
c 4 tens will be circled.

2 10, 20, 30, 40, 50, 60, 70, 80, 90

3 a 20 b 90 c 50

4 a 6 tens b 8 tens

5 a 13 b 27 c 4 tens 7 ones 47 d 95

6 a odd, 9 b even, 16

7 14

8 a 5 b 9

9 a 5 b 7 c 6

10 a 16 b 12

11 a 17, 16, 15, 14 b 14, 13, 12, 11 c 11, 10, 9, 8

12

13 a
b bottle, 2 cups

14 Answers will vary. Some answers include blocks, books, handspans, pencils or glue sticks.

15 Answers will vary.

16 a 10 o'clock b 2 o'clock
c 3 thirty, half past 3 or 3:30
d 11 thirty, half past 11 or 11:30
e f

17 a apples b 4 c 13

Copyright © Pearson Australia 2018 Australian Signpost Maths NSW 1 Teacher's Book ISBN 978 0 6557 0895 7 143

## Remediation records: Progress tests

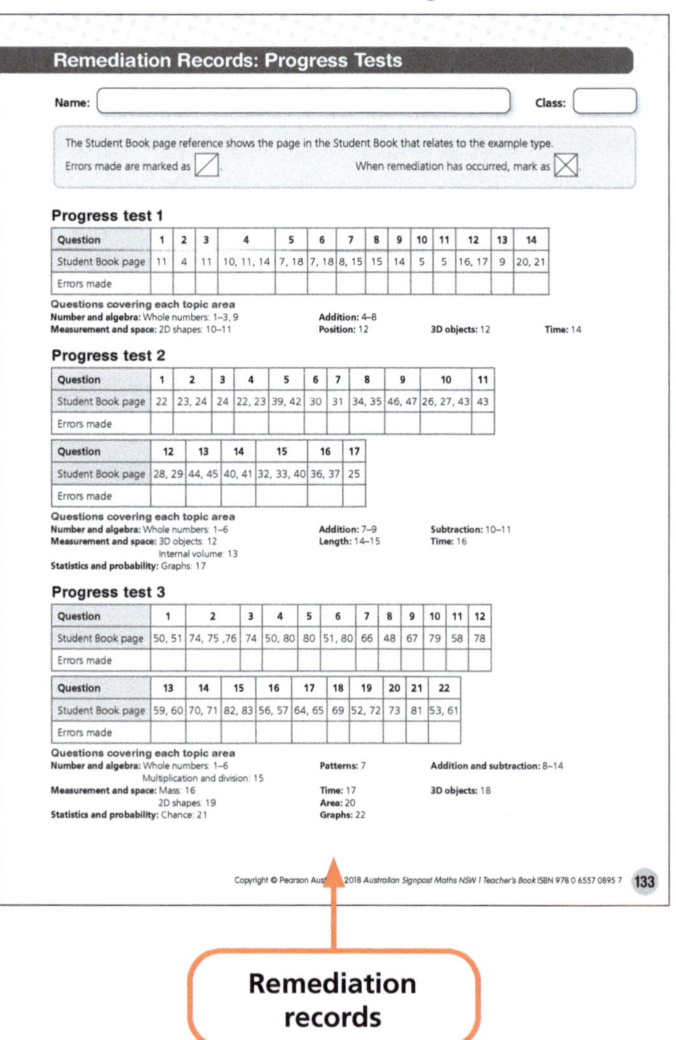

Remediation Records: Progress Tests

Name: Class:

The Student Book page reference shows the page in the Student Book that relates to the example type.

Errors made are marked as ⧄. When remediation has occurred, mark as ☒.

**Progress test 1**

| Question | 1 | 2 | 3 | 4 | 5 | 6 | 7 | 8 | 9 | 10 | 11 | 12 | 13 | 14 |
|---|---|---|---|---|---|---|---|---|---|---|---|---|---|---|
| Student Book page | 11 | 4 | 11 | 10, 11, 14 | 7, 18 | 7, 18 | 8, 15 | 15 | 14 | 5 | 5 | 16, 17 | 9 | 20, 21 |
| Errors made | | | | | | | | | | | | | | |

**Questions covering each topic area**
**Number and algebra:** Whole numbers: 1–3, 9 **Addition:** 4–8
**Measurement and space:** 2D shapes: 10–11 **Position:** 12 **3D objects:** 12 **Time:** 14

**Progress test 2**

| Question | 1 | 2 | 3 | 4 | 5 | 6 | 7 | 8 | 9 | 10 | 11 |
|---|---|---|---|---|---|---|---|---|---|---|---|
| Student Book page | 22 | 23, 24 | 24 | 22, 23 | 39, 42 | 30 | 31 | 34, 35 | 46, 47 | 26, 27, 43 | 43 |
| Errors made | | | | | | | | | | | |

| Question | 12 | 13 | 14 | 15 | 16 | 17 |
|---|---|---|---|---|---|---|
| Student Book page | 28, 29 | 44, 45 | 40, 41 | 32, 33, 40 | 36, 37 | 25 |
| Errors made | | | | | | |

**Questions covering each topic area**
**Number and algebra:** Whole numbers: 1–6 **Addition:** 7–9 **Subtraction:** 10–11
**Measurement and space:** 3D objects: 12, Internal volume: 13 **Length:** 14–15 **Time:** 16
**Statistics and probability:** Graphs: 17

**Progress test 3**

| Question | 1 | 2 | 3 | 4 | 5 | 6 | 7 | 8 | 9 | 10 | 11 | 12 |
|---|---|---|---|---|---|---|---|---|---|---|---|---|
| Student Book page | 50, 51 | 74, 75 ,76 | 74 | 50, 80 | 80 | 51, 80 | 66 | 48 | 67 | 79 | 58 | 78 |
| Errors made | | | | | | | | | | | | |

| Question | 13 | 14 | 15 | 16 | 17 | 18 | 19 | 20 | 21 | 22 |
|---|---|---|---|---|---|---|---|---|---|---|
| Student Book page | 59, 60 | 70, 71 | 82, 83 | 56, 57 | 64, 65 | 69 | 52, 72 | 73 | 81 | 53, 61 |
| Errors made | | | | | | | | | | |

**Questions covering each topic area**
**Number and algebra:** Whole numbers: 1–6, Multiplication and division: 15 **Patterns:** 7 **Addition and subtraction:** 8–14
**Measurement and space:** Mass: 16, 2D shapes: 19 **Time:** 17 **Area:** 20 **3D objects:** 18
**Statistics and probability:** Chance: 21 **Graphs:** 22

Copyright © Pearson Aus[...] 2018 Australian Signpost Maths NSW 1 Teacher's Book ISBN 978 0 6557 0895 7 133

Cross-references

Answers

Remediation records

# BLM 1 Number lines / chart

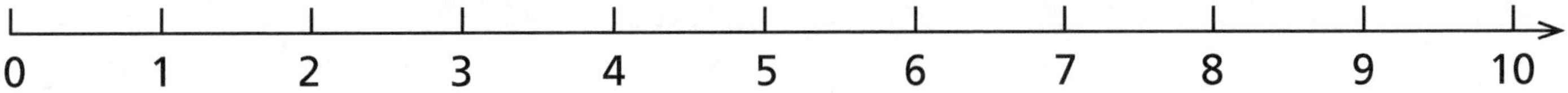

0 1 2 3 4 5 6 7 8 9 10

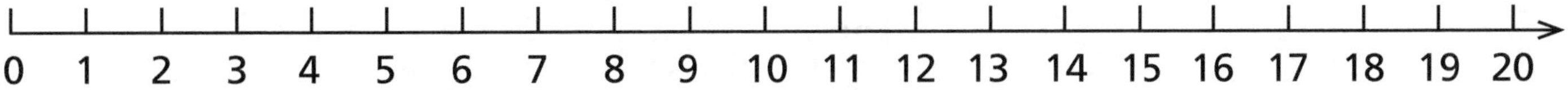

0 1 2 3 4 5 6 7 8 9 10 11 12 13 14 15 16 17 18 19 20

| 1 | 2 | 3 | 4 | 5 | 6 | 7 | 8 | 9 | 10 |
|---|---|---|---|---|---|---|---|---|---|
| 11 | 12 | 13 | 14 | 15 | 16 | 17 | 18 | 19 | 20 |
| 21 | 22 | 23 | 24 | 25 | 26 | 27 | 28 | 29 | 30 |
| 31 | 32 | 33 | 34 | 35 | 36 | 37 | 38 | 39 | 40 |
| 41 | 42 | 43 | 44 | 45 | 46 | 47 | 48 | 49 | 50 |
| 51 | 52 | 53 | 54 | 55 | 56 | 57 | 58 | 59 | 60 |
| 61 | 62 | 63 | 64 | 65 | 66 | 67 | 68 | 69 | 70 |
| 71 | 72 | 73 | 74 | 75 | 76 | 77 | 78 | 79 | 80 |
| 81 | 82 | 83 | 84 | 85 | 86 | 87 | 88 | 89 | 90 |
| 91 | 92 | 93 | 94 | 95 | 96 | 97 | 98 | 99 | 100 |

# BLM 2 Number bond houses

| 10 | |
|---|---|
| 1 | 9 |
| 2 | 8 |
| 3 | 7 |
| 4 | 6 |
| 5 | 5 |
| 6 | 4 |
| 7 | 3 |
| 8 | 2 |
| 9 | 1 |

| 9 | |
|---|---|
| 1 | 8 |
| 2 | 7 |
| 3 | 6 |
| 4 | 5 |
| 5 | 4 |
| 6 | 3 |
| 7 | 2 |
| 8 | 1 |

| 8 | |
|---|---|
| 1 | 7 |
| 2 | 6 |
| 3 | 5 |
| 4 | 4 |
| 5 | 3 |
| 6 | 2 |
| 7 | 1 |

| 7 | |
|---|---|
| 1 | 6 |
| 2 | 5 |
| 3 | 4 |
| 4 | 3 |
| 5 | 2 |
| 6 | 1 |

| 6 | |
|---|---|
| 1 | 5 |
| 2 | 4 |
| 3 | 3 |
| 4 | 2 |
| 5 | 1 |

| 5 | |
|---|---|
| 1 | 4 |
| 2 | 3 |
| 3 | 2 |
| 4 | 1 |

| 4 | |
|---|---|
| 1 | 3 |
| 2 | 2 |
| 3 | 1 |

| 3 | |
|---|---|
| 1 | 2 |
| 2 | 1 |

| 7 | |
|---|---|
| | 1 |
| 5 | |
| | 3 |
| 3 | |
| | 5 |
| 1 | |

| 8 | |
|---|---|
| 7 | |
| | 2 |
| 5 | |
| | 4 |
| | 5 |
| 2 | |
| | 7 |

| 10 | |
|---|---|
| 1 | |
| | 8 |
| 3 | |
| | 6 |
| | 5 |
| 6 | |
| 7 | |
| | 2 |
| 9 | |



 • *AUSTRALIAN SIGNPOST MATHS NSW 1* • ISBN 9780655709022

## BLM 3 Number bonds (addition)

Say the number bonds in a line, giving the answers as you go.
Line A would be 7 = 1 + ■, 6 = 3 + ■, 9 = 3 + ■, 8 = ■ + 5.

**A**

**B**

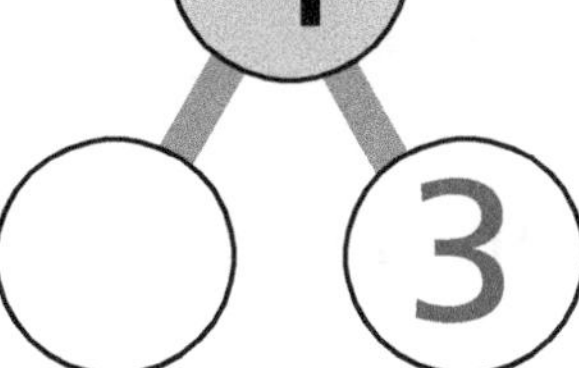


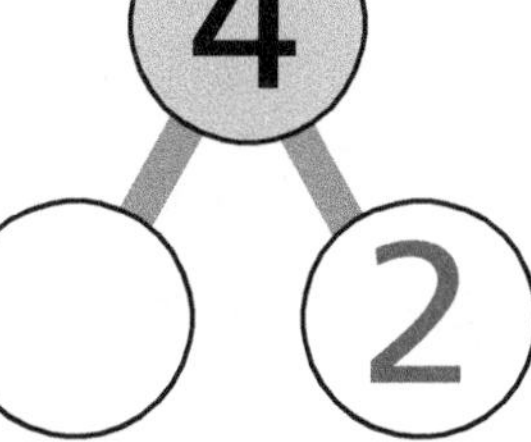


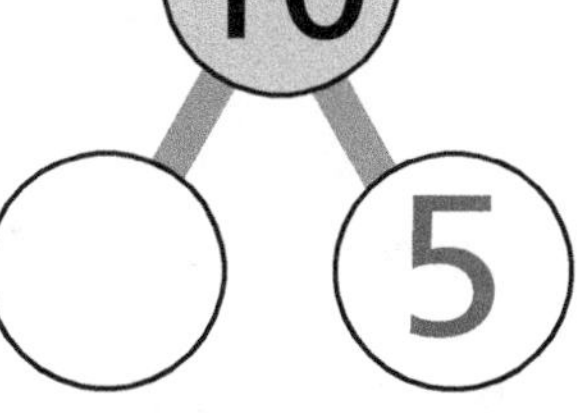


**C**

10
2

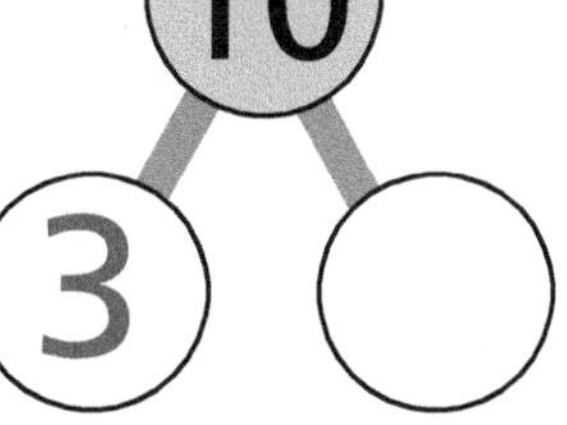

**D**

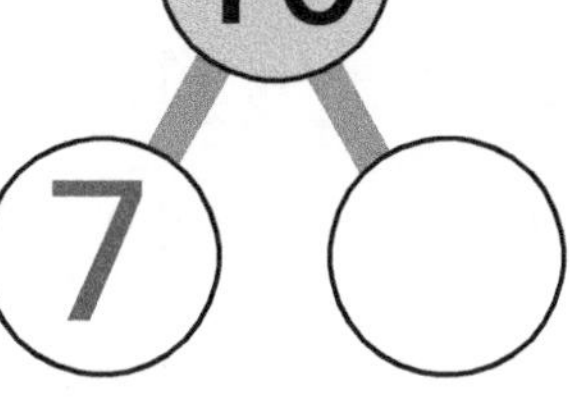


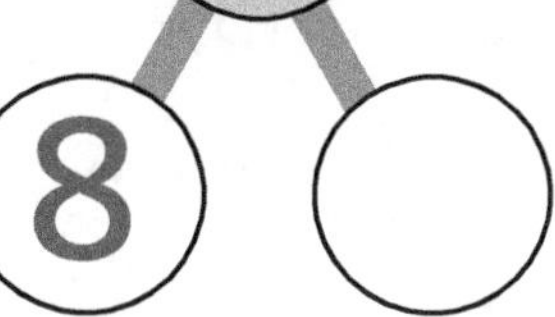

# Addition and subtraction facts

## Addition (Say the answers to each line as quickly as possible.)

| | | | | | | |
|---|---|---|---|---|---|---|
| **A** | 2 + 2 | 3 + 7 | 6 + 3 | 6 + 0 | 5 + 2 | 3 + 3 |
| **B** | 5 + 3 | 3 + 2 | 2 + 8 | 4 + 2 | 1 + 7 | 4 + 6 |
| **C** | 5 + 5 | 8 + 2 | 6 + 4 | 4 + 4 | 7 + 2 | 9 + 1 |
| **D** | 4 + 3 | 5 + 4 | 7 + 3 | 6 + 2 | 6 + 6 | 7 + 7 |
| **E** | 9 + 2 | 8 + 4 | 4 + 7 | 7 + 9 | 9 + 6 | 5 + 6 |
| **F** | 7 + 6 | 2 + 9 | 7 + 4 | 3 + 8 | 5 + 7 | 9 + 9 |
| **G** | 3 + 9 | 8 + 8 | 9 + 7 | 6 + 8 | 5 + 9 | 4 + 8 |
| **H** | 8 + 6 | 4 + 9 | 8 + 7 | 5 + 8 | 7 + 5 | 6 + 7 |
| **I** | 7 + 8 | 8 + 9 | 8 + 5 | 6 + 9 | 9 + 5 | 9 + 8 |

## Subtraction (Say the answers to each line as quickly as possible.)

| | | | | | | |
|---|---|---|---|---|---|---|
| **A** | 6 – 6 | 5 – 4 | 3 – 0 | 6 – 1 | 6 – 4 | 9 – 3 |
| **B** | 9 – 1 | 9 – 5 | 6 – 4 | 5 – 1 | 7 – 5 | 6 – 2 |
| **C** | 6 – 3 | 5 – 3 | 9 – 2 | 9 – 7 | 5 – 2 | 3 – 2 |
| **D** | 9 – 6 | 4 – 2 | 7 – 3 | 5 – 5 | 6 – 5 | 9 – 4 |
| **E** | 8 – 3 | 8 – 2 | 7 – 2 | 9 – 8 | 3 – 2 | 4 – 3 |
| **F** | 12 – 5 | 15 – 6 | 12 – 6 | 10 – 2 | 10 – 1 | 14 – 9 |
| **G** | 10 – 2 | 12 – 9 | 16 – 9 | 13 – 4 | 11 – 3 | 13 – 8 |
| **H** | 16 – 7 | 14 – 8 | 10 – 7 | 12 – 4 | 10 – 4 | 11 – 4 |
| **I** | 10 – 3 | 13 – 7 | 10 – 5 | 14 – 7 | 16 – 8 | 10 – 8 |
| **J** | 15 – 7 | 10 – 6 | 12 – 7 | 17 – 9 | 11 – 6 | 13 – 9 |
| **K** | 14 – 6 | 17 – 8 | 13 – 5 | 14 – 5 | 13 – 6 | 11 – 7 |
| **L** | 12 – 8 | 15 – 8 | 12 – 3 | 11 – 5 | 15 – 9 | 18 – 9 |